W9-BZJ-171

WITHDRAWN

The Theater of Politics

The Theater of Politics

Hannah Arendt, Political Science, and Higher Education

Eric B. Gorham

LEXINGTON BOOKS
Lanham • Boulder • New York • Oxford

LEXINGTON BOOKS

Published in the United States of America
by Lexington Books
4720 Boston Way, Lanham, Maryland 20706

12 Hid's Copse Road
Cumnor Hill, Oxford OX2 9JJ, England

British Library Cataloguing in Publication Information Available

Library of Congress Cataloging-in-Publication Data

Gorham, Eric B., 1960–
    The theater of politics : Hannah Arendt, political science, and higher education /
Eric B. Gorham.
        p.   cm.
    Includes bibliographical references and index.
    ISBN 0-7391-0048-3 (cl. : alk. paper) — ISBN 0-7391-0049-1 (pa. : alk. paper)
    1. Education, Higher—Political aspects. 2. Arendt, Hannah—Contributions in
political science. I. Title.

LC 171.G56   2000
378'.01   99-045672

Printed in the United States of America

♾™ The paper used in this publication meets the minimum requirements of American
National Standard for Information Sciences—Permanence of Paper for Printed Library
Materials, ANSI/NISO Z39.48–1992.

à Luce

Contents

Acknowledgments

I want to remember Hannah Arendt, whose words are a constant source of learning to me. Her ideas have challenged me to think in ways that have helped me appreciate the joy of understanding.

The book was written in places in the world very different from my home in New Orleans. Thanks to those people of Florence, Montréal, St.-Irénée, Calpe, Aix-en-Provence, and Claviers who have taken the time to get to know an itinerant American/Canadian couple, and who have opened their homes and their lives to us. Our friends in New Orleans have also made our life in the city that care forgot something to remember.

Chapter 7 was realized through a summer grant from the National Endowment for the Humanities and the resources of the European University Institute's library at the Piazza Edison in Florence. Loyola University provided me with a sabbatical leave in the spring of 1998. Thanks to Serena Leigh and her colleagues at Lexington Books for showing confidence in my work. Professor Phillip Hansen gave a 1995 lecture on the political theory of Hannah Arendt at Concordia University in Montréal that started me thinking about the ideas of Arendt. Jenny Rubick helped in the late stages by preparing the manuscript for publication. I am grateful to Jim Hobbs, Trish Del Nero, and Deborah Poole of Loyola University's Monroe Library for giving me access to its PCs. Connie Rodriguez contributed the cover photo.

The department of political science at Loyola has provided me with a most congenial and peaceful environment in which to work. Phil Dynia, Conrad Raabe, Ed Renwick, Stan Makielski, Mary Troy Johnston, Alex Reichl, and Gayle Mumfrey have treated me with a great deal of respect, friendship, and fairness. Special mention goes to Alex Reichl, who took pains to read different parts of this manuscript and who has been a great source of encouragement.

Colleagues and friends have taken the time to read parts of the manuscript and have offered considered and helpful advice and encouragement. Catherine

Guisan-Dickinson, Adolf Gundersen, Mark Bower, Rob Pirro, Rick Parrish, Jim Ascher, Gary Remer, Suzanne Dovi, Rick Erickson, Dan Levin, Jim Moore, Mary Dietz, Joan Tronto, and Suzanne Jacobitti have all made time for my work. Thanks to each of them. Thanks as well to my good students, past and present, for teaching me how to learn. My teacher and colleague, Charles Anderson, has been a friend, critic, supporter, and counselor. I continue to learn from him, and I value both his intellect and his wonderful temperament.

Of course, my immediate family has been an unending source of support. To Howard, Sue, Jim, Roger, Bev, Sam, Eleanor, Jeffrey, and Minna—your love and understanding have made all my efforts worthwhile. I would also like to remember Alan, who has been with me in spirit for the past few years.

Finally, my wife and constant companion for many years now—Luce Mélançon—has been the most profound source of love and inspiration in my life. Her daily gestures always remind me how fortunate I am to know her, and it is to her that I dedicate this book.

Introduction

In the spring of 1968 students and workers took to the streets in France to demonstrate against institutions of higher education, low wages, the society of consumption, and the French political establishment in general. It was a moment in time that left legacies from postmodern thought to the spread of *tutoyer* and warmer public greetings among acquaintances. At least that is how it was recalled by the French press in the spring of 1998, on the occasion of the thirtieth anniversary of the uprising.

In the spring of 1998, students took to the streets in France, Spain, and Indonesia. The issues were different in each country, and the students in France and Spain, at least, were lucky not to have to fight for their immediate survival in the way their counterparts in Indonesia did. But all these students called for changes in the way their universities were governed, the way higher education was structured, and, in the case of Indonesia, the very structure of the government itself. In France and Spain the inflexible character of the public university systems has been under attack for thirty years by those brave enough to raise their voices. They are systems that guarantee success for a few, exclude the vast majority from that success, and provide a handful of lucky professors with working conditions unparalleled in the western world. Of course, this is not so different in the United States, where success on standardized exams and personal wealth can ensure students places in the most prestigious universities. Professors at prestigious universities have working conditions that rival those of their peers in Europe.

But students are not taking to the streets in the United States, at least not to change the system of higher education in America. Why should they, in the age of Clinton's America, where jobs are plentiful in comparison with the rest of the world, and where the stock market can provide these future investors with the means to an early retirement? Professors do not seem to be complaining too much about their condition either. Many of them are locked into jobs that are hardly utopian, but given the downsizing taking place at most of our institutions of higher learning, who can complain if they have a job? Few professors are going to leave their positions at a university defending freedom of speech, or affirmative action practices, or multiculturalism, or corporate interference in university governance (except for those fortunate enough to have large reputations and even larger retirement plans). All of this relative peacefulness is remarkable given that these institutions seek to instill critical thinking in their members. Indeed, a central component of a doctoral education is in learning how to criticize.

Both professors and students complain about the conditions of study, work, and politics at both their universities and universities elsewhere. For students, it may be the problem of meaningless classes, or too many requirements, or not enough financial aid, or even the vital importance of having a basketball team on campus. For professors, complaints center invariably around salaries and benefits, working conditions, and, more rarely, the political actions of individuals within universities. In critiquing the institution, many students and professors seem to agree on a few points—university classes can be a waste of time, administrative tasks can overwhelm and alienate all members of the institution, injustices occur in hiring and firing professors and administrators, teaching is far from being as important as research in considering the purposes of our largest and most prestigious universities, learning is becoming relatively less important to the institution, and grades are becoming relatively more so. (This is true at all levels, from marking papers of individual students to teacher evaluations and public rankings determining the prestige of the university and its departments in sources such as *The New York Times* or *U.S. News and World Report.*)

More than any other individual factor, American institutions of higher learning seem to be at the mercy of a bureaucratic imperative. Members of these institutions have reasons to conform to bureaucratic practices in universities at the cost of actually teaching or learning, or thinking about and judging university life itself. Students need jobs and want to succeed, and so accept their programs for what they are and their teachers for who they are, suffer intolerable waits on line at the financial aid office, live in what can only be described as prison-like conditions their first year away from home, and seek just enough knowledge to pass the exam with the grades necessary to carry them into their future careers.

In pursuing their own paths to success, professors publish ever-increasing quantities of material in the appropriate journals, and serve on many committees—most of which are deemed a waste of time by many of these same professors. A few of them serve on committees that reward them with satisfaction or, more likely, power. More than a few of these professors have never learned how to teach because they were never given the opportunity to learn the skill from those who have mastered the art. Nor do they have much incentive to energize their classrooms because either their other tasks take them away from this one, or they do not see material, moral, or educational rewards in doing so. Perhaps they recognize rationally that it is not a stepping stone to either personal success or happiness, however defined.

Administrators are administrators. That is, their jobs involve performing bureaucratic tasks in order that the university operate in as efficient a manner as possible. Their *raison d'etre* is not political thinking, teaching, or even critical thinking; it is, to borrow common parlance, "to get the job done." The administration is judged by the outside world—parents, lending institutions, governments, and corporations—according to how well they manage the institution and support the purposes each desires. Are students finding work and happiness? Are bankers investing securely and profitably in the university? Are universities legitimizing the claims to power of governments? Are university administrations increasing the profitability of corporations investing in them?

Yet these concerns do not speak to the ultimate political purposes of higher education. I will offer an alternative political justification for universities and colleges. At universities there exist possibilities to create what Hannah Arendt termed "spaces of appearance"—spaces where individuals appear to others as members of a political society, and where individuals are permitted to express themselves as distinctive identities.[1] Many who belong to universities yearn to be noticed in institutions of higher learning. Students want recognition for giving the correct answer or making high grades, professors want to be praised for their teaching or research skills, administrators want to be given credit for managing their campuses well. But universities are places where individuals often do not think they act politically on a regular basis. Students attend class, they wait in line at the registrar's office, they drink with friends at the rathskeller, they sit in seemingly interminable committee meetings—though they do not necessarily attach political significance to these activities. Faculty members and administrators do likewise. When was the last time you considered a daily academic practice a political act?

Beyond this desire to announce one's identity, there is also a need to communicate and deliberate with others, an activity that can be rare at universities (of all places!). Think, for example, of the various factions on campuses who do not deliberate but who hurl epithets at their opponents concerning a wide variety of issues (from the most mundane, such as faculty salaries, to the most abstract, such as freedom of speech or multicultural rights). A common complaint that one hears from friends and colleagues is that so little deliberation occurs at universities. Yet so many channels of communication are open; multiple committees have been created for professors, students, and administrators to talk to each other and exchange ideas. In theory, the institutional means do exist to permit individuals to act politically as university citizens and convey both their identities and practical wisdom to each other. So what is the problem?

At universities, individuals have not lost the ability or the means to communicate; they have lost the sentiment to learn from each other. Put more commonly, professors and administrators talk a lot, but they do not listen so well, because they do not respect the other deliberators sufficiently to pay attention to what is being said. This of course is particularly ironic within institutions of higher education, because by refusing to listen and learn, professors contravene the purposes of these institutions. Thus they act hypocritically, but in a manner patently evident to both their students and the public at large.

In *Politics*, Aristotle comments that a mark of the good citizen is one who knows both how to rule and how to be ruled. I would modify his observation here to say that a good university citizen is one who learns how to teach and how to be taught. It has been my experience that many professors can do the former, a few can do the latter, and even fewer can do both. Unfortunately for the institution as a whole, too many professors believe that they can only be taught by other experts in their particular field of study. They do not approach other members of their university as if they were people who might enlighten them. Of course, some professors audit the courses of their colleagues in other departments, and others publish research jointly with their students in a spirit of cooperation and equality, but they are exceptions rather than the rule. If we want to help our universities and colleges realize their purposes as institutions of education and of higher learning, then all of their members must be able to both teach, and learn from, a variety of different individuals. I will suggest ways in which university teachers can learn by listening, and ways in which students can learn by speaking.

I have learned a great deal about learning from Hannah Arendt, and I employ her ideas in this spirit. In this book I apply the concept of the space of appearance to universities in a manner that Arendt herself may not have, by emphasizing the importance of learning to the human condition. Following the distinction she makes in *The Human Condition* (Arendt 1958b), I discuss learning in the context of action, or public participation, and not in the contest of either labor or work. Though learning involves hard labor, and though it produces bodies of work, it is a political activity. Learning is a public, collective activity; this fact characterizes educational institutions and distinguishes them from other communities. Learning in universities and colleges is inseparable from expressing one's identity, communicating one's thoughts to others, influencing public policy, or collectively raising a voice for or against a particular issue.

Political participation concerns learning, and in the university being an active participant means learning about learning. Our educational decisions—over curriculum, instruction, and governance—are inherently political because they occur through communal deliberation and public decision-making. Universities (save mail-order or "adult" universities such as the University of Phoenix) are non-profit institutions, and, at least in theory, decisions about curriculum, instruction, or governance are not made for the material benefit of one or two individuals. So collective participation determines who will learn and how they will do so (Anderson 1993).

I also consider at many points in the book the problem of judgment, both in general and as it applies to the university community. When individuals accede to the bureaucratic imperative at universities they often demonstrate, however momentarily, a lapse in political judgment. By this I mean that they do not act in accordance with common sense, and in some instances they do not follow their own experience. They permit others to treat them as functionaries. This is ironic because the bureaucracy in which we work becomes the "common" that we must "sense." Bureaucratic reasoning and administrative action substitute for the common sense that individuals cultivate as active members of democratic communities. Of course, all who work in large institutions accede to the bureaucratic imperative. But universities can help make their members more aware of these lapses. Because the university or college is an institution of *higher learning*, it has, by definition, a political obligation to make possible the learning of political judgment. This is not simply a moral or intellectual obligation. It is political because university professors and administrators extract material and intellectual benefits from educating the public. Following Arendt, I call those places where universities fulfill their political obligation to the public "spaces of appearance."

Universities provide these sorts of spaces occasionally, but I will argue that they ought to incorporate this justification more frequently into their everyday practices, and I will suggest how universities can do so consistently and practically. I am not arguing that this is the principal purpose of universities, or even necessarily a central one. But it must be one of the most important public, political functions of institutions that consider themselves schools of civic education. Any justification of American universities and colleges on democratic grounds must necessarily consider them as schools of political judgment. Where judgment is not considered, the purposes of institutions of higher education cannot be politically justified in a democracy.

Therefore, I want to give a political justification for universities, based not on democracy, or citizenship, or participation, or community ethics, but based on notions I have learned from Hannah Arendt—the space of appearance and political judgment. I conceive of the university as a theater of politics where individuals are permitted to act publicly and create a sort of enduring story together. But it is also a space where they must withdraw from action periodically in order to judge the performance in which they may have participated. Through this theater members of a university can satisfy public institutional purposes—democracy, citizenship, community ethics; so the theater metaphor represents a means to political ends. Faculty, students, and administrators are all actors in this theater, but they are also spectators to the action surrounding them. If they are to be good university *citizens*, then they ought to accept *both* these roles, and learn to both participate in and judge the academic community immediately surrounding them. It is not the only theater of politics, but it is the one most readers of this book have entered, and within which they remain, either backstage, on stage, or in the audience.

Notes

1. In the words of Arendt, "the space where I appear to others as others appear to me, where men exist not merely like other living or inanimate things but make their appearance explicitly" (Arendt 1958b, 177). Many of Arendt's commentators have discussed Arendt's relevance to the contemporary world of politics (see, for example, Isaac 1996, Disch 1994, Canovan 1992, Wolin 1994, Honig 1995, Ricoeur 1991, or Benhabib 1996). All have rendered judgment on her idea of the space of appearance, the importance of the political, and their relation to democracy. But I have seen no mention of her ideas to the space most immediately political to their concerns—the university. This condition is not simply ironic but strikes me as antithetical to the spirit of Arendt's work. For Arendt, creating a durable, *civil* public world was of utmost importance, and people accomplished this by acting with others in spaces that were accessible to them. Clearly, most interpreters of Arendt's work act and work within institutions of higher education, so it would seem obvious that within them academics might try to create the sort of civility in public life of which Arendt speaks in *The Human Condition* and other works.

Of course, Arendt herself did not speak of the university as a site of spaces of appearance, save for a few instances in *Crises of the Republic* and *On Violence* where she discusses the spontaneous nature of the student revolts of the 1960s. One reason for this was her concern for the world, as she would often write in her correspondence to friends. The daily actions of people at universities were local, not the world she had in mind when she wrote about the Hungarian Revolution of 1956, civil disobedience in the United States, school integration in Little Rock, or Watergate. But Hannah Arendt was never employed full time as a university professor, so, though she was obviously close to universities all of her life, they never sustained her as a site of work and action. She had the privilege of being able to think about the world at large, because she could dissociate herself from universities frequently, and could leave behind the bureaucratic imperative I have mentioned above. An example of this came in 1960 when, after being awarded a foundation grant for study, she chose to give it up and attend the Eichmann trial as a reporter for the *New Yorker*. The typical professor would never have had the freedom to do this—first because he or she would not have been awarded a grant freeing him or her from teaching and service responsibilities, and second because even given such an attractive option, some professors would not think to give up such a grant *because* it would free them from precisely these responsibilities. The "burden" of teaching and service was not a continual one for Hannah Arendt (though, without doubt, she bore her own). So it is understandable that the everyday functioning of universities was not on her mind.

Because interpreters of Arendt's work often examine in minute detail her books and essays, instead of applying her ideas to contemporary life, it is also understandable that these problems are not on their minds either. In this sense I am writing a different sort of political theory. Instead of analyzing the text of the author and her critics, I hope to bring out meaning in her work by applying it to situations immediately relevant to both author and reader alike. I think that I do so in the spirit of what Arendt, following Kant in the *Third Critique*, called "exemplary validity."

Chapter 1

Acting in Politics

For most people, most of the time, politics is an activity that is observed, not experienced. We read the newspapers and we watch television and we gaze upon a world that we very rarely enter. When we do enter it, we spend a good deal of time discussing the sites around us with our friends and colleagues. Many, if not most, people understand politics as spectators, watching some act, and others direct the activity.

What a peculiar notion this is, especially to those of us who have grown up in the United States, where political participation is ingrained in the psyche of the young citizen from the time he or she can recite the Pledge of Allegiance. Indeed, good citizenship is constituted by active involvement in a wide variety of community activities. Political life is not some spectator sport, our active citizens say; it is part of the energy and privilege of being an American.

Being an American, though, means more (and often less) than participating in "politics"—that is governmental activities or campaigning for or against those people in government and their legislation. Tocqueville's justly celebrated analysis of America reminds us of this. For Tocqueville democracy in America means that our civic mores go beyond the traditionally political. We engage with each other in communities, we join societies and formally apolitical civic associations quickly, we recognize the fundamental equality between ourselves and our neighbors. We, in short, create a kind of *isonomia*, a condition of no-rule, in our social relations by constantly acting socially (if not always politically) with those around us. The American experience, then, is precisely one of activity and action, a regular movement within and among communities of citizens designed to bring life to the public sphere and meaning to ourselves as citizens.

Yet, since the 1920s, academics have decried the lack of civic engagement with the community. Charles Merriam, John Dewey, and others wrote textbooks on the matter, and after the end of World War II, a new generation of political scientists lamented the dangers this behavior posed to democracy in general and to the United States in particular. In the past thirty years, while some have re-emphasized this point, others have praised civic disengagement, judging it necessary to the health of a polity—from the philosophical (Walzer's and Schumpeter's claim that individuals ought to have rights not to participate, rights to be left alone) to the practical (the early Dahl and others who have argued that democracies function best when left in the hands of political leaders and policy experts).

Consequently, even if democracy is practiced by many Americans politics is not. Treating people equally in our daily lives is a difficult task that most of us fulfill at least some of the time. Running for office on an egalitarian platform, lobbying for equal rights legislation, demonstrating for the fair treatment of minorities—all these things are a different matter, and engaging in these activities takes time, money, interest, and effort. Many Americans do not have any or all of these privileges, and so do not or cannot involve themselves at a level broader than the personal. As a result, a common political experience for Americans is as spectator to the performance of political action.

This may be what pundits lament when they note the poor voter turnout during elections, or the high numbers of individuals who mark "don't know" or "don't care" on opinion polls. It may be the result of what Elisabeth Noelle-Neumann has termed the "spiral of silence," a vicious circle of fear and passivity distinct in mass societies that renders citizens relatively more quiescent and politicians relatively more powerful (Noelle-Neumann 1993). It may also be a political condition created by an atomized society, individuated participants, immense bureaucracies, multinational corporations, weakened civil associations, or the anesthetic of our media culture. Regardless of its genesis, the passive observer on the American political scene—the common citizen—is considered a problem by numerous academics and critics.

Yet are observers simply passive, non-participating non-citizens? When one is "relegated" to the role of spectator, can one be said to be doing politics? What role does the observer play in the political drama? How important is this role? Can we speak properly of spectators as in some sense second-class citizens, or even non-citizens? In this book I will analyze some of the ways in which people act in politics and the ways in which they observe political action. I will examine the connection between observation and action, and I will argue that the political or social scientist plays a distinctive role at this nexus. The political scientist observes political action from the viewpoint of the educated spectator, but, I will argue, only as one sort of educated spectator among many. His or her position is one of a spectator-critic, who ought to render judgment analogous to that rendered by an educated critic of the performing arts.

I will further contend that, contrary to the instincts of many American political scientists, activists, and leaders, spectatorship not only is essential for political thinking, but is a necessary, if not sufficient, condition of good citizenship. A central aspect of this civic practice is education. Political education requires impartiality and good judgment, two characteristics of good citizenship that can be nurtured (among other places) in higher education. But to do this requires a rethinking of the purposes of higher education and the strategies for permitting students to learn how to think about politics in ways different from traditional academic concerns. One rethinking can begin by bringing together two disciplines traditionally distant from each other—drama and political science. In analogizing politics to the theater, I am interested not only in the actors themselves, but also in those who observe the action, and I will examine political action from the standpoint of one who observes a performance.

Theatrical Politics

The idea that the world is somehow analogous to the theater has a very long history, if we recall Pythagoras' parable that "life . . . is like a festival," or Jacques' (possibly mistaken) observation in *As You Like It* that "all the world is a stage." Enlightenment thinkers, such as Diderot and Rousseau, considered the man on the street to be an actor, and modern poets and playwrights such as Bertolt Brecht and Dario Fo (among many others) have effaced the line between theater and street in their art. Even twentieth-century political theory has sometimes treated politics as a spectacle or performance, and a few theorists have built their analyses, and their reputations, on making close analogies between politics and acting.[1] Though their understandings of theatrical politics differ to a great degree, all share certain premises: political action is based upon performance (of roles); when we act politically we put on certain masks both to hide our private selves and to present our political selves to the world; acting effectively requires practice and training; political acts ultimately depend upon the presence of spectators; and thus these spectators in some fashion determine truth in political action and regulate in some way the standards of that action.[2]

In this chapter I examine different ways of conceptualizing politics as theater in order to suggest its importance in contemporary political and social theory. I introduce four distinct manners in which political action has been characterized theatrically—as role-playing, as plot development, as recreation, and as spectacle. Each theory is celebrated among political and social theorists, and I analyze the ideas of their most important proponents (Erving Goffman, Richard Sennett, Jean Piaget, and Michel Foucault, respectively). While each theorist illustrates political action in an original manner, each also leaves certain questions unanswered about the relationship between theatrical and political action. I hope to answer some of these questions by introducing gradually the political theory of Hannah Arendt in this chapter, and in chapters 2 and 3 I argue that her theory of theatrical politics frames action in particularly useful ways.

In presenting different theories of theatrical politics I also raise issues I develop in future chapters, and I ask questions about the role of the political and social sciences in both civic training and higher education. The pedagogical role of political science has something to do with a certain kind of civic education. Training undergraduate and graduate students to think carefully about politics and society is tantamount to cultivating in them civic judgment. If institutions of higher education want their students to be good citizens they must first consider permitting them to act, in accordance with that judgment, more politically within those institutions. (I develop this last argument in chapters 7 and 8.)

Action as Role-Playing

The most widely known analyst of social and political theater is Erving Goffman. In *The Presentation of Self in Everyday Life*, Goffman reports, not on political life per se, but on the everyday activities that constitute both public and private worlds. He derives his principles from theater and considers "the way in which the individual in ordinary work situations presents himself and his activity to others, the ways in which he guides and controls the impression they form of him, and the kinds of things he may and may not do while sustaining his performance before them" (Goffman 1959, xi). His form of analysis has been employed by a wide variety of social and political analysts, and I would refer the reader to other works in order to learn how it has been used in political science and social theory (e.g., Cohen 1987). However, I would like to raise particular issues relevant to the subject matter of this book.

Goffman's text is, as he repeatedly remarks, a report (xi, 4, 15, 206, 239, 252, 254), a monograph that relies on observation, story-telling, and set-description. Growing out of his own research in a Shetland Island crofting community, Goffman appropriates sociological research, informal memoirs, interviewing techniques, literary descriptions, and personal remembrances to construct an analysis of social action as dramaturgy. In doing so, he offers the academic reader alternative means by which he provides evidence for his claims, and he investigates and analyzes his subject matter by different means (as interviewer, literary critic, etc.). He takes the position of an educated critic, and suggests ways in which others can take that position as well.[3] In this sense, he offers instruction on the phenomenology of studying social activity—how to construct social truth (through a dramaturgical perspective) from a multiplicity of research standpoints. He also self-consciously distances (though does not detach) himself from social action insofar as he employs a method of reportage. As the writer of a report (and as a member-observer in the crofting community), Goffman only rarely comments upon his own actions, though repeatedly admits that he was physically close to members of the community.

Goffman claims that the dramaturgical perspective can fit into the "analytical context" of sociological fact-finding, as a "*final* way of ordering facts" (240, emphasis added). Considering it "end-point analysis" Goffman hoped that his method would supplement, and complete, the array of means sociologists have at their disposal to analyze "establishments." All forms of social organization can be viewed technically, politically, structurally, and culturally. The dramaturgical view would not only complement these other four methods of understanding the social world, but cohere them into a sociological whole. In this sense, Goffman uses his method as a means by which facts are not (merely) presented to the world, but ordered.

The Presentation of Self in Everyday Life is about appearing in the world, presenting oneself to the world. It does not concern how individuals represent themselves to others or how they represent things in their own minds. Indeed the act of thinking is often absent in Goffman's report. He is concerned primarily with the methods used to stage one's behavior in the public sphere, where one needs to manage the impressions others have of him or her. As an observer, Goffman makes no pretenses to understanding how people actually think, for as a reporter he can only recount their actual behavior. What people do when they manage impressions others have of them is evident. What they are thinking is not, and Goffman does not intend to read their minds, so to speak (nor does he indicate that he is capable of that).

Goffman notices that when people act in public, they attempt to control the impression others have of them. The actor determines which actions are governable and which are ungovernable, and he or she attempts to define a situation (and thereby govern it) through his or her expressive activity. Actors do this by presenting fronts, offering idealized impressions of themselves, working with others to perform as teams, and marking out regions where certain behaviors become appropriate or inappropriate. Goffman describes the "art of impression management" and indicates the numerous ways actors in their everyday lives dominate others through theatrical play. An end of human behavior, then, is self-control and control over others. Theatrical expression becomes a means by which one can accomplish this end, and to be human means to understand the panoply of human expressions and the dangers and possibilities inherent in them.

Of course, actors rarely have complete control over any scene or situation, and quite often disruptions occur that challenge the actor to reassert control. Goffman details those individuals who play the "discrepant roles" that disturb the play itself, and he notes those frequent times when we are forced to go "out of character" to reestablish control over the situation. Ultimately we learn how to save face and re-define the situation in a comfortable and secure fashion. We strive constantly to fix our stages and direct our scenes, yet those very stages and scenes produce the selves that define our characters. Goffman concludes that the self is a sociological construct resulting from a lifetime of theatrical action (253).

Though Goffman uses drama to model daily social activity, he mentions its political significance in a number of places. For instance, theatrical action is a fundamentally individualist and democratic form of behavior.

> Whether the character that is being presented is sober or carefree, of high station or low, the individual who performs the character will be seen for what he largely is, a solitary player involved in a harried concern for his

production. Behind many masks and many characters, each performer tends to wear a single look, a naked unsocialized look, a look of concentration, a look of one who is privately engaged in a difficult, treacherous task (235).

Actors perform in equal conditions—each hides his or her efforts behind a front that differentiates each person from the other. Goffman's theory suggests a radically egalitarian, mass society of primarily undifferentiated human beings striving to display particularity and character. But Goffman acknowledges that one's character results from the performance of the scene, it does not determine that performance. So individuals are left tragically seeking to control something over which not only do they have no control, but that renders them powerless to determine their own lives. In seeking control, the human actor engages in situations that disempowers him or her. For Goffman, this is the paradox of democratic action.

Politics further intrudes into action, and vice versa, "in regard to the capacities of one individual to direct the activity of another." Politics is power and "power of any kind must be clothed in effective means of displaying it, and will have different effects depending on how it is dramatized" (241). Dramatic action serves as a conduit to power and helps communicate a powerful message to an audience. Thus rulers display coercive practices not only to define and control a situation, but to express the extent of their power to the citizenry (the audience). Both leaders and citizens play roles that express not only their parts in a drama but the relationships of power among them.

Political action conceals as much as it reveals, and this is an important merit to Goffman's theory of action as dramatic. In presenting ourselves in everyday (and political) life what sort of selves do we present? We hide much from others, both because we choose to do so and because others have coerced us into hiding those selves. The selves that we hide are those we feel powerless to express (for whatever reason), and those that we (choose to) express are the result of the situations in which we act. In this case, we do not always present our authentic selves, but rather the selves we deem acceptable or safe or comfortable for public consumption. Politics, then, becomes a deceptive activity, one filled with actors forced upon a stage who create personas defined by the scene, and who mask their true intentions for the purposes of impression management and the expression of power.

But what of people who do not act? Goffman calls them the audience, but he implies that even they act as members of an audience. Performance teams relate to audiences in particular ways that render them actors as well. These spectators to the performance act as spectators, and as such are performers themselves. Furthermore, in everyday life, those who the actors consider members of their audience are actors themselves, and thus attempting to define a situation and control a scene of "their" making as well. It may not be the same situation or the same scene as other actors, but Goffman's theory suggests that everyone is acting some part in some way, even if the plots are talking past each other, so to speak. But is this really the case? What would it mean to perform as a spectator? Are spectators doing more than observing, are they acting, and acting out, performance-observations?

Note the implications of Goffman's theory here for the political and social sciences.[4] Certainly, political research based on detached observation becomes impossible, because the researcher cannot simply observe action, he or she too is engaged in the activity of research. As such, he or she must put up fronts, define regions, and consider discrepant roles. So there is no finding an Archimedean point from which to perceive, organize, classify, and reproduce data. Beyond a critique of traditional positivism, Goffman's theoretical perspective precludes the possibility of a researcher rendering impartial and considered judgments about action. Not only can there be no possibility of an eye "outside" the action, but consequently there can be no possibility for criticism of that action. Were the actors in a scene to engage in morally questionable behavior, would the researcher, under this perspective, truly be able to judge the ethics of that behavior? Or would the researcher be forced into the following dilemma—either the activity is merely theatrical, as part of the human situation (and whose ethical content is irrelevant to the observer), or precisely because the spectator is engaged in his or her own theatrical action, he or she cannot be at a place where he or she can render a fair and impartial judgment? After all, if he or she makes a judgment on a scene he or she observes, the actors in that scene, as spectators of the theater of research, can also maintain that the researcher's judgment has been perverted by his or her own actions.

More fundamentally, I have noted Goffman's belief that his dramaturgical theory orders facts ("finally"), and that his theory displays a concern for appearances, presentations (and not re-presentations). Yet in applying this theoretical perspective Goffman does not merely order facts, he creates them. Viewing action as theatrical, Goffman establishes an ontology to each bit of social and political reality created by actors. Individuals, or in this case "performers," create facts by means of the events in which they and their fellow performers portray themselves and (by virtue of this) create a scene. The reality of this scene, however, is based on the existence of the drama (and the dramaturgical perspective) itself. That is, the "facts" that the researcher observes would be considered in light of the play in process, and as such the researcher would be looking for plot development, character dialogue, and ultimately an ending to the play. But how can anyone predict the ending to the play of everyday life?

Goffman forgets that plays have narrative, and that narrative drives the action. In everyday life, we do not present ourselves either with an ending in mind, or with an ending imposed upon, not only us, but society in general. It is only by looking at the end of a play, by having the whole of it in front of us, finished, that we not only make judgments about the play, but that we understand the significance of every scene, and thus every action. If we view everyday social and political life as drama, we must necessarily impose some sort of meaning on action, based upon what we, as researchers, deem an appropriate ending to the drama. But we cannot know this because the ending remains out of our hands, and because everyday dramas never end. Therefore, we, as researchers, impose endings on dramas in order to give significance to the lives and actions of the people we have been fortunate enough to observe. We create plays as we watch them. This blurs the distinction between actor, spectator, and author, and makes questionable Goffman's claim that the dramaturgical perspective can be a *final* ordering of the facts. Or at least it indicates that a final ordering of facts makes a dramaturgical *perspective* or *theory* impossible to validate or confirm. The best we can say is that the book represents a sort of libretto to accompany actions or works (*le opere* in Italian) that the author has observed. In that instance, the self cannot be a sociological construct, as Goffman claims (253), but rather a literary one.

In order to render impartial judgment on action we need to consider not merely how people act, but how they tell a story by their actions. We can observe, as a reporter might observe, the external behavior of individuals, but we must also be able to order that behavior into a coherent narrative. In writing narrative, we render judgment upon actions, because we impose a teleology on them. By doing this we exercise what Aristotle called our basic human capacity, that of making choices, and thus prove ourselves to be ethics-creating animals. Political and social science, as a means by which some of us can render ethical judgment, becomes a stance through which we can learn to understand others impartially. In so doing, we are no longer simply observers, we have become critics, and the eye of the critic is something very different from that of a sociologist or political scientist doing traditional field work.

We can teach others how to inhabit this standpoint. To be a social and political researcher does not merely mean understanding, reporting, and even defining facts, nor does it mean simply creating narratives through which facts can be ordered coherently. It also means teaching others how to take an impartial standpoint in order to comprehend both facts and narratives, and how to think about the world in such a way as to render good judgment. Social and political research can be pedagogy, the researcher shows others how to judge the world. This does not mean telling them what or how to think about the world, but setting an example for others to follow if they choose, and giving reasons why following the example would be a good choice for the student. In Goffman's words, it can mean providing a "guide worth testing" for the novice researcher. The greater value of the guide is not in the perspective supplied, but in the judgment gained in engaging in that research activity.

This can be what acting-as-role-playing is ultimately about—a means by which some individuals teach others how to act appropriately given a particular set of circumstances (or scene). To act, in the theatrical sense of the term, is not merely to put on a performance, but it is to present to the audience an exemplar by which its members can judge themselves or others. It is also a way that the spectator can observe the world from the standpoint of someone else (namely the character or characters in the play). The didactic, exemplary nature of theater encourages individuals to step outside of themselves, if only for a few moments, and glance upon either some other world, or some other view of the world in which that spectator lives. In either case, political and social researchers ought to encourage this thinking in teaching others.

Action as Plot Development

Richard Sennett complains that Goffman's work is a "picture of society in which there are scenes but no plot" (Sennett 1974, 36),[5] that in Goffman's perspective people's lives do not change, they merely adapt to situations. They behave, but they do not experience life. In contrast, Sennett develops a dynamic theory of society as theater, one that accounts for the transformation of the actors themselves. Sennett grounds his theory of the social psychology of modern man on the idea that the public life of such a man has somehow "fallen." In so doing, Sennett begins his history of the public man at its end—the decline of public action from the city stage.

We live in a world where intimate relations have become the way in which people relate to each other "authentically," and yet in the process they have become less expressive, less theatrical. "With an emphasis on psychological authenticity, people become inartistic in daily life because they are unable to tap the fundamental creative strength of the actor, the ability to play with and invest feeling in external images of the self" (37). We have arrived at a time and place in the narrative of Western urban man where our ability to act publicly has been greatly diminished, where we have acted ourselves out of our public roles and into the private domain. In Goffman's terms, we, as modern-day actors, have fled the front regions of our action into the security of the back regions, and most of our *significant* daily activity now takes place there.

Sennett analogizes the city to the theater and examines the transformation, over time and space, of the urban actor. Cities share with theater four fundamental problems: (1) how to arouse belief in one's appearance among a milieu of strangers, (2) how to discover and maintain continuity in those appearances, (3) how to produce a public geography, that is how to define scenes and situations and how to move comfortably within diverse social circumstances and among strangers, and (4) how to express to others one's feelings that signify in and of themselves, that present one to others and not represent one's feelings to others. In each of these ways, public man has declined—we are less capable of solving these problems effectively, and we are less able to present ourselves in public in a real and authentic manner.

To make his case, Sennett examines three moments in the history of modern urban society and culture—Paris and London in the 1750s, 1840s, and 1890s. As the "plot" develops over these two centuries we begin to see a story emerge of privatization, internalization, and loneliness. His analysis begins with the advent of the city of strangers, eighteenth-century Paris and London where the poor were arriving daily, thus adding to the population and to the sense of estrangement long-standing residents of the city experienced. He recounts the means by which people comprehended and managed this strangeness—by dressing and talking in certain ways that acted as signs to others of one's class or status (65-87), by differentiating the public, cultural space from the private, familial one (89ff), and by creating what can be called the "public actor"—the man who presents emotions on the public stage. This sort of public actor was not a classical one, as represented in the theater of Dionysos (see chapter 2), but rather one who played in the streets of Paris and London as a character might, drawing attention to himself (in both good and bad senses).

Diderot imagined this sort of action to be vital to the nature of modern, enlightened individuals. He wrote that performing was an art unto itself, unconnected to speech or rhetoric, and actors self-consciously fake emotions on the public stage in order to express nature in a more concise, precise, and comprehensible manner. Diderot's paradox is that exaggerated, histrionic expressions of emotion convey human nature better than "true" emotions do. So to truly express one's nature to others one must act as an actor does on the stage, performing theatrically in order to communicate to others one's authenticity as a human being. This is not the *flâneur*, who displays himself for the benefit of a detached, wholly observant audience; it is a society of display, where individuals portray themselves as actors in order to convey and elicit true emotions from all members of society. Given the strangeness of urban surroundings, Diderot and others considered theatrical display an essential corrective to an otherwise profoundly impersonal experience.

The transformation of the idea of the city occurred with Rousseau, who viewed just this sort of acting as pretentious and ultimately barbarous. According to Rousseau, the theater is dangerous because it "promotes the vices of men and women who do not have to struggle to survive. It is the agent of loss of self" (Sennett 1974, 117; see also Strong 1990, 55). The cosmopolis corrupts the nature of true human beings by forcing them to put on masks, and to hide their true feelings from each other. This does not reveal the individual to others in a world of strangers, as Diderot had hoped, it conceals one's true self from the public sphere and makes the world even stranger to the individual. This results in cruelty and violence in a so-called civilized world, ironic for Rousseau given that enlightened European opinion preferred the urban, pretentious European way of life. For Rousseau, expression was achieved through honesty, simplicity, and genuineness. It is Rousseau's romantic vision that helps guide the nineteenth-century urban dweller, and in the process, transforms the nature of urban relations.

The nineteenth century sets a scene of city dwellers withdrawing from public display in order to secure private needs and personal desires. The rise of the retail trade, department stores, and a consumer society rendered city dwellers more passive (Sennett 1974, 142ff), as they were now members of an audience observing the display of consumable items in their infinite variety. People became more concerned with their appearances, and flamboyance declined in the general population. The urban dweller was to be conscious of one's own body and one's own self, and this meant a turn inwards. No longer was public display in dress or behavior appropriate, and the man and woman in the street were taught to conform.

Out of this emerged a new kind of urban dweller—the spectator. The spectator did not participate in urban life so much as he tried to steel himself in order to observe it. In Benjamin's terms, the modern urban citizen was one who would parry the shocks he or she would encounter in living daily with millions of others. In the process, spectators now demanded that others put on displays through which the emotions of the spectators would be aroused, in order that they might experience those lives vicariously. The emerging public persona (such as the *flâneur*) was meant to shock the spectator into feeling, and this shock was necessary because the spectator, the simple observer, was skilled only in the art of seeing.

Sennett's plot culminates in the "intimate society" of the late nineteenth and early twentieth centuries, one whose ideology promoted intimacy as the most authentic form of human relationship. As a result, public life was enervated.

> Personality in public was a contradiction in terms; it ultimately destroyed the public term. For instance, it became logical for people to think of those who could actively display their emotions in public, whether artists or politicians, as being men of special or superior personality. These men were to control, rather than interact with, the audience in front of whom they appeared. Gradually the audience lost faith in itself to judge them, it became a spectator rather than a witness. The audience thus lost a sense of itself as an active force, as a 'public' (261).

Such a development triggered a rise of narcissistic personal relationships, as we eliminate boundaries between ourselves and others and try to impose ourselves on others. Narcissism itself had two consequences—first the social consequence of the loss of civility ("the activity that protects people from each other and yet allows them to enjoy each other's company" [264]); and second the technical or aesthetic consequence that individuals become actors deprived of their art (i.e., they forget the techniques of acting in the social and political theater). Moderns are told to uncouple the mask from their face in order to reveal their true selves and in order to lose their pretensions. But in the process we burden each other with ourselves and this results in a decrease in sociability. After all, who wants to maintain a relationship with many people who constantly and unremittingly reveal themselves to others? Our energies are often consumed by this sort of relationship with those closest to us; if one suffers this in public, one can become intellectually and emotionally exhausted. For this reason (among others) we withdraw from the public realm and privatize ourselves in order to parry these very sorts of psychological, interpersonal shocks.

The public danger here is that those who do not privatize themselves, who accept uncivil interpersonal relationships in their public lives, participate in authoritarian political action. For example, Sennett presents the charismatic leader who destroys the distance between his own emotions and those of his audience as one who creates incivility in political life. Another perversion comes in the form of communal experiences that require too much intimacy— communities that become exclusive and that create strict rules for membership and communal citizenship. Nationalism in its many different, and especially extreme, varieties reflects this, as do religious cults, survivalist movements, and ethnic blocs. Its effects can be seen in barricaded cities, the need for crowd control, the rise in crime, the emergence of *ressentiment* politics, and the rise of the therapeutic sciences (social work, psychotherapy) in the service of the welfare state.

I would add that incivility prevents public learning because it erases the distinction between actors and thus eliminates the possibility that one can learn *from* someone else. Our experiences are no longer learning ones, but rather shared moments of intimacy. If we are concerned with sharing intimacy with others we become less concerned with treating them as separate and separable individuals. This prevents us from learning how to take their position, how to understand their reasoning and their perspective, in order to develop our own capacities of impartiality and judgment. Judgment comes when we detach ourselves sufficiently from the experiences of others so that we can, indeed, come to experience them by taking their position. If we are constantly seeking unity with another person, our capacity to take the position of that person, reflect upon it, and teach ourselves a different way of looking at the world becomes impossible. With the rise of intimacy, then, comes the loss of political and social judgment. How political and social scientists can recognize the loss of judgment and teach impartiality are central concerns of this book.

Sennett concludes that public man has fallen and that public culture is weakened through these transformations.

> The expectation is that when people are close, they are warm; it is an intense kind of sociability which people seek out in attempting to remove the barriers to intimate contact, but this expectation is defeated by the act. The closer people come, the less sociable, the more painful, the more fratricidal their relations (338).

Need this be the case, however? His narrative is only one narrative among a possible choice of many. For instance, how does the "decline of public culture" thesis account for women, who have been relegated to the private realm, and not just in the past 150 years? Is the idea of a public culture one that excludes much of the culture? Is the decline of such a culture necessarily a bad thing? The intimacy he excoriates is a quality that some feminist critics (e.g., Gilligan, Ruddock) admire in women's lives, thus is his criticism an implicit attack on the very public values women have contributed to society? If the notion of a public culture is a patriarchal deception, then maybe the narrative of, and lament for, its *decline* is a misleading one.

How do individuals act in public? How do they play roles and develop the plot? Sennett is not merely observing, then; he is not a mere historical spectator to the narrative of urban life in the eighteenth and nineteenth centuries. He is actually the playwright. In beginning at the end, in tracing back our current malaise to the eighteenth century, Sennett forgets that history is a science with no end. How people performed in the nineteenth century helps explain their lives. But the researcher must always remember that those actors enact dramas that signify in and of themselves that they are not tools for the recreation of an historical sequence concluding one way or another.

Teaching political science and political judgment requires the sort of thinking that refuses to end stories. Certainly we can try to understand events that occur in a time or place different from the one in which we currently live, but we need to be conscious that when we recount historical narrative or explain political phenomena that we engage in a form of story-telling. We re-create a scene, on paper or in our minds, to exemplify other ways of living or acting, to grant our students the privilege of participating in the lives of others who are not present to them in "everyday" life. We illustrate action to our students so that they may draw from it their own conclusions, or, if they are to be future storytellers, an understanding that history and politics does not end.

This is an approach to political and social science dramatically different from that practiced in many universities at present. It is an approach to political science that begins with the education of the student, not the research agenda of the social or political scientist. It presumes that the first consequence of thinking is education, that when we engage in analysis and investigation we are doing so primarily to enlighten our students. Enlightening our students means teaching them impartiality and the capacity to judge particular events and particular acts with acuity and good sense. Dramaturgy enlightens because it exemplifies facts or events to students, it puts narrative before their eyes, and permits the student to become the knowledgeable critic. The student learns not only about the events themselves, but how to make sense out of those events. Thus he or she learns skills of observation and interpretation. In this fashion, political action becomes truly theatrical in the ancient Greek sense of the term—an object for observation, based on *thea*, a seeing.

Understanding a theatrical representation of political action requires an *eye* for the expressive qualities of human activity, as well as for "plot development" (the ways in which the action transforms both actor and scene). But we cannot always determine what the end of that development is, and if we attempt to impose our own endings on the narrative we cannot understand the truth of that narrative (though we can get at its meaning). What remains is education and learning—namely, how we understand the scenes of human activity and communicate them to others in order to teach impartiality, judgment, and the importance of political thinking.

Action as Recreation

The play is the thing. How people learn has much to do with how people play, especially as children, but as adults as well. Childhood play serves a variety of functions. First, it teaches children social conventions.

> Social relations can be aesthetic relations, because they share a common root. That common origin lies in the childhood experience of play. Play is . . . a certain kind of preparation for a certain kind of aesthetic activity . . . by teaching [children] to treat conventions of behavior as believable. Conventions are rules for behavior at a distance from the immediate desires of the self. When children have learned to believe in conventions they are ready to do qualitative work on expression by exploring, changing, and refining the quality of those conventions (Sennett 1974, 266).

Play distances children from themselves and their own actions in the world and helps them act out in the world that they perceive. Consequently, they are able to take the position of others (e.g., the mommy, the daddy, the policeman, etc.) and learn perspective through the faculty of the imagination. After playing, children can imagine how the world must look to adults, and this act of imagination prepares them to live in the world. It also teaches them how to think about social conventions by imagining how adults act in them. This is an important prerequisite for judging whether or not those conventions are, for example, fair or efficient or even significant.

This capacity literally socializes children to the world. As children learn to distance themselves from their own immediate needs and interests, they learn about the voluntary character of the self, and they learn how to follow rules. In following rules, the desire to master others is put off, because the child must learn to master himself for the sake of the rules. As they grow older, this can lead some adults to obey rules thoughtlessly, but it also teaches children equality. Rules equalize the conditions of play for all (by, for instance, giving handicaps to the "superior" players), and it teaches children the expressive quality of rules and conventions. Sennett calls this developing a "third ear"—the ability to hear oneself practicing rules (of music, of games) so that one does not woodenly repeat the same pattern again and again. It also accustoms children to the idea that expressions can be repeated. When individuals learn to express themselves, they learn how to appear to others, how to appear in public, and this has the additional virtue of allowing individuals to create their world(s). In educating youth, we might consider more closely ways in which we cultivate creativity through play, and ways in which we might use rules as commands for our students to follow thoughtlessly. The same holds true in educating our young researchers.

Piaget believed that childhood play possessed a symbolic function. Because the child struggles in making a balanced adaptation to reality, Piaget suggests that the child play-acts in order to develop his or her powers of deductive reasoning. These powers can then place for the child "the real in a matrix of possibles and which is an essential complement to the empirical examination of things" (Taylor 1985a, 158). Piaget believed that we come to greater sense of objectivity by acting out as children—we develop the ability to detach ourselves from ourselves, overcome egocentrism,[6] and develop ourselves cognitively along the lines he maps out in his famous theory of learning.

Childhood play has another symbolic function, above and beyond the one described by Piaget, according to Charles Taylor. By pretending or playing make-believe, children lift themselves out of their situation, and this disengages them for another purpose than achieving objectivity. In disengaging in this fashion, children can live the scene from

> a different vantage point; not, in other words, to remain inextricably trapped in the primary experience. And this stepping out of our situation may help us to come to terms with it, to see it as something different, and hence to live with it in a different way (159).

It permits us to "build up a capacity to live on several levels, which the adult normally has." To do this is not to detach oneself completely from the world or achieve objectivity, an Archimedean point, but rather to develop "our capacity to step out of our situation and 'play it back' from a different vantage point . . . where we cannot loosen the affective link with our situation, we can still live it through play in another perspective" (159). This is important, I would argue, because it helps us cultivate a capacity for impartiality—an understanding of how others live, not to take on the other's personality as a component of our own, but to use that vantage point as our reference point when we judge a particular scene of action.

Both Piaget and Taylor suggest that this capacity for disengagement is also a critical tool for learning language. Play does not merely help us learn the particulars of the language—rules of grammar, syntax, etc., as adults might use them, but the very disengagement in the act of playing parallels the process of using language.

> [T]o be able to talk about things is to be potentially aware of them outside any particular transaction with them; it is to be potentially aware of them not just in their behaviour relevant to some activity we are now engaged in, but also in a "disengaged" way (151).

In talking about things, we in some sense detach ourselves from those things in order to comment upon them. Play-acting cultivates this ability; it is a means by which we can learn the skill of conversation—how to engage with others as distinct others. This requires that we recognize the autonomy of others within our conversational circle, a skill necessary for any form of democratic deliberation.

I would suggest that play can also help students learn social and political observation. Play can nurture the skills necessary for astute spectatorship, and from this, good judgment. In playing roles, in experimenting with the positions of others, students learn, not only disengagement from their immediate interests, but other languages from which they can understand the world. In taking the position of others, they learn both to see from a different vantage point and to articulate what they have seen from that vantage point. They learn a language of "perspicuous contrast," as Taylor calls it, one in which two or more perspectives are weighed by the inquiring student in order for him or her to think about the event more actively (Taylor 1985b, 123-130, 236-244). It is not a kind of Gadamerian "fusion of horizons," however, for the object is not to fuse the perspectives of different observers. Rather it is a matter of comprehending different perspectives in order that one be able to make a balanced judgment about the significance, meaning, and ethical import of a scene or event. In contrasting two or more perspectives, the student learns that impartiality is possible. In comprehending those perspectives perspicuously, the student takes steps toward thinking impartially.

Finally, playing functions as a means by which humans recreate social reality.

> Acting out the social drama we keep pretending that these precarious conventions are eternal verities. We act *as if* there were no other way of being a man, a political subject, a religious devotee or one who exercises a certain profession—yet at times the thought passes through the minds of even the dimmest among us that we could do very, very different things. If social reality is dramatically created, it must also be dramatically malleable (Berger 1963, 138-139).

It is a means by which we can understand our capacity to recreate alternative worlds, which is presumably the first step to doing so. Though more often than not our play carries with it the pretense that something is necessary when it is really the result of our conscious choice or bad will. In playing we can thus learn to accept those eternal verities almost all the time. Indeed, even the "least dim" among us conform to a wide variety of social conventions.

But play reveals the possibility inherent in the human capacity for change. In this sense, playing is a way we learn, not to recreate reality and the world, but to create it. Playing reveals the innate abilities of human beings to innovate and initiate action that was not there before. That the child recreates something he or she sees in his or her life is obvious; what is not always so is the ways in which that play is actually a creation. Children are capable of bringing into existence something that was not there previously—a drama, a narrative, a plot line. Insofar as adults can do the same, we can admire their ability to create the world, and we can use our informed judgment as adults to determine whether or not those creations have social or political significance and value. The creation of worlds is something that actors do, and those people with dramaturgical skills develop powers of giving birth to new activities.

In letting go of oneself, in acting histrionically, in standing outside of one's routine in society, one becomes, literally "ecstatic" (*ekstasis*—the act of standing or stepping outside the taken-for-granted routine of society). The actor, playing a role that is not himself, can transform his or her awareness so that givenness can become possibility. In taking another part than one's own self, one creates for oneself openings to other worlds, and so when one returns to play the part of one's self, one now has enlarged his or her mentality about him or herself and the world at large. This is part of the self-creation of character, a possibility that Goffman, for one, thought restricted to social interaction. Yet humans need not simply adapt themselves to the situations in which they act; they transform, or rather they *form*, themselves by acting.

How they form themselves, not how they transform or reform themselves, in the political world is one subject appropriate to the political scientist. It is a task of the political researcher to explain how the individual human creates the world in which he or she lives, and yet too often we teach our students that it is our task to explain how the world creates the selves that live within it. Trends, hypotheses, modeling, correlation—these are often the tools of researchers who wish to explore how worlds are shaped and reshaped, not how actions create that world. By returning to a classical understanding of theater, I will be arguing that individuals create their own worlds, that this is a proper object for political science, but that it is only so where we are willing to view the disciplines of social science as primarily educational activities, and not as activities of research.

Role-playing creates action where there was none previously, and creating unprecedented action initiates learning. The political researcher employing a dramaturgical perspective comprehends the creative possibilities lodged within action. To do this one must be open to learn from those whose actions create possibilities within the social and political sciences. But, and this is crucial to my argument, those who create possibilities are not simply the researchers/professors/teachers who instruct their students. If all are capable of action, and if all action is a kind of creativity, then we must respect the creativity inherent in the action created by our students. We must learn from our students as they learn from us, and so the enterprise of political and social research ought to be a fundamentally educational one. This will have, as I will argue in the final two chapters, profound implications for the governance and structure of American universities.

Action as Spectacle

In the modern world citizens must be concerned with how stages are constructed, and how people appear in them, for they are important where individuals are permitted to display themselves. Political spaces permit citizens to display themselves in various forms and in various ways, and they permit actors and audience to associate with each other. In theaters public displays and social bonds are momentary—actors, audience, and stage settings appear at one place and at one time, for the next night there will be a different performance, with different participants, possibly in a different venue. The audience members will attend a different play in a different theater. Very few see the same play twice. So it is in politics—citizens, institutions, and history appear only once together, for then citizens transform both institutions and history, and the stage is set for a new performance. Neither history nor institutions ever repeat themselves exactly so citizens are confronted with new stages, new props, and new audiences every day they act. This is an opportunity for citizens to discover their own powers and identities, associate with other actors, and, if they are skillful, impress the critics.

Yet are there conditions of modernity that stage political space in such a way that actors, audience, and stagehands cannot initiate action, portray themselves, or meaningfully associate with others? Where political spaces are representational or where they are constructed spectacles, those spaces frame action as if in a theater. How can one participate in civic space where that civic space has been constructed as a spectacle, where the space itself is representational? Under these conditions is direct action illusory? Citizens believe themselves to be displaying themselves and associating with others, but in fact they take on identities conditioned by that space of representation.

Moreover, spectacles prevent spectators from ever becoming performers— the audience beholds the action before them and cannot participate in that action. During the performance of a spectacle, the audience cannot interrupt the action and redirect its meaning. So actors and spectators are clearly divided. Political action as spectacle is meaningful not for what it achieves but for what it signifies. Consequently, the political spectacle is by definition both undemocratic and theatrical in only a narrow sense of the term. I will argue in chapter 2 that another conception of theater—as Dionysian experience— promises greater participation on the part of spectators. Spectators are audience members whose activities as spectators are essential for the cultivation of collective political judgment.

I am adapting here an argument made by Michel Foucault in *The Order of Things* (1970) and developed by others since its publication. Foucault reveals that his book originated from a reading of Borges, who wrote of a Chinese culture "entirely devoted to the ordering of space, but one that does not distribute the multiplicity of existing things into any of the categories that make it possible for us to name, speak, and think" (xix). In what follows, Foucault analyzes the ordering of Western space through the disciplines of biology, economics, and linguistics. He presents the "system of elements" classifying this space, and looks for the "fundamental codes of a culture" that "establish for every man, from the very first, the empirical orders with which he will be dealing and within which he will be at home" (xx). His study is "an attempt to analyze . . . the pure experience of order and of its modes of being" (xxi). Foucault concludes that in Western thought "representation has lost the power to provide a foundation—with its own being, its own deployment and its power of doubling over on itself—for the links that can join its various elements together" (238). The space of order "which served as a common place for representation and for things . . . is from now on shattered" (239). In its place emerged ideology, which "situates all knowledge in the space of representations, and by scanning that space it formulates the knowledge of the laws that provide its organization . . . [it] superimposes all knowledge upon a representation from whose immediacy one never escapes" (241). Modern theaters are representational orders, and are irreplaceably so.

Timothy Mitchell (1988) supports empirically Foucault's argument through an analysis of colonial Egypt and elaborates Foucault's theory. In examining the European "understanding" of Egypt in the nineteenth century, Mitchell concludes that Europeans represented Egypt in ways that re-made the country in an image they held of themselves. The colonial world was represented, and recreated, as an exhibition, and the French attempted to rationalize Cairo and other cities into a Cartesian order. Mitchell develops Foucault's notions of power and representation and argues that they are compatible with authority and sovereignty of the state (a position Foucault himself never took).

> [D]iscipline and representation are two aspects of the same novel strategies of power, linked by the notion of enframing. Disciplinary powers acquire their unprecedented hold upon the body by methods of distributing and dividing that create an order or structure in which individuals are confined, isolated, combined together and kept under surveillance. This 'order' is, in effect, a framework that seems to precede and exist apart from the actual individuals or objects ordered. The framework, appearing as something pre-existent, non-material and spatial, seems to constitute a separate, metaphysical realm—the realm of the conceptual. It is such 'order' that the modern and colonial state claimed to have introduced into Egypt; what was introduced, with this order, was the effect of the world's division into two realms, the material and the conceptual. In the same way as it divided the world, this division separated the human person into two distinct parts, a body and a mind. The power of representation worked in terms of this correspondence between the division of the world and the division of the person (176-177).

Mitchell's notion of "enframing" describes an ordered space and challenges the belief that politics is about direct action. An enframed space is one that is fundamentally representational and one within which political action must be representational as well. The Foucauldian argument questions whether individual actors can even present themselves on the public stage at all. For maybe in the contemporary world, our public presentations are mere re presentations of who we otherwise are. In this fashion, the Foucauldian position challenges the positions of both Goffman and Sennett that through (theatrical) action we present ourselves to the world, whether as we are or as we would like to be seen.

Take for example the case of Ralph Nader's bid for the Presidency in 1996. Did Nader challenge the American system of political representation in running as the people's candidate? Or, in challenging the system in this fashion did he, however unintentionally, strengthen it? Insofar as he offered an alternative to traditional party politics, Ralph Nader, presidential candidate, legitimated the system of electoral politics that orders American public space. Indeed, in 1996, he presented himself to others as the "non-candidate," and thus provided voters with the opportunity to register an objection to Clinton, Dole, and Perot. But this was only *possible* because Nader himself adapted the consumer and environmental movements to representative, and not direct, democracy.

Certainly Nader's candidacy exemplifies a challenge to the system of electoral representation but it also reinforced a system of political representation that itself represents politics. Similarly, "anti-system" groups in Canada, such as Alliance Quebec, have not only run candidates in Quebec elections, but they have also promoted themselves in mainstream media outlets, such as *Maclean's*, and to institutional powers such as the Congress of the United States and Wall Street.[7] Alliance Quebec has, in short, worked within the enframed institutional order of North American politics, as well as sought to represent itself to the (anglophone) electorate in certain ways. Thus it, too, plays the game of representation, and *dis*plays itself in the Quebecois theater of politics.

Murray Edelman (1988) has expressed "enframing" in terms of the construction of political spectacles. He rightly challenges the possibility of a theatrical space where people can appear as themselves, or as they *want* to be seen in modern politics. Most people do not even try to appear on the political stage.

> Most of the world's population, even most of the population of the 'advanced countries,' has no incentive to define joy, failure, or hope in terms of public affairs. Politics and political news are remote, not often interesting, and for the most part irrelevant. This indifference of 'the masses' to the enthusiasms and fears of people who thrive on public attention to political matters is the despair of the latter group (6-7).

Edelman is skeptical about the prospects for true politics in the modern age and laments its increasing irrelevancy. But he applauds those citizens who do not participate and who abdicate "power" because in refusing to attend to the desires of their representatives they subvert the power of those representatives. He argues that indifference is "a paramount political force," and that it has prevented mass slaughter and terror, as well as having permitted it (8). For this reason, Edelman argues, it is important to recognize that political symbols construct what I have (following Mitchell) called an enframed, or representational, space.[8]

Here we have a serious challenge to a dramaturgical theory of political space. For such spaces might be symbolic, in which case actors present themselves symbolically (and thus merely representationally). Edelman's theory presents a problem to the modern actor: how does one engage in theatrical political action within a public realm that is constructed spectacle? In Sennett's terms, how does the actor maintain his art in a constructed spectacle? Must not his or her very action be representational itself? For example, how is the citizen to be sure that direct action is not just another representational position within the broader public realm, a realm that is viewed indifferently by those citizens because it too is perceived as merely symbolic? How are citizens to associate with others whose purpose may be to simply further their own material interests?[9] The citizen searching for civic friendship must always be aware that his or her fellow citizens necessarily "misrepresent" themselves because on a representational stage of politics, they cannot present who they are, but portray themselves as something. They don a mask. For their part, why are political elites in, for example, the Democratic Leadership Council or the Commission on National and Community Service, to be taken seriously by either the public or politicians and bureaucrats? In both organizations, politicians perceive themselves to be engaged in a "revolutionary" struggle of resistance against entrenched (political and bureaucratic) interests. So how are citizens to understand the "reality" of their public displays when elite politics itself is part of an ordered world of appearance?

Where politics has become representational and symbolic, what permits individuals to appear as themselves? How do citizens truly appear in a space that is already enframed? The challenge is to disrupt the order and thus an order to appearance.[10] Yet without participating in public action of the kind offered by the consumer, feminist, and environmental movements, how can we be sure that these disruptions will be political? In theatrical terms, how can citizens act without being accused of merely acting? Where they are *all* actors, where they all place similar masks in front of their faces, differences between citizens are effaced, and their plurality becomes irrelevant. Yet it is in action that citizens differentiate themselves from each other, express their plurality, and create the possibility for civic friendship and association. How can citizens maintain political equality, and retain the distinctive, plural nature of the public theater at the same time? This is the dilemma presented by the dramaturgical theory of politics.

But this is also the potential inherent in postmodern approaches to politics. For the work of scholars such as Foucault or Edelman create for the student the spectacle of politics. In *Discipline and Punish*, for instance, Foucault sets stages, literally, of men being drawn-and-quartered, or prison activity, and so on. These stages serve a heuristic purpose of exemplifying to the student framed political action, action on a stage, so to speak. I will argue in the next chapter that the sorts of stages with which we are familiar in the modern world are not the only kinds. If we were to consider classical notions of theatrical action we might consider other sorts of political action as possible. For classical theater can teach us not another way of looking at performance, but another way of looking at politics. As political scientists we examine ways in which we can teach others how to look at politics.

I will try to argue, in contrast to, for instance, Edelman's argument presented here, that viewing the political spectacle need not be equated with passivity. I will make the claim that there is a positive, civic role in helping students learn how to be spectators of the political theater, and that teaching political thinking is a means to encourage good citizenship. I have already indicated the first lines of this argument—namely that in being a political spectator, one is in a position to be impartial and to make judgments about the fairness or ethical content of policies. This does not mean that people are impartial or that they analyze judiciously what they see, but that they place themselves in relationship to the action in a position that is necessary (if not sufficient) for sound judgment. For in observing politics, they must first disengage themselves from the play of politics, and this permits them to perceive the play in its entirety.[11] To teach disengagement or observation is not to teach passivity, however, and I shall try to make this distinction in chapters 3, 6, and 7.

Political Theater and the Space to Appear

To anyone even remotely familiar with her work, it will be obvious how much I have been influenced by Hannah Arendt in these pages. So much has been (and is still being) written on Arendt's ideas that it is daunting to even consider presenting yet another interpretation. My fear is, to appropriate her metaphor for Benjamin's method (Arendt 1968b, 193), that in diving for pearls I will find that the ocean floor has been scavenged and no oysters remain. Yet I have found that one can read her works repeatedly and by doing so, find the ocean floor re-bedded almost infinitely.

In this book I want to bring together a number of ideas gleaned from her pages and combine them with concerns that I have developed as both a graduate student in, and now professor of, political science. I emphasized these repeatedly in the pages above: impartiality, judgment, political learning, "scientific" learning, and the structure and governance of higher education, at least in the social and political sciences. As both a student and teacher of political science I have been interested in, and have become troubled by, certain understandings political scientists have concerning the vocation of college teaching. I do not mean to suggest that there is a crisis in higher education, that is too dramatic a term. But I share the concerns of many both inside and outside the university community that the practice of teaching has been denigrated unfairly by institutions that purport to be educational.

My general argument in the book is as follows: higher education in the social and political sciences ought to focus more consistently on teaching both undergraduate and graduate students how to make fair, reasonable, and effective political judgments. In making these sorts of judgments, students will learn both how to be more active, more informed citizens, as well as how to be more active, more informed observers of political life. The two educational tasks are inseparable, and good civic judgment, a prerequisite for political action, depends on how observant students can be of politics. This will permit those students to be more effective and reasonable teachers of the art (and maybe science) of politics. But observing politics is quite like observing live theater, and it behooves political scientists, or any academic concerned with cultivating good citizenship, to at least present politics to their students as a theatrical art. I am not claiming that politics is only theater, or that only a theatrical understanding of politics helps create citizens. I am suggesting that political judgment, as a characteristic of citizenship, can be fostered by analogizing politics to theater. In theater, as in politics, actors learn to play roles, and role-playing contributes to political thinking (and therefore, following Arendt, judgment).

As an example, let us take an object of political science research—say the Canadian parliament. A traditionally empirical political scientist will look at the structures, functions, offices, rules, folkways, and behavior of legislators in the parliament. A formal political scientist might model political behavior in parliament along game-theoretic lines. A postmodern political scientist might examine discourses that emerge from that parliament. All of these political scientists may be concerned with, say, how power is accumulated, distributed, mapped, or produced by and among parliamentarians. All of their methods bring a good deal of insight into the ways in which Canadian parliamentarians act politically.

Following Arendt, however, I would present a vision of the Canadian parliament as a theater of performance. I, too, might consider power to be an object of the performers, but in this case power is revealed as performers display themselves. On this Arendtian model, power does not come from, say, examining in whose interests a bill is passed, or in how parliamentarians work the spoils system, or even in how the discourse of the parliamentarian represents power to a disengaged public. Rather power generates itself in the ways in which one can display oneself, as well as in the ways one associates with other parliamentarians as actors (and spectators) do in a theater. Ultimately, this perspective may not be more meaningful or truthful than any of the others. But, I am arguing here, it serves an important pedagogical function because it teaches the student to observe actors performing and spectators observing. It imagines Canadian parliamentary politics as, not a stage, but a theater,[12] where actors and spectators meet, engage, and disengage with each other. It presents politics in a heuristic manner, as a means of educating students toward political thinking and ultimately judgment. By presenting the Canadian parliament as a theater, students are permitted to view the institution in a variety of fashions, much as different vantage points in the theater afford spectators different sights.

For instance, we can perceive parliamentary action as dynamic interplay between regional and linguistic protagonists and antagonists, as a spectacle where native legislators dramatize their communal concerns, as a theater dwarfed by the larger theater to the south. As students any or all of these dramaturgical perspectives (and there are certainly more than these), they can learn not only the facts of Canadian parliamentary politics, but how to imagine the ways in which parliamentarians act by acting out themselves the drama either in their minds, on paper, or in the classroom. Higher education can teach students—as spectators—to take a different seat each time they watch the performance, and it can also teach them to engage with the actors in much the same way classical audiences enjoyed the Theater of Dionysos. Professors can help students learn what Arendt, following Kant, called "enlarged mentality"— the capacity of the thinker to consider the position of others in rendering informed judgment on a topic. This capacity I believe to be the end of an education in political science, and a fundamental consideration in the teaching of any social science.[13]

Consequently, I imagine Arendt's method, not as a means of coordinating a research program or agenda (in either the Kuhnian or Lakatosian senses of these terms), but as a means of incorporating research and political analysis into a pedagogical "agenda." I am suggesting that Arendt's insights recommend to the political and social scientist ideas by which they can think about and communicate ideas, but more importantly facts, with which they concern themselves. Moreover, this way of thinking emphasizes learning in a Socratic manner—understanding how teachers can help students draw out knowledge by exposing them to facts and ideas and by posing examples from which they can make sound judgments. I am not proposing, then, a new methodology by which social and political scientists can frame their theories and hypotheses. I am considering ways in which teachers help students create meaning concerning action.

I will make this argument by interpreting Arendt's ideas in a particular manner. Her work teaches us the importance of a theatrical approach to political science, she has something to contribute to the so-called methodology of political science; and we can recreate this methodology in the examination of case studies. In chapter 2, I introduce an important Arendtian concept concerning political action, the "space of appearance," and argue that we can root this concept in her classical understanding of theater. In remembering the classical roots to her understanding of theater, I hope to clarify contemporary debates concerning her theory of political action and the public realm (though I leave this to the Appendix). In chapters 3 and 4, I note that Arendt approaches her political studies with the eye of a reporter, but a particular kind of reporter— a theater critic. In *Eichmann in Jerusalem*, and to a lesser degree *On Revolution*, I see a kind of nascent method of political reportage and criticism. More importantly, I emphasize lessons that we can draw from these analyses in teaching our students how to observe and judge political action. In learning from Arendt's later work, most prominently *The Life of the Mind*, I argue that political thinking has something to do with judgment which has something to do with good citizenship.

Political judgment and citizenship ought to be central public concerns for institutions of higher learning, and in chapters 5 through 8, I connect these concerns to the three pillars of such institutions—research, teaching, and service. In chapter 6 I give an empirical example of at least one kind of Arendtian research method[14] in comparative politics and international relations. In chapter 7, I consider some broader questions concerning strategies of graduate and undergraduate education in the social and political sciences, and their implications for classroom pedagogy. I connect these issues with the creation of civic virtue among university students. In which ways can university students exercise good judgment and civic responsibility in the university community? Finally, in chapter 8, I discuss the issue of community service for professors and students, and re-think its political grounds, based on Arendt's theory of the space of appearance, not a communitarian or civic republican conception. Thinking in Arendtian terms, higher education can reconceptualize its pillars—research, teaching, and service—and integrate them by creating sometimes radically different institutional structures, but structures that might help people learn and exercise political judgment.

Notes

1. Contemporary theorists, following Aristotle, have commented on the close relationship between political theory and theater. Both, for instance, are concerned with identity and community—how one comes to understand and encounter oneself in the presence of others. Both also concern "self-contained action." Dana Villa (1996, 17ff) claims that this fact permits an analogy to be made between theater and political action, while Tracy Strong (1990, 46) argues that ordinary life is not self-contained, but that we are attracted to theater because it is self-contained. Theater's appeal is many-sided, but primarily it shows us something accomplished and performed, and so transcends ordinary life. This can show us the "true meaning" of activities in which we engage (Strong 1990, 49). In Strong's words "drama...makes available a world about which all questions can be answered and in which we see the perfection of our reasons and understanding" (50). We are attracted to perfection.

This may or may not be true. After all, many theatergoers attend bad performances religiously, or enjoy drama that does not answer questions, but leaves us hanging, or takes us away from a consideration of our own lives because that has become too boring, or difficult, or painful for us to do. We ought to value theater not because it answers questions, but because it raises them. It introduces us to ideas or perspectives we had not yet considered previously, and which may in fact trouble us. This demands that we learn other ways of viewing the world. Consequently, attending dramatic performance cultivates our skills of impartiality and judgment, whose political relevance is most evident in the art of citizenship.

For example, Strong sees Oedipus as a character who has perfected himself by recognizing himself at the end of the play (52), and that in the presence of perfection, the audience admires this awakening. Yet one could interpret the Oedipus drama as a display of imperfection, in which the audience is relieved to experience its own distance from the troubles Oedipus brings upon himself. It is the fact that multiple interpretations are open to the audience member that makes theater relevant for politics and political theory. Because, in attending the performance, the spectator learns how to judge the play. The theater may help individuals recognize themselves and others as persons, but the *political* importance of this is obscured by the civic importance of learning how to think about performance itself. I elaborate this argument throughout chapters 1 and 2.

2. Tracy Strong (1990) claims that political theory and theater have been hostile to each other historically: "But what is the source of the age-old hostility of political theory to drama?" (40). Yet is this conflict truly "age-old"? After all, Plato wrote in the form of dialogues, Aristotle lectured on aesthetics and politics, Cicero presented "characters" in his works, and Machiavelli wrote farces. Certainly Rousseau criticized theater, but was "lured" by aesthetics nonetheless in writing *Emile* and *Julie, ou la Nouvelle Héloise* as narratives. Politicians are often threatened by theater, individual political theorists have critiqued the theater, but whether political *theory* is antagonistic to it is another question.

3. "The justification for this approach...is that the illustrations together fit into a coherent framework that ties together bits of experience the reader has already had and provides the student with a guide worth testing in case studies of institutional social life" (Goffman 1959, xii).

4. And, consequently, his own research method. Consider the problem that if Goffman as a sociological observer of the Shetland Island crofting community is also an actor, he, like the members of the community he observes, engages in theatrical behavior. If the members of that community knew this, would they alter their behavior to either influence or accommodate Goffman in this case? For whatever reason, members of the crofting community might have become, in Goffman's terms, either discrepant role-players or actors who caused Goffman, in his role as a researcher, to communicate out of character. This in turn would make it difficult, if not impossible, for him to get a true reading of the play of the community. Social scientists have termed this the Hawthorne Effect.

5. Sennett's reading of Goffman is not always so accurate. He complains on the very same page that Goffman has "no ear for, indeed no interest in, the forces of disorder, disruption, and change which might intervene in" the arrangements of society. Clearly Goffman's treatment of discrepant roles and communication out of character refutes this claim. Goffman has an eye for disorder and disruption, but his theory does not describe the ways in which people learn from these disruptions. Learning helps actors not simply to manage future scenes more effectively, but transform the very situation in which they find themselves. It also permits them to develop more sophisticated means of impression management.

6. Sennett (1974) comments that we have lost our ability to play in the modern world and that this retards the development of the self. "To lose the ability to play is to lose the sense that worldly conditions are plastic. The ability to play with social life depends on the existence of a dimension of society which stands apart from, at a distance from, intimate desire, need, and identity. . . . The ability to be expressive is at a fundamental level cut, because one tries to make one's appearances represent who one is, to join the question of effective expression to the issue of authenticity of expression. Under these conditions, everything returns to motive: Is this what I really feel? Do I really mean it? Am I being genuine? . . . Expression is made contingent upon authentic feeling, but one is always plunged into the narcissistic problem of never being able to crystallize what is authentic in one's feelings" (267). Without play, then, individuals are in danger of being thrown back into (or of never growing out of) a condition of primary narcissism. Sennett contends that adults who have lost the skill of playing withdraw from sociability into themselves, into a narcissistic attempt at discovering their deeper selves. This deprives the actor of his art, of his skills as an actor.

The political symptoms of this are twofold (327-340): (1) the rise of a technical, bureaucratic class that defines itself as a part of large institutions. Bureaucracies are then enlarged for the purposes of self-promotion, not functional selection. Functionaries are also promoted on the basis of their "people" skills—their ability to be intimate with others, not on their ability to labor. The corporate experience pacifies men and women into receiving the actions of their institution, and rarely challenge its rules. This is the opposite of children at play, individuals who are constantly testing and challenging rules. (2) The rise of a new Protestant ethic, which escalates our expectations so that our present behavior is never fulfilling, and this makes us fear that we will never achieve closure. In both symptoms, a basic narcissism triggers ascetic thoughts and practices.

The problem with Sennett's claim here is historical. Clearly both these symptoms could easily apply to industrial and even pre-industrial societies. Bureaucracies pre-date the 1840s and industrial workers were often as passive as service sector workers are today. Indeed, given the strength of service sector unions in many countries of Western Europe, his claim that bureaucrats are passive in relation to their industrial forefathers is questionable. Though industrial workers are not promoted on their people skills, they are promoted on their "obedience" skills—namely, their willingness not to combat the employing class. Furthermore, what differentiates a new Protestant ethic from an old one? Bureaucracies are also not necessarily narcissistic, given the ethic of service upon which they are theoretically based. Rather contemporary bureaucracy, as Weber was the earliest to note, conditions us to follow rules thoughtlessly. This enervates our capacity for creative thinking, and thus creative action (a function of action-as-play that I discuss below). Where creative action is weakened, the human ability to innovate is weakened as well

This, I would argue, is a greater danger to our undergraduate and graduate students than instilling narcissistic behavior in them, for it is this capacity to create that may in fact teach them how to think and act independently. This is a threat to many faculties, because thinking independently endangers the social system upon which much of higher education is based, namely the ability of the graduate student, for instance, to "get along" with his or her advisor or advisors. Thinking and acting independently can often disrupt otherwise "harmonious" graduate school training.

7.   *Maclean's*, 23 September 1996, 18-19; *Maclean's*, 7 October 1996, 38-39.

8.   Edelman (1988) employs examples from a variety of political topics to illustrate his point—social problems, political leadership, the enemy, news, and political language. Political concerns in all of these subjects are constructed spectacles.

9   Or in Benhabib's (1996) terms how do citizens avoid a public space "constituted by an anonymous public conversation taking place in multiple spaces in society and in which potentially infinite voices can participate"? (204). How are democratic deliberation and political learning possible among a faceless public in either an undifferentiated or radically differentiated space? How is deliberation possible where either space is formed representationally—where people are not permitted to appear to others as other appear to them, but where they represent themselves as something other than they are? In short, how can we understand political spaces where people do not always appear to be what they are, or more pointedly, what they seem?

10.   Such has been the task of postmodernism, and theorists such as Foucault, Lyotard, and Derrida (Villa 1992b, Honig 1993).

11.   I have already suggested above that it is important for people to have learned how to play in childhood in order that they be able to disengage. A political analogy might be drawn here—namely, that it is important for the political spectator to have engaged in political action at certain points in his or her life, in order to be able to take the position of others that one meets while engaging in such action. It teaches that actor, following Taylor, how to disengage him or herself from the action. So political action may also be a necessary, if not sufficient, condition for political spectatorship.

12.   Consequently, I do not consider the actual Parliament buildings in Ottawa as the only scene of parliamentary politics or governance. The theater includes spectators who engage with the parliamentary actors—namely, the media, interest groups, and the general citizenry.

13.   See Jun-ichi Kyogoku, *The Political Dynamics of Japan*, Nobutaka Ike, trans. (Tokyo: University of Tokyo Press, 1987): 37-95. At the time of publication, Kyogoku was both an actor and spectator in Japanese politics, and he examined it in dramaturgical terms. In so doing, he presents different "codes" and "paradigms" to the reader (in theatrical terms, scenarios and role-playing). This permits the reader to develop his or her own judgment about Japanese politics—something Kyogoku intends (150-152).

14. I do not claim that there is only one method of political understanding that can be gleaned from Arendt's work. Indeed, a variety of scholars have explored other avenues (e.g., Disch 1994, Pirro 1996, Gottsegen 1994, Benhabib 1996).

Chapter 2

The Theater of Politics and the Space of Appearance

Though she asked "what is freedom?" in a famous essay, Hannah Arendt also asked "where is freedom?" and "when is freedom?" throughout her work. In reply, she pointed to particular eras and locations where freedom ruled, places she termed "spaces of appearance."[1] Spaces of appearance were rare in history, though celebrated—for example, they existed in fifth century Athens, during the American Revolution, and the Hungarian Revolution of 1956. They are characterized by human action, and they permit human beings, as citizens, to present and represent themselves to others and to participate in the creation of human immortality. They are spaces where humans can be free existentially in place, as well as in time. Spaces of appearance, then, are the geographical location of those activities in which human beings build civic relationships that transcend the particular time that each human being is on the earth. They are places where citizens may express themselves directly over time and initiate collective action that sustains itself over a certain history and geography. They are the places, and the moments, when the history and geography of citizenship merge, unite, and reproduce themselves.

But the notion of a space of appearance is not as simple as all this. For at what point does a space emerge? How do people, as citizens, appear, and appear to each other? When does an appearance count as an appearance, and at what point do appearances end? What is the relationship between the where and the when of appearance? How can one visualize a political space, and can one visualize a space without reference to a specific historical/geographical instance or without recourse to metaphor? How does our understanding of history and geography, and our representation of language, influence the way we can comprehend a space of appearance?

I hope to explore at least some of these questions in this chapter. Employing Arendt's metaphor of the theater, I will suggest that a dramaturgical representation of the space of appearance accounts for plurality in her theory, and that the concept of theatrical space permits theorists to apply Arendt's notion to the real world of politics. I root her understanding of theater in her understanding of classical Greek theater and observe that her concept of the space of appearance is colored by that understanding, if not derived from it. But it is an understanding of politics that can be useful to political and social scientists because it represents the political world in an innovative manner. Such representation lends itself to a sort of analysis different from the type normally practiced in these disciplines. I will elaborate this analysis in chapter 3. In the appendix, I discuss the relevance of the classical conception of the space of appearance to contemporary disputes over the meaning of her concept, and I advise readers interested in the academic drama that has played out over this term to look there for explanation and argument concerning it.

The Political Ontology of the Stage of Appearance

What is appearance? How does one appear? Politically, how does one present oneself as a citizen? Arendt, though concerned with the concept for most of her intellectual life, actually wrote about it most pointedly during the late 1950s and the early 1960s. Her reflections on appearance are developed most thoroughly in "What is Freedom?" (Arendt 1961, 151-156) and *The Human Condition* (Arendt 1958b, 155-223). I want to examine the concept of appearance, and its relevance to politics, in these texts and suggest continuities and differences in Arendt's thinking on this matter through the 1960s.

Political space is free space. Free actions transcend both motives and goals, and thus are independent of the will or the notion of choice. Freedom is specifically that which calls "something into being which did not exist before" (Arendt 1961, 151). Following Montesquieu, Arendt argues that political action originates in principles that inspire from outside the human will and that become "fully manifest only in the performing act itself" (152). Indeed, action manifests principles only so long as that action lasts, and no longer. Montesquieu distinguished between these types of principles while categorizing governments as monarchical, aristocratic, or republican and noted that they were guided by honor, glory, love of equality, distinction, or excellence. Corrupt governments were characterized by principles such as fear, hatred, or distrust. Freedom appears where citizens perform political action, for this permits principles, as virtues, to be actualized (Arendt 1968b, 9; see also Canovan 1992, 205-208, and Heather and Stolz 1979, 11).

Because freedom demands the very performance of an act (and is irrelevant to its motive or purpose), its accomplishment requires virtuosity, "an excellence we attribute to the performing arts" (Arendt 1961, 153). Consequently, Arendt characterizes politics metaphorically as art, and political institutions require the ongoing practice of the political arts, upon performance. In the creative arts freedom does not appear in public, because the sculptor, composer, or novelist does not create in public. Nor does that creative artist reveal the freedom with which he or she accomplishes the act of creation.[2] On the other hand, the performing arts require the presence of others to show their art and the process of creation itself. Actors, musicians, and dancers must be present before others to perform and rely on a publicly organized space for their art to appear. Citizens, like performance artists, require spaces of appearance to create freedom and to express the actions which are their own purposes, and the earliest political space was the Greek polis. The Greek polis was theater, the space in which free acts were permitted and encouraged to display themselves. The end of the polis was, thus, "to establish and keep in existence a space where freedom as virtuosity can appear" (154), and those actions remaining outside the polis were, by definition, non-political. Ironically, but also tellingly, Arendt recognizes foreign affairs as the only "purely political" domain extant in the modern world—ironic because in ancient Greek times foreign affairs were outside the polis and thus extrapolitical, telling because this domain is often referred to as "theater" (e.g., the nuclear theater, the European theater, the Asian theater, etc.).

Who is the actor? George Kateb (1977) depicts him or her in three ways: as performer, as persona, and as principled liberator. The actor, by displaying virtuosity, "reveals himself as a distinctive performer" who is "less deliberate, more self-surprising, and more personal" than the other two depictions (150). The actor is also one who hides certain things about him or herself in order to reveal other things about his or her identity, and so dons a mask. Here the actor plays a persona. We don masks, Kateb argues, to appear composed so that the truth of our words may resound on other actors (151).[3] Here one is more deliberate, less spontaneous, and imbued with what I term below "civility." Finally, Kateb argues that the political actor can "escape the self" and act from principle in a depersonalized way. These Montesquieuan principles differ in different spaces. Thus, political actors themselves play different roles and act out their parts within different spaces. Political acting is a plural enterprise.

All political performance, however, requires courage, "demanded of us by the very nature of the public realm" (Arendt 1961, 156). For in politics,

> it requires courage to leave the protective security of [our private domain] and enter the public realm, not because of particular dangers which may lie in wait for us, but because we have arrived in a realm where the concern for life has lost its validity. Courage liberates men from their worry about life for the freedom of the world. Courage is indispensable because in politics not life but the world is at stake (156, see also 166).

The analogy to theater remains, for the one thing preventing the performer from appearing is stage-fright. This must be overcome not by denying one's insecurities about appearing on stage, not because there is actual danger out there in front of hundreds, possibly thousands. But because the show must go on, the very existence of the theater rests on the performance, and the actor must draw on a great deal of courage to perform.

In politics, then, appearance is constituted by those actions, freely taken, characterized by performance. The space in which this takes place can be analogized to a theater. Indeed, this is how Arendt develops her argument in *The Human Condition* (1958b). She begins her discussion of action by suggesting that the agent discloses him or herself in speech and action, yet does so on a "stage" of human plurality and otherness (*alteritas*). By acting within a theater of diverse human beings we reveal our own uniqueness,[4] we "set something in motion," we take initiative, we begin. By inserting ourselves into the human drama we enact our own creativity, and for this reason Arendt considers "natality" to be a fundamental condition of humanity.[5] Action and speech are revelatory, however; they disclose who we are, our identity (Honig 1993 and 1995). Indeed, just as in theater action is, and must be, accompanied by speech, for

> speechless action would no longer be action because there would no longer be an actor, and the actor, the doer of deeds, is possible only if he is at the same time the speaker of words. The action he begins is humanly disclosed by the word, and though his deed can be perceived in its brute physical appearance without verbal accompaniment, it becomes relevant only through the spoken word in which he identifies himself as the actor, announcing what he does, has done, and intends to do (Arendt 1958b, 158).

This characterized, if not all theater or acting, then at least classical theater, which relied on characters articulating their positions to make sense out of the themes or purposes of the drama. In identifying him or herself, the political actor displays who, and not merely what, he or she is, and that identification occurs in a space "where people are with others and neither for nor against them—that is, in sheer human togetherness" (160). Again, this space can be something like a theater where people are brought together, not as friends or enemies, but as participants in a common experience, in the "roles" of actors, stagehands, and audience. For its full appearance action needs "the shining brightness we once called glory" (160), and the act of glorification is the finding of a "who," that "identifiable somebody." The presence of an excellence such as glory serves as the sort of lighting for the stage (Arendt 1968b, viii); thus Montesquieuian virtue contributes to the recognition of identity, if not its creation.

Actions produce stories that are their own purposes. Though these stories may be recorded for posterity, "they are not products" (164), and the agent is neither author[6] nor producer. Each human life is also the result of action, and this gives rise to the "great perplexity" that has baffled political philosophy from its beginning in antiquity—that though we can identify an agent who initiated action, a story, we cannot point to that agent as the author of the story's outcome. Between the time of its creation and resolution that story has been transformed by the stories and the actions of other actors. The story can be "represented and 'reified' only through a kind of repetition, the imitation or *mimesis*, which according to Aristotle prevails in all arts but is actually appropriate to the *drama*." The story, the play, "comes fully to life only when it is enacted in the theater," and its direct and universal meaning is revealed by the chorus in Greek theater,[7] while the identities of the characters can only be conveyed through an imitation of their acting. This is why, Arendt insists, "the theater is the political art par excellence; only there is the political sphere of human life transposed into art. By the same token, it is the only art whose sole subject is man in his relationship to others" (167). The space of appearance, then, is best analogized to a theater, even a stage of appearance, but most directly to the theater of classical antiquity.

As actors, citizens in ancient Greece sought to leave behind a story and an identity which would bring them immortal fame. Acting was performed in an agonal spirit, "the passionate drive to show one's self in measuring up against others" (173). Indeed as statesmen, citizens "acted like craftsmen," and lawmaking was analogized to city building. But both city builders and lawmakers were actors, and their tasks were brought together by the theater. Thus the "work" of citizens—the laws made and the civic institutions built— were a product, but a product made possible by action itself, actions whose own meanings are destroyed in the acting. Fame was achieved and meaningful action was made possible in ancient Greece through the polis. The polis multiplied the opportunities to disclose oneself, win fame, and be immortalized; it offered "a remedy for the futility of action and speech" (176). The polis became a stage of remembrance, a theater where both actors and audience left without forgetting the drama that had just been presented and without forgetting their own experiences at that theater. The polis was that space between participants "which can find its proper location almost any time and anywhere. It is the space of appearance . . . where I appear to others as others appear to me, where men . . . make their appearance explicitly" (177).

Political action, then, is worldly theater, a drama that may occur at any place where citizens meet and at any time individuals think and conduct themselves as citizens. To Arendt, then, politics is theater because actors disclose themselves on stage as citizens do in the polis, and actors and citizens can disclose themselves in various ways and in different venues. Just as there are multiple stages for actors to portray a self, so there are multiple spaces for citizens to present and re-present themselves. Spaces of appearance, then, are fundamentally plural because they *can* be located "anytime and anywhere." Because "this space does not always exist" (177), individuals are not always citizens, just as dramatic actors are not always in plays. Moreover, each play possesses a distinct narrative, actors take on different roles, stages are designed differently, members of the audience do not always take the same seats nor are they always in theaters that are built exactly alike. So it is for politics.[8] Political space changes not only its content but also its form each time citizens act together.[9]

The space of appearance, then, pre-forms all "constitution of the public realm and the various forms of government"; it is a potentiality that sometimes realizes itself but always disappears as citizens disperse (178). According to Arendt, power, as potentiality, keeps this space in existence, but only actualizes that space, and does not fully materialize it. The space of appearance is called to existence by the power of citizens acting together, but it is always exhausting itself in the process, and as soon as those citizens choose not to act, as soon as they retire from acting, that space will dissemble itself. Theatrical and political spaces are momentary.

They are also spaces that fill and empty simultaneously—political space places itself between citizens by bringing them together and separating them at the same time. This, I would argue, requires "civility"—that glue or bond cementing society. But in bonding people together, civility keeps people apart; for to be civil means to at once be willing to participate in society, to respect others as fellow citizens, but also to keep one's fellow citizens at arm's length.[10] To be "civil" to another means to recognize that other as worthy of toleration, but it also implies that one recognizes the other as a separate individual and that that separation is both good and necessary for political community. For to be "civil" is not necessarily to be friendly, welcoming, or nurturing.[11] Civility creates associational friendship within the polis and arises or emerges where citizens empower themselves and each other through political action.[12] Power, in the form of civility, is "what keeps people together after the fleeting moment of action has passed," and by remaining together citizens keep power alive, and with it, civility, the political virtue apposite to citizenship (180). In doing so, the space of appearance is both full and empty; it is a space that unites people as well as separates them.[13]

Tyranny, which attempts to substitute violence for power, destroys civil society and the public realm by eliminating spaces where people can both come together and hold each other at a distance. In mass society individuals have great difficulty both connecting with others and maintaining their individuality. This situation permits pathological, totalitarian governments to rule, for these sorts of governments abolish the public realm. Arendt traces this calamity, in part, to utopian thinking, which originated in Plato's substitution of making for acting where he provided "blueprints for action" (203), and argues that we ought to view politics, not as product or process, but as the capacity for human initiative to make possible a realm where people can aspire to immortal fame.[14]

This, she concludes, is possible because humans possess the power to forgive and the power to promise. Promising is "the force that keeps [citizens] together" within the space of appearance (220), while forgiveness, in the political form of respect, keeps a regard for citizens "from the distance which the space of the world puts between" them. Forgiveness and promising, then, are those human capacities that, in spite of all possible crises, may create, and sustain, the space of appearance. They bring people together, yet permit individuality and separateness.[15] They allow humans to act and through action to create miracles that will destroy tyranny (222). Consequently, they are essential to maintain the plurality of human spaces, to permit actors to portray themselves in the theaters of their choice.[16]

The theater can only be comprehended, in its entirety, by the spectator, and this is the role of the theorist. One must withdraw from the space of appearance to understand its significance: "only the spectator, never the actor, can know and understand whatever offers itself as spectacle" (Arendt 1978, 92). The scholar abstains from ordinary activities determined by our daily wants in order to leisurely observe human action. Thus the term "theory" implies looking upon something from the outside, "from a position . . . that is hidden" from the actors themselves (93). Only the spectator occupies a position that permits him or her to see the entire play and is the only one who can understand the play's meaning. The actor himself is only a part of the play, and thus does not possess the perspective necessary to comprehend its total significance. The political theorist plays the role of the drama critic, who steps outside the theatrical space in order to judge the meaning of the space and spaces generally.

But the spectator, in another theater, can become an actor; we are both actors and spectators because we disclose ourselves and interpret the meaning of the world on the multiple stages in which we choose to appear or observe (Biskowski 1993, 872). Sandra Hinchman (1984) argues that spectators, by judging, influence the action itself; actors who are watched while acting are disinclined to do beastly things (333). Where an actor knows he or she is being observed, then he or she will try to give his or her best performance. Tracy Strong (1990) notes that the audience actualizes the performance, by recognizing the speech and action of the dramatis personae. "[It] is the *acknowledgment of the performance* of the action by the other that gives it actuality. You have to show me. . . . Then there is a 'we'" (53). Thus, spectators[17] do indeed act, and shape, the actions on the stage (see also Taminiaux 1996, 220).

The Classical Theater of Appearance

A dramaturgical theory of the space of appearance emphasizes the plural nature of the classical theater. The theater of ancient Greece reflected an interplay between actors, audience, and chorus to a greater degree than occurs today, and such interplay enabled the space of the theater to take on different forms. That theater could be public spectacle, civic stage, and performance scene. While theaters can function like that today, the technical devices of the classical theater (e.g., *parabasis*, its emphasis on oratory or delivery) and its conditions (e.g., festival judging, stadium construction) rendered the theatrical experience both dramatic and participatory, agonal and deliberative. Arendt assumes the plural nature of the classical theater, and this gives rise to some of the interpretive battles over, not merely her intention, but the significance of her theory of the space of appearance (see the appendix).

Arendt admired most things classical, and her references to theater in *The Human Condition* are classical as well (Arendt 1958b, 149, 166-167, 169, 172-

173, 307 n. 8, 353 n. 18, 354 n. 33). Indeed, it is remarkable how few, if any, citations of non-Greek theater Arendt offers in characterizing the performing arts.[18] We know how central the arts were, not merely to her conception of action, but to the very heart of justice and, ultimately, judgment (Arendt 1961, 210). Arendt, in her lectures on Kant's philosophy, highlights the importance of taste in judgment, and there is good reason to believe that she would have developed an argument along these lines in the final part of *The Life of the Mind*, had she lived to complete it (for a hint of this, see Arendt 1961, 222). Finally, we know that Arendt most certainly did not mean the crafts, or even what Nietzsche (1993) called the Apollonian arts, in analogizing politics to art (Arendt 1961, 217). Clearly Arendt looked to Greek theater (and possibly, following Nietzsche, to its origins in music) as the artistic paradigm for politics.[19]

What might she have seen in looking at the Greek stage, in the Theater of Dionysos? What could the City Dionysia and its rural counterparts teach her? I will argue that, whether she realized it or not, the metaphor of the theater was useful because it represented performances and events that displayed themselves in a variety of ways. The striking characteristic of Greek theater was that it was so difficult to characterize, as the multifarious debates over its nature can surely attest.[20] But this difficulty strengthens Arendt's analogy, because were one to observe a theatrical performance, one might very well observe politics.

The space of theatrical appearance was plural. By this I mean that Greeks performed both in various spaces throughout Attica and in varied theatrical venues. However Greek theater emerged—through religious ritual, through dance and music, through a broader performance culture, or through the tradition of Homeric bards—by the fifth-century B.C. Greeks were performing not only in Athens, but at theaters across the peninsula. In the sixth-century B.C. there is evidence suggesting that these performances were often held in the agora and in the city and village streets of the Dionysian festivals. During these festivals avid theatergoers would attend many different performances, often spending days walking from one venue to the next. These festivals would be theater themselves—participants in the City Dionysia, for instance, enjoyed themselves as if in a carnival. But, as in Carnival or Mardi Gras, there were always rules to be followed, and so the City Dionysia was also characterized by formal rituals and political spectacles. The theatrical *event*, then, was one where citizens (and, presumably, non-citizens alike) could appear as anything they chose, while following rules of decorum. The City Dionysia, then, was a space of appearance itself, a radically plural space of appearance, where individuals might take on identities they would not "normally" present to others, but where participation was thought to have strengthened the bonds of the polis.[21]

Individuals made their appearance as citizens during the City Dionysia because its very creation was considered a civic responsibility. The festivals were organized in great detail by citizens responsible for finance and production (Walton 1990, 65-73; Pickard-Cambridge 1968, 94-98; Henderson 1990, 286). Rush Rehm (1992) argues that the production of plays was a participatory political act, not only because it was a civic duty, but also because so many citizens were involved (20-30). The opening ceremonies included the Dionysos Eleuthereus, a religious ritual whose name includes *eleutheria*, or freedom in ancient Greek. The ceremonies first took place after the democratic reforms of Cleisthenes (508-507 B.C.), and so signaled democratic liberation for the Athenians (Rehm 1992, 15). Thus the Dionysia rooted itself in political freedom. Furthermore, the Dionysian festivals were organized around political themes and purposes. John Winkler (1990) maintains that such festivals were "occasions for elaborate symbolic play on themes of proper and improper civic behavior" based on the military training of young males (20). Indeed the Theater of Dionysos was given over to hoplite military maneuvers and close-order drills in front of the assembled citizen body. Many of these trainees were also chorus members (*ephebes*) whose dances were military in step. Consequently, Winkler traces the origin of tragedy to a coming-of-age-ritual in the development of citizens (58-60, see also Goldhill 1990, 107-113). Simon Goldhill (1990) suggests that the Dionysia and tragedies presented the key terms of civic discourse as essentially contestable to the citizenry. The Dionysia itself, he argues, represented the "interplay between norm and transgression" and played out difference and otherness to the city (126-127). Such practices indicate the essentially Arendtian purposes of the theatrical festivals and their fundamentally plural nature.

But the spaces *within* the theaters, most specifically the Theater of Dionysos, were also plural. The Theater of Dionysos was divided into three parts—the theatron, the orchestra, and the skene. The theatron was the bowl-shaped seating arrangement for the audience to "see" the performance. It could hold up to 14,000 spectators, and seating was arranged by tribes, with priests, high officials, and other honored citizens taking their place in the front rows. The orchestra was the circular space at the bottom for choral singing and dancing, and the skene (a later development) was the stage upon which the actors (usually, but not more than, three) performed. The theater was outdoors, built into the south side of the acropolis, and lit naturally. The conditions of the theatron permitted a Dionysian experience within the theater, and the patrons engaged in multifarious acts during the performances.[22] Attending theater in ancient Greece might remind modern readers of their experiences at professional sporting events, rather than the constrained, more formal modern theater or symphony.[23] To borrow from both Aristotle and Rousseau, it was a space where political animals could be "natural," and could present themselves to others as they really were, in all their glorious and diverse humanity.[24] Thus, there were multiple performances displayed at the theater, one in the skene and orchestra, but many in the theatron. If actors were to grab the attention of even half of these unruly theatergoers, they had to distinguish themselves—by their dress, their gestures, but especially their voice. Thus a crucial part of acting was distinction—making one's appearance as an identity, even if a purely representational one. So the architectural conditions of the theater itself explain to some degree how Arendt might have conceptualized the space of appearance.

The audience must have been sufficiently earnest to have paid some attention to the events on stage. When they did pay attention, they experienced a theater of appearance, in ways that we no longer experience in the modern theater. First, the architecture of the theater created a spatial continuity among actors, chorus, and audience. No special lighting highlighted the stage, which was situated below, not above, most audience members, and seats came up to the edge of the orchestra. Both audience and performers entered and exited from the same gates and passageways, and many of them had already "met" each other at the *proagon*, held immediately before so that the playwright could introduce the play and the actors to the audience. Consequently, not only could the playwright, actors, and chorus present themselves to the audience, the audience could—literally—present themselves to the playwright, actors, and chorus! Thus many modern interpreters recognize that Greek theater focused its energies on the audience, because they were a part of the performance (Rehm 1992, Arnott 1991, Simon 1982, Meier 1993, Longo 1990, Goldhill 1990).

Second, the stage itself was a participatory space of appearance that permitted the audience members to stage the plays they saw in diverse ways. Employing sparse stage design and descriptive dialogue and song, Greek drama permitted the audience to create their own stages of appearance. This, too, was necessary given the architecture of the theater and the technological constraints of ancient Greece. Ruth Padel (1990) argues that the Greek theater required the audience to understand and interpret the performance space in multiple ways. First, the drama allowed audience members to observe the interior space of the characters, one not normally available to the average person or citizen. Second, plays made visible "invisible" spaces—either by presenting the audience with locales to which they had never been or by suggesting those locales in the dialogue (usually through Messenger speeches or the use of the *ekkuklema* or *mechane*—stage props designed to permit gods to enter the performance).[25] Third, the stage facade and stage painting provided an illusion of spatial depth (346-354; Simon 1982, 20-27). This compelled audience members to construct their own personal spaces with the actors and chorus and framed their relationship to the action.

The audience shares the theater and the experience with the performers and yet is distanced from them. They can "go into" that feigned world, enticed in by the structure they see . . . or draw back from it. They can be objective and feel pity. They can be subjective and feel fear. The relationship is encapsulated in Aristotle's statement that tragedy works by creating pity and fear in its audience (*Poetics* 1449b27). You simultaneously enter into and retreat from the tragic world. There is a doubleness in your relationship to its frame. In one sense, tragedy's "frame" is the theater itself. But its emblem is the *skene* front with its revolutionary portrayal of a three-dimensional facade on a two-dimensional wall (Padel 1990, 353-354).

In the terms I used above, the theatergoing experience inculcates the act of civility in the practices of the patron. Padel suggests that the audience "makes the space speak" in the theater, engages in a kind of dialectical exchange with those on stage and in the orchestra. In so doing, I would argue, audience members learn an important civic lesson—how to unite and distance themselves with others in a given communal space.[26]

Third, because the space is a relatively empty one, the audience must fill in the action themselves, given what the playwright has written and what the actors are doing. Before the building of the skene, plays required the audience to fill in almost every detail of the space of appearance themselves with help from the dialogue, but even after the skene became a part of the theater, audience members still needed to imagine scenes outside their direct vision, and they had to imagine places in more detail than the scene painting displayed (Ley 1991, 30). The theater space can, more often than not, become every and any space, and it does not create the locale, only the actors can and do that (Arnott 1991, 136).[27] Theatrical space was anonymous and undifferentiated, and actors made the space appear by acting and carried those spaces with them as the plot developed (Arnott 1991, 137-138; Walton 1990, 131). This sort of challenge exists for audiences in modern drama, but it is not common. Consequently, classical actors literally made space appear in ways that modern actors, who perform on a detailed stage, cannot.[28]

So it was up to the playwright and his actors to maintain the appearance of the performance space, and this could only be done in their coming together (as Arendt hypothesizes citizens do in creating civic spaces).[29] Theatrical power is, in this sense, plural, because actors create different theatrical spaces given the plot and given their skill in holding the audience's attention. For without the audience, there would be no theatrical space of which to speak, only some masked men gesturing in front of thousands of partygoers. A great burden falls upon the actors—the need to create and recreate the space of appearance. In modern theaters, the bored audience member can fixate on the scene and never lose track of where the play "is" topographically at any point in the drama. Classical actors did not have this luxury, and space depended very directly upon their actions. Arendt notes that the American and French revolutionaries of the eighteenth century were also aware of their responsibility to create a space where the civic might appear, and they too were burdened with the responsibility of continually re-creating that space. They failed, but, as Jefferson realized in suggesting a ward system, it was possible. The analogy is limited because theatrical performances end, but politics does not; this may suggest why Arendt's theatrical metaphor ultimately insufficiently represents her arguments for council democracy.

Finally, Greek theater was a space where the spectators could take the position of gods and judge the actors who make their appearance before them. Arendt (1978) describes the theatron as a place with "ascending rows" where the spectators "could look down godlike on the game of the world" (140). The very structure of the building placed great responsibility on the spectator, first in rendering judgment upon the actors. But more fundamentally, the presence of spectators, in such a "godlike" position, permitted the actors to appear.[30] The "ascending" quality of the theatrical space transports the spectator into the world of the gods—a world that, in pre-Platonic Greece at least, created the very conditions for human appearance (129-141).

Beyond the spatial form of appearing in the theater, the plot, costumes, actors, and chorus also contributed to the performance, and an aesthetic representation of the civic relationship, by establishing a rapport with the audience. In the words of James Redfield (1990):

> Theater . . . is unique among public events in that it is not only *for* the audience but it is *directed to* the audience. Through theater the poet communicates with his audience; at Athens he was said to "teach" the chorus. There is thus no obvious answer to the following question: who, in the theater, makes a public appearance (324).

The actors, chorus, characters, and poet all appear, as does the audience. Furthermore, the plot and the costumes are written and designed in such ways as to involve the audience in the acting, thus guiding them, through the theatrical experience, in a kind of civic practice.

The plot itself elicited action on the part of "the city." Peter Arnott (1991) notes that many plays (e.g., Aeschylus' *The Eumenides* and *Prometheus Bound*, Aristophanes' *The Archanians*) included the audience as part of the dramatic narrative of the story (14, 16-21, 34). Because there were also no stage directions in the dramas, the audience was forced to actively imagine the space of theatrical appearance through the words of the playwright (Arnott 1991, 49). The dialogue between the actors was necessarily stylized to permit characters to distinguish themselves on the stage, thus actors would be forced to exaggerate their speech or gesture and talk in hyperbole in order to make themselves appear to an audience that might otherwise overlook them. The content of the plays were also "political" in a number of ways. First, there were many public speeches in the theater. Second, playwrights used debate to dramatize political or moral issues (*Antigone* is probably the most well-known to political theorists here), thus establishing the theater as *agon* (Arnott 1991, 105, 108, 112-113; Rehm 1992, 64-65, 73-74; Nietzsche 1993, 24). As agon, audience members "become" a jury and learn aesthetically the political judgment necessary to them as citizens. But this engagement also communicates issues to the audience and educates them civically. In comedy, Jeffrey Henderson (1990) argues, this meant subjecting political leaders to ridicule and criticism, championing the underdog, and airing minority viewpoints. The audience also learned to identify themselves as Athenians by being presented with an imaginary, oppositional space, most often Thebes, in the plot (Zeitlin 1986). The character of the hero offered the audience members an exemplar of greatness, of one willing to defy convention and distinguish oneself from the community (Knox 1964, 5, 57; Strong 1990, 45, 49, 54; Nietzsche 1993, 80).[31]

More importantly, in playing many different characters, the actors (including the one playing the hero) taught the audience *that* appearance is crucial, and *how* to appear (and distinguish oneself) at different times and places. The Greeks, Peter Arnott (1991) contends, were "trained to see character as a series of disconnected appearances" (192, see also 182-183), thus reemphasizing the significance of appearance itself. The actors themselves were a plural group with some specializing in comedy, others in tragedy, and still others in the satyr plays (Ley 1991, 28). Because their costumes, shoes, and masks expressed character type, and not the individual character,[32] actors learned to distinguish themselves through gesture and voice, and for this reason delivery also contributed to the appearance of the character.[33] The increasing importance of the actor to Greek drama signified a change in the polis, according to Oddone Longo (1990):

> The reduction of the choral element in favor of the actor's debates might be seen as the product of a progressive integration of the drama into the more pluralistic system of the polis, where division of labor, social stratification, and class struggle reduce precisely the area of unanimity in the community. As a result, dialectical distinction increases, and along with it the opposition of roles and parts (17).

In other words, the very use of actors represented a more plural, socially differentiated city, a fact unlikely to be lost on the audience.

The chorus, too, functioned politically in Arendtian terms. Beyond the tie with the *ephebes* that I mentioned above, membership in the chorus was considered a civic responsibility (Arnott 1991, 23). The nature of this chorus was plural, however. First, the chorus "represent[ed] the ideal spectator, the city, the common man/woman, the heroic characters, the voice of the poet, and so on" sometimes all in the same play (Rehm 1992, 60). Second, the chorus changed their appearance over the course of some plays, for instance *Choephori*, *Oresteia*, or *Helen*, and so reemphasized the very significance of appearance in the theater. Thus, to use the term I have used before, the choral space was flexible (Rehm 1992, 59; Walton 1990, 177) and opened up possibilities for action in many different directions. The chorus performed in different ways throughout the play through poetry, song, dance, movement. The chorus also engaged the play "in an ongoing dialogue with itself" and so helped the play take shape (Rehm 1992, 52). So the chorus was crucial in helping the narrative unfold and in communicating the messages of the play to the audience. One means of doing this was through the *parabasis*—a "turning around" of the chorus to face the audience and address it directly (Arnott 1991, 12-13, 27, 115; Walton 1990, 73-74; Ley 1991, 24, 56). The chorus leader was probably the individual who addressed the audience, in order to clarify the narrative and suggest issues upon which the audience ought to reflect. This practice was most common in the Old Comedy of the sixth and fifth centuries B.C., and was a technique by which the playwright could speak with audience members.

Nietzsche (1993) argued that the chorus functioned agonistically, touching the metaphysical heart of the citizen.

> [T]he Greek man of culture felt himself annulled in the face of the satyr chorus, and the immediate effect of Dionysiac tragedy is that state and society, the gulfs separating man from man, make way for an overwhelming sense of unity that goes back to the very heart of nature. The metaphysical consolation (with which, as I wish to point out, every true tragedy leaves us), that whatever superficial changes may occur, life is at bottom indestructibly powerful and joyful, is given concrete form as a satyr chorus, a chorus of natural beings, living ineradicably behind all civilization (39).

The Greeks, sitting in the Theater of Dionysos, were able to "overlook the whole of the surrounding cultural world, and, in satisfied contemplation, to imagine themselves members of the chorus." Thus, the early chorus was "a reflection of Dionysiac man for his own contemplation" (42). Strong (1990) argues that the Dionysian state to which Nietzsche refers rests on the fact that the chorus does not act and only beholds the action on stage "in rapt contemplation" (57). The tragic chorus is thus the means by which the audience "is swept up onto the stage and taken out of itself" (57). I have tried to suggest (in the above paragraph) that Nietzsche's theory is not strictly true for tragedy, and that comic choruses presented festivalgoers and audience members a multiplicity of choral forms and functions. This, I would argue, is crucial to remember as we try to understand the theatrical dimension of the Arendtian space of appearance, because that space can possess different form and content on different occasions. Such is the nature of politics as I have understood Arendt to argue.[34]

In conclusion, the plural spaces of appearance *of* the theater and *in* the theater had multiple effects on the audience. First, the audience received an education in democracy, as office holders and members of a jury (Ley 1991, 35; Arnott 1991, 22-24, 129; Meier 1993, 215; Euben 1990, 51, 58). Second, it reinforced their skills of listening and memory, skills vital to the practice of democratic politics (Arnott 1991, 75-76, 78, 99; Ley 1991, 43). Third, such skills helped the city to reflect upon itself and taught audience members aesthetic, *and thus political* (Arendt 1961, 1978), judgment (Nietzsche 1993, 109; Euben 1986, 23, 29; Euben 1990, 56; Meier 1993, 3, 42; Longo 1990, 13-14; Salkever 1986, 295; Ober and Strauss 1990, 249, 270). Finally, the theater encouraged the city to act politically, institute reforms where necessary, and check democratically the political leadership (Ley 1991, 61; Henderson 1990, 293-307). To use terms currently in vogue in contemporary Arendtian scholarship, the theatrical agon functioned politically by communicating the human condition to the audience members.

Arendt's conception of politics, then, is grounded in her notion of the space of appearance, and this space reflects a classical understanding of theater. It is an understanding of a theater that involves both the actor and the spectator as participants in the drama together, and thus is superior to those theories I reviewed in chapter 1. In like manner, politics, from an Arendtian perspective, becomes a practice that involves both actors and spectators, and political understanding blends both participation and observation. In the next chapter I will piece together a political science from this conception of politics and argue that if we view politics as theater, then the political scientist becomes a sort of theater critic. More importantly, though, if politics is theatrical, in the Greek sense, then teaching citizenship is a matter of combining action and political thinking, and I argue in chapter 4 that Arendt elaborates this idea in *Eichmann in Jerusalem*.

Notes

1.   On the importance of the spatiality of appearance for Arendt, see Parekh 1992, 632-634; Passerin d'Entreves 1994, 146-148; Taminiaux 1996, 215-220; and Villa 1992b, 714.

2.   Arendt is clearly mistaken here if we consider the authorial performance of writers such as Mario Vargas Llosa or Paul Auster. In novels such as *The Real Life of Alejandro Mayta* or *The Storyteller*, Vargas Llosa narrates not only a story, but displays the process of writing that creates that narrative. This sort of self-conscious writing suggests that the creative artist can also display publicly the freedom experienced in the act of creation. Auster has recreated an authorial space of appearance in *Leviathan*, his narrative of a writer writing.

    Following Austin's insight that speech is performative, Henry Sayre (1990) argues that writing can also be performative (see also Honig 1993, 89-96). Roland Barthes (1974) characterizes those texts as "writerly" which render the reader "a producer of the text" (4). Barthes, however, notes the inherently plural nature of writerly texts, for they require the reader to interpret them, which means "to appreciate what *plural* constitutes it" (5). Barthes describes plural texts as those with "a galaxy of significrs . . . [they have] no beginnings; [they are] reversible; we gain access to [them] by several entrances" (5). In short, the plural text is one that requires the reader to insert him or herself in the beginning and/or creation of the text. I believe this to be consistent with Arendt's sense that a plural space demands the insertion of human creativity and the capacity for initiative. In contradistinction to writerly texts Barthes posits readerly texts, and a method of writing "at the zero degree" (Barthes 1967). In "zero degree" writing the writer slavishly imitates style and writes in a colorless, mechanical, stale manner. In other words, the "writer degree zero" is anything but creative, who, in Arendt's terms, might prevail in mass society.

3.   Arendt argues that appearances "never just reveal; they also conceal" (1978, 25), and suggests the importance of masks in political theater. In *On Revolution* (1965), Arendt also notes that masks protect by analogizing the theatrical mask to the Roman legal construct, the *persona* (106-108). Susan Bickford (1995) interprets the mask as operating "as a neutralizing device, perceptually dispersing certain kinds of sameness and equalizing certain kinds of difference" (319). Though if we assume that Arendt thinks of theater in the classical Greek form, I agree with Rush Rehm (1992) that masks teach the audience to "fill out the fixed visage of a tragic character caught in radically changing situations" (40-41). So even in concealing, masks taught the Greek audience to imagine difference and otherness. Concealment, in this sense, not only protects the actor, but reinforces human plurality, by attuning the audience/the citizenry to the voice.

4.   As Jacques Taminiaux (1986) observes, the sharing of the world permits "a life to be the life of some*one*" (32, emphasis added).

5.   Natality is the word Arendt uses to describe the birthlike condition of acting in the world. As Françoise Collin explains, "to be born is to appear for the first time, and all

acts of appearing in public—in order to share in the human collectivity—recollect this original act. It is because I have appeared once that I can make my appearance [again] in public. Being born is to affirm that presence by speaking and acting in the collectivity, the *inter-esse*" ("Du privé et du public," in Collin 1986, 56).

6. The Arendtian subject is one who "is never the *author* of acts, but rather the *agent*, or the *actor*—in the sense of the Roman *persona*" (Françoise Collin, "Du privé et du public," in Collin 1986, 58).

7. Though Arendt suggests that meaning of actions collected into a story can only be revealed to the storyteller, or in political terms, the historian. Indeed, "what the storyteller narrates must necessarily be hidden from the actor himself, at least as long as he is in the act or caught in its consequences, because for him the meaningfulness of his act is not in the story that follows" (1958b, 171). Again, writers like Vargas Llosa have demonstrated that the act of storytelling itself is, in Arendt's terms, part of the performance.

8. By the early 1970s Arendt seems to have broadened her conception here, and employs the theater as a metaphor for all forms of sentient activity, not just human political ones. "Living things *make their appearance* like actors on a stage set for them. The stage is common to all who are alive, but it *seems* different to each species, different also to each individual specimen" (Arendt 1978, 21). She also tries to determine a psychological basis for our urge to appear as a natural innate impulse in all beings (29). She notes, however, that only humans present themselves for display, only humans choose what to show and what to hide, "up to a point" (34). I am only interested in the relevance of theatrical appearance to politics, but she raises the point here that theater depends ultimately on the spectator, that each species perceives the stage differently. I return to this point in the text.

9. Jennifer Ring (1991) notes that Arendt depicts the polis, and the capacity for political action, as "portable"; the polis "is not, after all, a specific physical place" (439-440). I argue that "portability" reflects Arendt's metaphor of the theater. For while Arendt may have viewed the polis as portable, and in analogizing it to the theater, she certainly recognized that action can take place in different scenes and on different stages. The theater itself is not portable, but the drama can be moved from venue to venue, and so political action is certainly portable. This is one reason why Arendt's metaphor is so apt and insightful.

10. "Respect…is a kind of 'friendship' without intimacy and without closeness; is a regard for the person *from the distance which the space of the world puts between us,* and this regard is independent of qualities which we may admire or of achievements which we may highly esteem" (Arendt 1958b, 218, emphasis added). In her essay on Lessing, she concludes that civic friendship occurs between people who speak truth to each other. It requires community, "an area in which there are many voices and where the announcement of what each 'deems truth' links and separates men, establishing in fact those distances between men which together comprise the world" (Arendt 1968b, 30-31).

11 Margaret Canovan (1992) notes the "cooler" nature of the public realm, as "civilized values, such as objectivity, [grow] only among people who have space between them" (248). Maurizio Passerin d'Entreves (1994, 146) and Jacques Taminiaux (1996, 217) highlight the same point.

12. On civic friendship, see Arendt 1968b, 24-25, 29.

13. For this reason, I argue in the appendix, a space of appearance can be *both* associational and aporetic at the same time, and so those who characterize political space as one *or* the other are mistaken. The "civilized" space created theatrically is also

confirmed by classical rhetoric. Gary Remer (1996) notes that classical rhetoricians, such as Cicero, proposed rules of civility for conversation (35). "The decorum of conversation...impels speakers...to seek an emotional equilibrium in the conversations, that is, to produce a condition of tranquillity that would permit reason to come to the fore" (36). Cicero's rules of civility effect tranquillity, and in doing so "control the relationship between the interlocutors." Ultimately, conversational rules exist to facilitate associational friendship, the foundation of citizenship. Conversation unites people, while it "controls" them (that is, separates them). "This stands in stark contrast to oratory's agonistic ideal, where orators confront one another as adversaries" (37, see also Vickers 1988). So Arendt may be appealing to two different rhetorical traditions in her characterization of public space, or at least the speech in that space. This may be a source of the interpretive debates surrounding the concept (see the Appendix for an analysis of these debates).

14. In other words, the space of appearance is not the common world (Arendt 1968b, 4, 10; Passerin d'Entreves 1994, 143).

15. Promising, in the form of a contract, is how citizens maintain the connective space, while Arendt seems to argue that forgiveness helps citizens maintain a distance from each other. Forgiveness is a human action that is new and unexpected, "unconditioned by the act which provoked it," and for this reason frees both the forgiver and the forgivee from that act (Arendt 1958b, 216). In this way, forgiveness helps detach citizens from each other by liberating them from the (unfortunate) bond that the provocative act created. This is why punishment is an alternative to forgiveness, but not its opposite. For men "punish what has turned out to be unforgivable," (217) and so functions as forgiveness does—to detach and separate citizens after a transgression has brought them together.

16. Arendt emphasizes in *The Life of the Mind* that the contemplative life is quite opposite to that of action in all its forms. In contemplating, the philosopher explicitly withdraws from the world of appearances (1978, 74-78), and asserts that indeed philosophers do not only withdraw from action, but stop action in order to think ("All thinking demands a *stop*-and-think," 78; see also Beatty 1994). Moreover, "thinking annihilates temporal as well as spatial distances" (85) and so is irrelevant to space in which people appear, and can be seen by others (e.g., a theater). Thus the contemplative life is radically different, even opposed, to the life of action. She implies here, however, that the life of action, however variegated, is characterized by appearance. Where citizens appear, they are acting, regardless of the form of that action. On this account, the philosopher-as-philosopher cannot appear. When the philosopher-as-philosopher attempts to appear on the stage of the world he is often subject to ridicule (82).

17. The "representatives of the world," according to Arendt 1968b, 7.

18. This is also true in "What is Freedom?" (Arendt 1961, 154, 159, 239n. 14), and *On Revolution* (Arendt 1965, 103, 106-108, 281). Bertolt Brecht, another dramatist who played a central role in the development of Arendt's thinking (Arendt 1968b, 207-249), is rarely, if ever, mentioned in her texts. Even her main thesis on his life—that "a poet's real sins are avenged by the gods of poetry" (242)—reflects classical imagery.

19. Taminiaux (1996) notes that Arendt criticizes Plato for privileging pocisis over praxis in characterizing the polis, which explains Plato's preference for the model of craftsmanship instead of performance (220-221). In doing so, Plato misrepresents the polis, *as a space of appearance*, because he (falsely) assumes that philosopher-experts (and especially Socrates) dissociate themselves from politics in the same manner that artisans differentiate themselves from their product. This view is not only incorrect (as

Taminiaux (1996) argues, 229-230, and as I have mentioned above), but has colored the way political theorists have viewed the public space ever since. Villa (1996) maintains that Arendt conceives of politics aesthetically (and emphasizes *performance*) by deconstructing Aristotle (42, 52), who, obviously, analyzed only classical theater.

20. For just a sampling of these, see Meier 1993, Rehm 1992, Arnott 1991, and Walton 1990.

21. Meier 1993, 49. To anyone who has lived in New Orleans for at least one full year, this assertion hardly needs justification. With 750 artists and performers, and up to 14,000 theatergoers each of the three days of the festival, the Dionysia involved many, if not most, of the citizens and residents of Athens.

22. Including eating, drinking, shouting, hissing, booing, talking, cavorting, and urinating into the drainage canals of the theatron. See Pickard-Cambridge (1968), 149, 272-273, and Arnott (1991), 5-6, 60.

23. For this reason, it is strange that Strong (1990) assumes that the audience focused its attention completely on the stage itself (57). He justifies this claim by assuming Nietzsche (1993) as the voice of authority here, and that in using the word "overlook" (*ubersehen*), Nietzsche was using the term in its double meaning. Not only historians of classical theater (some of whom I cite in this chapter), but spectators who have attended open-air events, would disagree with Strong here. It is simply too difficult to overlook the performances in the audience itself. Maybe Strong misread Nietzsche's object. In "overlooking the whole world of culture around him" the audience might be distracted by itself and overlook the dramatic action on stage (which may be the "whole world of culture" to which Nietzsche refers). It is difficult to be careful in reading Nietzsche and misleading to render him authoritative on Greek theater. It does, however, point up the importance of learning judgment in attending performances.

24. Nietzsche (1993) explains this as an "intoxication" effect, where "subjectivity becomes a complete forgetting of the self" (17, see also 19-21).

25. Zeitlin (1990) argues that stage settings offered views of the "other" by presenting interior and exterior scenes simultaneously through architectural design (76-79).

26. Graham Ley (1991) notes a "controlled proximity" between the actors in tragedy (46), so audience members might have been able to visualize an artistic/formal representation of civic space. See also Rehm 1992, 46-47. Strong (1990) notes Aristotle's observation that in the theater the audience "does not experience the distancing from the aesthetic object that is found in other art forms" (41).

27. See Walton (1990), 107-108. Rush Rehm (1992) notes that "the early theatre was conceived more as a space than as a building. It lacked the inherent controls of programmatic construction and architectural order that defined, for example, the temple and the stoa, the most formally fixed of Greek buildings. Put in dramatic terms, it was not the precise shape of the cavea and orchestra but what happened there that mattered in the fifth century" (33). In Arnott's words (1991, 145, 162), Greek theatrical space was flexible. Jennifer Ring (1991) makes this very point regarding Arendt's theory, as I indicate above.

28. Note Rehm (1992): "Epitomized by the frame of the proscenium-arch, the modern theatre supports the central assumption of theatrical realism, namely that the spectator is a hidden observer looking in on a specified location through an invisible fourth wall. The Greek theatre aims at precisely the opposite effect, a sense that the audience has gathered in a public place to be addressed, and confronted, by the play. The

empty space of the Greek theatre encourages us to imagine the scene for ourselves, guided by the word and gestures of the performers" (37).

29. In Peter Arnott's terms, Greek theater was, at least until the time of Euripides, presentational, not representational (1991, 37-38).

30. I elaborate this argument in the next chapter.

31. Strong (1990) seems to have the Shakespearean hero in mind when he writes that "the desire for immortality is allure which leads us to confuse the stage with ordinary life, precisely the same urge that lies at the source of original sin. *It is not that perfection and immortality cannot be attained, but that they can, that forms the human problem*. The stage shows us what we might be like were we accomplished and perfected, were we gods" (69). I believe that Arendt, imagining classical Greek theater, would object to this statement in a number of ways: (1) The desire for immortality is not the same as the Christian concept of perfection, and the Greeks recognized that they need not be perfect to be immortal. Thus the audience is well aware of the failings of Odysseus or Oedipus, but they admire his capacity for action. (2) Greek theater does not show us what we might be like if we were gods, but rather how citizens can maintain the public space in the face of obstacles, portrayed dramatically. (3) Theater shows us not the dangers of trying to make ourselves perfect, but why humans should celebrate their plurality and difference, for this is what makes a life worth living.

32. But, as Rehm (1992) reminds us, the use of standard long dress, *Kothornos* (an exaggerated, big, flat shoe), and masks required the audience to participate in the construction of the character, thus involving them in the creation of the play as it appeared (40-41). Furthermore, different masks not only signified different characters, but different periods and places in a single character's life, so they too required the audience members themselves to make the character appear.

33. Arendt (1965) comments on the dual purposes of the mask; "it had to hide, or rather to replace, the actor's own face and countenance, but in a way that would make it possible for the voice to sound through" (106). She uses the theatrical metaphor to explain the protections afforded by Roman law to the *persona*, or legal personality. Consequently, masks were essential to sustain the appearance of rights-bearing citizens.

34. It is also important to understand the plurality in her theory in considering the very definition of the space of appearance. In the Appendix I argue that academic disputes over her public realm theory are misguided because the participants do not consider the very plurality of perspectives engendered by Arendt's position.

Chapter 3

A Mode of Being Alone: Reporting Truth in Political Science

"The facts, ma'am, just the facts."

Jack Webb

Hannah Arendt begins her prologue to *The Human Condition* (Arendt 1958b) by referring to the Sputnik launch of 1957 as the technological answer to man's quest for escaping the earth. She remarks that, though the earth is the very "quintessence" of the human condition, scientists have, for some time, designed to make life on earth artificial, and this too reflects our desire to escape from our terrestrial imprisonment, "the wish to escape the human condition" (3). Indeed, it seems possible that scientists will create a "future man," which we can then exchange for our own lives. This possibility, Arendt laments, signals a "crisis within the natural sciences . . . the fact that the 'truths' of the modern scientific world view, though they can be demonstrated in mathematical formulas and proved technologically, will no longer lend themselves to normal expression in speech and thought" (3). The modern scientific enterprise, no matter how unintentionally, has begun to divorce itself from the everyday language of human beings, and in doing so renders us potentially enslaved to "our know-how," our scientific and technological desires. This situation created by the sciences is of great political significance, because language is what "makes man a political being" (4).

We must be skeptical of the judgment of scientists because they "move in a world where speech has lost its power," so they endanger the very possibility of politics. As she said many times in her writings, politics is the means by which we create freedom and permit ourselves to appear as distinct, plural beings. Thus, we are presented with an early indictment of some unintended harmful consequences of the scientific enterprise—its potentially anti-political character.[1] Another, she continues, is the advent of automation, which seeks to eliminate another aspect of the human condition—the burden of labor. The danger here is that laborers, though freed of labor, will remain just that—mere laborers—and they will be deprived of "the only activity left to them. Surely, nothing could be worse" (5). Science and technology are not Arendt's concerns in this famous work, the "most elementary articulations of the human condition" are—labor, work, and action.

But it is important to note that she frames these articulations against the so-called achievements of science and technology. Her final chapter, "The *Vita Activa* and the Modern Age" counterpoises the human capacities for labor, work, and action against the modern scientific tradition and the world which it has created. In this chapter, I argue that she does not leave these concerns at the end of the last page. Rather, she maintains a concern for understanding reality in later essays published in *Between Past and Future*, as well as *On Revolution*, and *Eichmann in Jerusalem*, she relates that concern to social action and partially articulates an alternative means by which political scientists can understand the world.

We can glean at least one common, unarticulated theme, among many others in texts produced in the period 1958 to 1966, namely the search for a method of describing, analyzing, and judging the political world. I will first describe the problems Arendt has with science and then argue that she formulates a political methodology based on her understanding of "factuality" and the connection she makes between theater and politics.[2] I will reconstruct a nascent theory of reportage from different sources in her work, and I will suggest that during this period, Arendt played reporter on the public stage. But she played a particular kind of reporter—a drama critic. We can ground an Arendtian political science in her understanding of the relationship between theater and reportage, as this emerges in her later work. Out of the ideals of a good theater critic—one who reports what one sees, one who situates the drama historically, one who adeptly recounts narrative, and one who makes astute judgments about the performance—Arendt offers us a model of political research that lends itself "to normal speech and thought."[3] This model of research challenges the understandings and interpretations of more commonly accepted empirical and mathematical traditions in political science. It is also a model of research that can be incorporated rather easily into both an undergraduate and graduate teaching agenda.

The Problem with Science

The problem with modern science begins with the story of man's fateful and futile search for an Archimedean point with which to observe his planet and himself. With the discovery of the new world and the advent of the Reformation, modern men were thrown back upon themselves, as their original understandings of the world, and their place in it, was turned around. Out of this emerged an early modern alienation from the world, a process abetted by truths revealed through modern science and Cartesian philosophy.

Copernicus and Galileo upset the sense experience of people, indeed challenged "the adequacy of the senses to reveal reality" (Arendt 1958b, 237). This triggered both despair and triumph, for Galileo's discoveries proved the ancient fear that our senses might betray us, and it gave hope in reaching an Archimedean point "outside the earth from which to unhinge the world" (237-238). Arendt argues that modern scientific discoveries result from handling "nature from a point in the universe outside the earth." Even though we are bound to the earth by our human condition, we have "found a way to act on the earth and within terrestrial nature as though we dispose of it from outside" (238). We learned how to think in terms of the universe while remaining on earth, "and perhaps even more astounding" we became able to use cosmic laws as guides to terrestrial action (240). With this comes "the modern ideal of reducing terrestrial sense data and movements to mathematical symbols," and a new language of science is born (241). The mathematical symbolization developed by scientists permitted man to "place nature under the conditions of his own mind, that is, under conditions won from a universal, astrophysical viewpoint, a cosmic standpoint outside nature itself" (241). Mathematics was a language unconcerned with appearance, but with "reducing all that man is not into patterns which are identical with human, mental structures" (242).

From all this emerged the physical sciences as truly universal, where earth was seen as only one example of processes and laws that held elsewhere. Corresponding to this was an attendant change in the human mind, though this change was for a long time restricted to scientists and men of letters. Cartesian philosophy emerged from the discovery of Galileo's telescope, "the decisive event of the modern age," and anticipated in part the perplexities inherent in the new standpoint of man. Cartesian doubt displaced the Greek *thaumadzein* or wonder at the world, and became "the self-evident, inaudible motor which has moved all thought" (249). Galileo's telescope disrupted what men for ages had believed true to their reason and senses, and a new method of revealing truth was thus born. Cartesian doubt appealed to the early moderns because it was universal—"nothing, no thought and no experience, [could] escape it"—and it was deployed against the presence of truth itself in our senses, our reason, and in the nineteenth century, our faith (250). But this gave rise to the fundamental problem that moderns would suffer—that the truth might not exist, or that we might be deceived by a *Dieu trompeur*, an evil spirit.

Cartesian doubt led to a fundamental uncertainty about the world with which modern moral philosophy would have to reckon in the decades to come. The philosophy of science turned away from the revelation of truth and ultimate reality and toward the ability of scientists to be truthful and to make their experiments reliable. Following Descartes, scientists and philosophers discovered that even if there was no truth and certainty, man himself could be truthful and reliable, and concluded that if there were to be answers to the questions of the world they had to come from man himself. It would be man's introspection, "the sheer cognitive concern of consciousness with its own content," that would yield certainty. In doing so, Cartesianism "used the nightmare of non-reality as a means of submerging all worldly objects into the stream of consciousness and its processes," which dissolves objective reality into subjective mental processes (256). Moreover, this method taught men that even if they cannot know truth as something given and disclosed, they can at least know what they make themselves. This ultimately supported technological invention and change, at an ever-quickening pace, for technology can be known, with certainty, to men.

But these developments led to the displacement of common sense—traditionally the one sense by which all other private sensations were fitted into the common world. After Descartes, men did not hold the world in common, but rather the structure of their minds, which "they cannot have in common, strictly speaking" (257). Men held the faculty of reasoning in common, but this was a particularly individualized mental process; and its results became the standard for what was to be called commonsense reasoning. Two-plus-two-equals-four became not a balance of self-evident harmony, but the result of play, a process that generated "truths" because all men, fitted with the same mental process, necessarily came to this conclusion. In reckoning with consequences, however, men lost their traditional understanding of common sense, and thus the sense that fits their animal senses into a common world with other men. Descartes had moved the Archimedean point into man himself, and the human mind became the ultimate "point of reference for the pattern of the human mind itself" (258).

This would ultimately be destructive to science. Every question the scientist puts to nature is answered in mathematical patterns to which no model can correspond adequately, because it cannot be shaped after our sense experiences. While technology can demonstrate the truth of man's abstract, and mathematized, concepts, it really shows no more than that man can apply the results of his mind under all sorts of scientific systems. Scientists formulate their hypotheses to arrange their experiments and then use experiments to verify hypotheses, and so the world of the experiment becomes a man-made reality. While this can expand our ability to make our world, it puts us back into the prison of our own minds. We remain limited to the patterns that we ourselves create. So the very idea of an Archimedean point is, ironically, proved false.

In the past thirty years philosophers of science have come to agree with Arendt that the search for an Archimedean ideal is misguided, but they take issue with the idea that modern science is destructive of common sense or even the truth. Thomas Kuhn, Imre Lakatos, and Larry Laudan have all maintained, in one form or another, that the scientific enterprise is very much a common enterprise and that scientists working together appeal to the world they share in common (both professionally and socially) with each other and the greater public.[4] Out of common research programs scientists construct contingent "truths" about the world which evolve into, or revolve around, commonly held truths about that world. Regardless of whether or not Arendt is correct on these matters, the point is that she structures a critique of modern science as an enterprise grounded on a misguided principle—the goal of "abstract impartiality" (Disch 1994, 20ff).[5]

In other essays written during the 1950s and early 1960s, she developed this critique into a sustained attack on social science. To some degree she was forced to do this because of the criticism leveled against *The Origins of Totalitarianism* (1973) that it was unscientific and subjective or that it relied on a poorly developed methodology (a concern particular to positivists and post-positivists).[6] To many of her critics she responds that in applying scientific methods to social action, social scientists attempt to achieve an Archimedean point that is impossible. Reflecting the temper of her times, Arendt also criticized functionalism as ignorant of the substance of historical and political phenomena. In establishing "objective" standards, Arendt lambastes functionalists for ignoring what different political systems say about their own practices. She finds the refusal to take political actors at their own word to be cavalier, for political truth is based on such facts (Arendt 1994, 374).[7] This argument is crucial to Arendt in explaining herself during the Eichmann controversy, and I will argue that it constitutes a central proposition in a theory of reportage.[8]

Moreover, in trying to find a rational language with which to describe social phenomena, social scientists assume jargon-laden discourse. This leaves behind a part of their own understanding (rooted in "common sense") and separates them even further from the layman (or the "common world") (Arendt 1968a, 268, 272). Jargon, for example terms such as imperialism, totalitarianism, and functionalism, is often used indiscriminately, so that social scientists cannot make distinctions.[9] None of these political phenomena is "understood with its particular historical background. The result is a generalization in which the words themselves lose all meaning" (Arendt 1994, 407). So even though social science may posit higher standards for scientific accuracy, "our standards and criteria for true understanding" seem to have declined (339).

I would add that this also distances the expert from the educated reader and makes the process of teaching political science more difficult. Because these concepts are not readily available to the educated student, some of them become alienated from the discipline. They either believe (wrongfully) that they do not possess sufficient skill in comprehending such concepts or that jargon renders their own studies meaningless. Arendt opposes this distancing as well in her nascent theory of reportage, for the reporter does anything but create or extend the gap between expert and layman. Indeed the reporter's success at attracting readers depends on his or her skill in bridging the gap between discoveries and events, and man.

In a larger sense, Arendt laments the loss of human dignity and pride in the social scientific enterprise. She concludes that the application of the Archimedean point to "the various activities of men" has led to a decline in the stature of man (Arendt 1968a, 265). As we look upon ourselves with the same methods we use to study the behavior of rats, "all our pride in what we can do will disappear into some kind of mutation of the human race" (279).[10] Our behavior falls under the rubric of necessity and our creativity and originality get lost in the process (or history of social systems, etc.).[11] In terms she uses elsewhere, modern social science originates in the rise of the social, where people's individual behavior, rather than their public action, signifies their collective reality (Arendt 1958b, 39-41).[12]

Where human action is understood in technological terms "speech and everyday language would indeed be no longer a meaningful utterance that transcends behavior even if it only expresses it, and it would much better be replaced by the extreme and in itself meaningless formalism of mathematical signs" (Arendt 1968a, 279-280). Even if formalism has not developed for the reasons she gives, a quick glance at the *American Political Science Review* suggests that political science has "come perilously close to this point." In Arendt's view, the application of the Archimedean ideal in political science has emptied politics of its space to appear. At the very least it has become a sign of "certain obvious trends in modern society," which may result in "the deadliest, most sterile passivity history has ever known" (Arendt 1958b, 295).

The Theory of Reportage

In contrast to the scientific enterprise, which seeks to determine what lies behind phenomena "as they reveal themselves to the sense and the mind of man," Arendt seeks to understand the actual appearance of such phenomena. She wants to comprehend the common world whereby people understand the reality of each other and, by virtue of this fact, of themselves. She turns away from the specialized jargon of the scientist, his discursive search for an Archimedean ideal, and interrogates reality in common language and through commonsense experience. In contradistinction to social scientists, who have "lost confidence in appearances," Arendt describes and explains the ways in which people act politically, in the world they create between them.

In *The Origins of Totalitarianism*, Arendt employed a kind of historical method, one she defends in her exchange with Eric Voegelin (Arendt 1994, 401-408; Barnouw 1990, 202). Contemporary theorists recognize her narrative method (Disch 1994, Benhabib 1996, Gottsegen 1994, Miller 1979), and one commentator argues that Arendt tells stories "from the plurality of its constituent perspective[s]" (Disch 1994, 163).[13] I will argue, however, that we see the rudiments of another method of political analysis emerging from the concerns rooted in *The Human Condition* and explored in her research on revolution and in her report on the Eichmann trial. Here she offers elements of a method that addresses directly the "problem of factual truth," whose opposite is not falsity, but the lie, a falseness told or spoken. I will suggest that this method specifies both the historical and narrative methods others have recognized in her thought and respects the understanding of politics as theater I have presented in the previous chapter. Finally, it is a method compatible with, and congenial to, modes of social and political research.[14] The method—theatrical criticism—emerges from a theory of reportage that I will develop in this section.

We know from both her personal life and her written comments that Arendt respected journalism generally and the profession of reporting in particular. While in exile in Europe and New York in the 1930s and 1940s she wrote many pieces for Jewish (and non-religious) periodicals and newspapers. She began her professional career in the United States as a freelance journalist, and was hired by the journal *Aufbau* as an editorialist. She reported "on assignment" often, including, for example, on the reconstruction of Germany after World War II (Courtine-Denamy 1997, 26). She was both pleased and proud to attend the Eichmann trial as a reporter for the *New Yorker* and published versions of many of her essays there and in other periodicals. Two versions of pieces upon which I will rely heavily to make her case for reportage, "Truth and Politics" and "Thinking," were originally published in the *New Yorker* before becoming part of *Between Past and Future* and *The Life of The Mind*. As she herself pointed out many times (and as others have noted as well), Arendt was always looking for an audience broader than specialists in political theory or political science, and publishing in newspapers and periodicals was a means to find this audience. Even selected essays published in academic political science journals, such as "Totalitarian Imperialism: Reflections on the Hungarian Revolution," often refer to information found only in press reports or wire services (Arendt 1958a, 26, 33).

She honed her skills as a correspondent in her many letters to close friends, such as Karl Jaspers and Mary McCarthy (Kohler and Saner 1992, Brightman 1995). In them, she continuously reported current events, cultural and artistic life, and economic changes wherever she or her friends were in the world. While many of these letters contained philosophical reflections and personal exchanges, her reports to her friends increased noticeably in the late 1950s and early 1960s.[15] This probably did not reflect an increased interest in the events of the day, because she had already been politicized in the 1930s as a result of Nazism (Young-Bruehl 1982), but rather a more conscious, and conscientious, effort to present facts and appearances as she experienced them.

While she does not discourse at length about the virtues of reporters or journalism, she reveals enough of her opinions in letters, essays, and books, to elaborate her ideas on the subject.[16] In piecing together elements of her understanding of "truth" and "factuality" with her assessment of the journalist's enterprise, one can reconstruct a methodology of political research

The Journalist's Enterprise

The journalist's enterprise begins with the coverage of "events," actions that occur out of the ordinary realm of daily life.[17] Arendt believed that events moved individuals to understand the world, themselves, and ideas, and we see repeated reference to their importance in all of her works. The central topics of many of her books and essays revolve around events: the discovery of Galileo's telescope, the creation and growth of totalitarianism, the founding of the Constitution of the United States, the French Revolution and its bloody aftermath,[18] the Hungarian Revolution of 1956, the publication of the Pentagon Papers, the forced integration of schools in Little Rock, Arkansas, the student movement and Moratorium against the Vietnam War. These are just a few events that feature most prominently in her writing, and as she reflects upon them she develops her theories of power, action, and appearance.[19]

Many scholars have noted these insights, but I would like to pursue other lines of inquiry. I do not suggest how "events" led Arendt to understand, world or appearance or the public realm, but how her world and the political appearances in them led her to understand events. That is, I would like to limn from Arendt's writings the means by which one comprehends the event, and this, I would argue, directly reflects her understanding of the reporter's role in society.

Independent journalism—reportage not beholden to any financial or partisan interests—is an existential mode of truth-telling (Arendt 1968c, 260). Journalists begin the process of telling factual truth and so provide a necessary (if not sufficient) means by which we can begin reflecting upon the human condition. Without independent reportage, Arendt asserts, we cannot find our bearings in the world. So in supplying information, reporters perform a vital function for both actors and spectators, they help people place themselves in the world they hold in common with others. In other terms, they provide crucial data by which our common sense can be invigorated.

The reporter supplies people with facts, and after they are in possession of facts the political event becomes possible (Arendt 1958a, 25).[20] Reportage helps people both "recognize facts as they are" (21) and reveals facts to the public that had been otherwise unknown or hidden from them.[21] Though Arendt herself relied often on stories from newspapers and wire services, she also regarded one form of journalism as analytical, what we know as the op-ed piece (36).

Though reportage supplies the public with facts,[22] and though it can occasionally itself be analytical, there are precise moral and intellectual limits on the practice. Journalism, as an existential mode of truth-telling, must engage in the disinterested pursuit of truth (Arendt 1968c, 262), which means that it cannot be beholden to any financial or partisan political interests. Journalists must be interested in human beings and the human condition. So they must be fundamentally interested in people as ends in themselves and in the collective action that constitutes the world (Brightman 1995, 161). But they must be aware of their own neutrality and have no right or responsibility to become involved in the event itself. "A simple reporter bears no responsibility whatsoever for what goes on" she replied to Karl Jaspers, after he suggested that she, as a reporter for *The New Yorker*, would be somewhat responsible for the events unfolding at the Eichmann trial (Kohler and Saner 1992, 414, 417). Reporters have the right to criticize aspects of the event—for instance, to analyze the judges' final determination at a trial—but not to make suggestions or otherwise influence events as they transpire.

Intellectually, there are boundaries to reportage as well. First, reporters have limits on what they can say about an event—they report only what is appropriate to the subject matter. For instance, in a letter to Mary McCarthy, Arendt commented that a reflection on the nature of evil would have been inappropriate to include in the Eichmann book because it was a report (Brightman 1995, 152). She emphasized to McCarthy that in reports there should be no "ideas," but rather simple facts with conclusions (148), and that reporters, for reasons of space, must often leave out of the account questions of why certain things happened the way they did (152). Most importantly, reporters must focus on the subject matter—they must devote all their energies to describing the events under question as accurately as possible to inform a world that can interpret those events in their own ways (Arendt 1964b, 285, 298).

Reporters play many roles according to Arendt. They are chroniclers caught between the past and the future. They recount history (e.g., her retelling of events in the Holocaust in the context of her report on Eichmann). They listen to people's stories (Arendt 1964b, 8), and they recount stories themselves.

> Since the times of Homer, great tales have followed in the footsteps of great wars, and great storytellers have crept from the ruins of destroyed cities and devastated landscapes. Newspapers today employ storytellers, calling them reporters or correspondents, and storytelling itself has become organized by modern techniques. Word by word, tales are brought home by telephone or wireless, and sometimes, buried in an abundance of reading material, they emerge as sparkling as precious diamonds from a heap of worthless stones (Arendt 1994, 85).

Thus reporters are (Homeric) storytellers and possess the power of narrative commentators have respected in Arendt herself (Miller 1979, 192; Disch 1994; Gottsegen 1994; Benhabib 1996, 87, 91-95). Moreover, reporters, because they are "buried" under so much material,[23] are in some measure genealogists—reconstructing a lineage of the truth from an array of sources and references. Finally, reporters, like painters, produce portraits of scenes and individuals. In June 1962, she wrote to Mary McCarthy that she was painting a portrait of Eichmann (Brightman 1995, 135), and *Eichmann in Jerusalem* is filled with both humorous and touching portraits of individuals caught up in the events of the Holocaust and the trial itself.[24]

In the *persona* of the reporter, then, we can observe many different roles—the chronicler, the historian, the storyteller, and the portrait artist. These roles will lead to two more roles Arendt emphasizes in her later writings—the Nietzschean spectator (called a "conscious pariah" by Disch 1994), and the judge (or the judging citizen). Certain reporters, we shall see, are detached spectators who, because of their detachment, grasp the "facts" of the event more fundamentally than the actors themselves.[25] These reporters combine detachment with a civic function—by sitting in judgment of the event. I will refer to one example of this kind of reporter—the theater critic.

Factuality

Arendt referred to independent journalism as "a mode of being alone" (Arendt 1968c, 260), and by this she observed more than that reporters, to do their job, must be self-reliant in the pursuit of truth. Like philosophers or judges, reporters confront facts in a solitary manner—they search for truth by understanding existentially its appearance in the world. Yet they do so by experiencing worldly events directly. In this manner, the reporter differs from the philosopher who withdraws him or herself from the world in order to think. The reporter actively seeks out facts by constantly engaging himself in the world of the event, a world that would otherwise distract the philosopher. Philosophers, judges, and reporters all confront facts as representations of (different) methods of seeing as well. As professionals, each group has learned a different approach to the facts. But all have learned to approach them existentially—that is, as bearers of truth and meaning in themselves.

The quest for factuality begins with experiences in the world. As Arendt put it at a conference in her honor in 1972:

> What is the subject of our thought? Experience! Nothing else! And if we lose the ground of experience then we get into all kinds of theories. When the political theorist begins to build his systems he is also usually dealing with abstraction (Arendt 1979, 308).

The first step toward truth is experience, a step diametrically opposed to those taken by political scientists, who, by working from theory, seek the Archimedean point and so abstract systems from the world. Indeed we are motivated to know the world from our curiosity about it, "our desire to investigate whatever is given to our sensory apparatus" (Arendt 1978, 58).

Following Leibniz, Arendt distinguishes between truths of reasoning and truths of fact and observes that truths of fact are contingent, yet "are as compelling for anybody witnessing them with his own eyes as the proposition that two and two make four is for anybody in his right mind" (59). Both sorts of truth compel, though while reasoning compels universally, factual truth compels in a more limited manner—"it does not reach those who, not having been witnesses, have to rely on the testimony of others, whom one may or may not believe" (59). Thus Arendt implies the vital importance of the reporter, who serves as the eyewitness to the event and whose independence from the event gives readers good reason to believe him or her as witness.

Arendt notes in *The Life of the Mind* that, historically, rational truths have been held to be "higher" than factual truths (Arendt 1978, 59-61; see also Arendt 1968c, 231). But she recognizes that factual truth pertains more appropriately to politics. The very contingency of factual truth—its momentary presence, its reliance on witnesses to corroborate it—corresponds precisely to the realm of freedom, because it, like freedom, is opposed to necessity (60).[26] Political truth, she concludes, cannot derive from reasoning or thinking, it must necessarily result from a confrontation with facts.[27]

But facts and events are vulnerable things—"infinitely more fragile things than axioms, discoveries, theories" (than, that is, the stuff of science), for "they occur in the field of the ever-changing affairs of men" (Arendt 1968c, 231). Arendt traces the different histories of philosophy and politics, arenas of activity corresponding to these types of truth (232-239) and notes the difficulty of those who must deal with the factual truths of politics. The reporter of factual truth

> does not return from any journey into regions beyond the realm of human affairs, and he cannot console himself with the thought that he has become a stranger in this world. If his simple factual statements are not accepted— truths seen and witnessed with the eyes of the body, not the eyes of the mind—the suspicion arises that it may be in the nature of the political realm to deny or pervert the truth of every kind, as though men were unable to come to terms with its unyielding, blatant, unpersuasive stubbornness (237).

But this is the bias of the philosopher, for in reality factual truth is always related to other people. "It is political by nature" (238), and it informs political thought "just as rational truth informs philosophical speculation" (238).

Even after matters have been discussed, theories formulated, and histories rewritten, what remains are the facts themselves.[28] This is what makes facts and the tellers of facts—so dangerous to political regimes. The facts cannot be changed, and so regimes can at best hope to muzzle their tellers. But censorship and repression cannot change those facts and if the reporters are muzzled, it will be up to future historians, storytellers, and poets to recount the facts to generations that will listen. Facts are thus hated by tyrants, "who rightly fear the competitions of coercive force they cannot monopolize," and even governments that rest on consent treat factual truth precariously.

Factual truth is not self-evident; it requires witnesses, testimony, documentation, monuments, and observation. Yet these can be unreliable or forged or coerced into lying. Thus, as Arendt observes through examples collected in *Crises of the Republic*, even republican governments have attacked the truth. The "hallmark of factual truth is that its opposite is neither error nor illusion nor opinion . . . but the deliberate falsehood, or lie" (Arendt 1968c, 249). Whether a politician or citizen, the liar is always an actor, because he distorts facts for political purposes.[29] The teller of truths, on the other hand, is not— indeed if the teller of truths even enters the political realm he "compromises on the only quality that could have made his truth appear plausible, namely, his personal truthfulness, guaranteed by impartiality, integrity, independence" (250). Arendt thus gives reasons why truth tellers, such as reporters, are vital to the establishment of a public realm, for they provide the facts necessary to combat the manipulative lies purveyed by politicians and other political actors. Furthermore, reporters do not themselves act, they merely observe as spectators, but in telling the truth they create the conditions necessary for political action, so that the truth can appear. Under certain circumstances, lies sometimes emerge to suppress the truth.

Another reason reporters are vital to the public realm is that they provide the sorts of factual truth necessary to manifest judgment. "The political function of the storyteller . . . is to teach acceptance of things as they are.[30] Out of this acceptance, which can also be called truthfulness, arises the faculty of judgment" (262). Judgment is a product of the truth that emerges from an impartial review of an event or a fact. Political thought is representative; it comes from considering the viewpoints of others as well as our own. One forms opinions by "making present to [one's] mind the standpoints of those who are absent; that is, [one] represents them" (241). The more people's standpoints a person has present in his or her mind the better that person can imagine how he or she would think about a given issue if they were in his or her place. This strengthens a person's capacity for representative thinking and renders that person's conclusions more valid. So political thought requires the powers of representation, imagination, and an "enlarged mentality" (Arendt 1968c, 241; 1982, 42-43; 1961, 220; see also Disch 1994).[31]

Thinking with an enlarged mentality differs from thinking at an Archimedean point. In the latter, one seeks a position outside an event in order to examine it in its totality and through so-called objective eyes. In the former, one imagines how others might view the same event in order to come to greater understanding of that event for oneself. Enlarged mentality corresponds to Charles Taylor's language of "perspicuous contrast" that I noted in chapter 1. Taylor argues that social scientists achieve understanding by developing such a language: a language in which we could formulate [different ways of life] as alternative possibilities in relation to some human constants at work in both. It would be a language in which the possible human variations would be so formulated that [all ways of life] could be perspicuously described as alternative such variations (Taylor 1985b, 125).

Taylor contends that through such a language the social scientist succumbs neither to the false objectivity of the positivist nor the radical subjectivity of the phenomenologist or ethnomethodologist. Instead, one takes the position of the other in order to better understand not only one's own position, but the truth of an event or situation.[32]

Such thinking is practiced in the method of reportage, for the journalist seeks truth by interviewing different witnesses or sources, each of whom may present a slightly different story. In fact, the reporter *seeks out* witnesses to action (more than, say, does the traditional social scientist, because it constitutes the very nature of his or her job).[33] The reporter must also know how to listen, and in his or her listening skills, he or she understands the facts.[34] It is the journalist's responsibility to sift through all the "material" and produce the truth. Consequently, the reporter employs an enlarged mentality in order to present the facts to an interested public. The reporter imagines a plurality of viewpoints in order to present the facts as accurately as he or she can.[35]

The only condition for the person who imagines is "disinterestedness, the liberation from one's own private interests" (Arendt 1968c, 242). In detaching oneself from one's own interests, the person establishes a place of "situated impartiality" that helps him or her to judge. So those who judge do so only because they are capable of separating themselves from their own personal material or political concerns or interests. But where do they find the "other's" point of view—especially if they live a rather solitary life? Here is where the role of the truth-teller looms large.[36]

The reporter, the historian, and the poet supply the citizen with facts and truths from which they can form judgments.[37] But the reporter is the only one of these truth-tellers who has been a witness to events, another observer of a political fact that the citizen may or may not have personally experienced. This gives the reporter a place of special importance in the story by which people's judgments come to be formulated and told. The reporter is another pair of eyes and ears to the citizen and whose power rests completely on his or her impartiality and integrity. The reporter is that *publicly recognized* individual who recounts stories from witnesses and data from original documents that permit stories to be re-told and judgments to be rendered. In doing so, reporters are the *first* individuals to bring facts *to* the world. Historians and poets re-tell stories composed of facts first discovered by reporters and witnesses.

Reportage then is a particular kind of storytelling—more often than not reporters are storytellers who have experienced the event at hand. This is not the case for historians or poets. For this reason the reporter might be a better model for the social scientist than these other two storytellers. Social science, after all, claims to present an understanding of empirical reality, and while it may not succeed (at least according to Arendt) in realizing its positivist self-image, reportage is the only form of truth-telling that can at least pretend to have encountered reality—in the presence of the event itself. Poets and historians organize facts and tell truths from afar (in both time and space). Correspondents live events, and so long as citizens believe that they possess integrity, citizens can employ the facts reporters render as part of the means by which they learn and by which they take the opinions of others into account before rendering judgment.[38]

Clearly the reporter is not one who should propagandize citizens with a viewpoint, with an opinion, though they often do (Edelman 1964). Reporters ought to provide the citizen with facts, not to influence that citizen, or even, many argue, to render judgment or opinions themselves even if their intent is not to influence.[39] Arendt admits that reportage involves opinion (Arendt 1958a, 36), and she believes that people ought to "think as though nobody had thought before, *and then start learning from everybody else*" (Arendt 1979, 337, emphasis added). But does this mean that it is the responsibility of the storyteller, for instance the reporter, to teach the citizen? If so, does this mean the reporter teaches the citizen facts about the world? Or can the reporter teach the citizen about judgment as well? Can the citizen, in "learning from everybody else," learn the arts of "situated impartiality," imagination, and "enlarged mentality" that Arendt recognizes as so vital for rendering good judgment?

In the next section, I will argue that the reporter can indeed teach civic judgment, if we consider a particular kind of reporter—the drama critic—and a particular method of reportage—theatrical criticism. For the theater critic combines the concern of a reporter (the truth), with the concern of a citizen (judgment)[40]—all from the position of a spectator who treats politics and political action as theatrical, as a dramatic performance of agonal display, communication, and public participation.

The Theater Critic: Toward An Arendtian Method in Political Science

The theater critic is a specific type of reporter.[41] Like any reporter he or she must present the "facts" of the event, in this case the play. Like any reporter this one must be interested in the human condition. But unlike most other reporters, the theater critic possesses an interest in the righteousness of the activity. The crime reporter can cover crime stories and yet not admire criminals or criminal activity; the business reporter can present economic issues while disagreeing fundamentally with the moral foundations of capitalism; the human interest reporter can report inconsequential stories about people without believing that human interest stories are interesting or important. But the theater critic, whether he or she likes or dislikes a particular play, must always defend the integrity and purposes of the theater as an activity. The critic does so for three reasons—first, to support him or herself with a job (the material interest); second, to recognize theater as a good (the moral interest); and third, to understand theater and theatrical performance as a representation of beauty in the world (the aesthetic interest). All reporters have material interests in the fields they cover (or to which they are assigned). But not all reporters need to defend these fields as public goods. To the critic, the theater is a good because it is a place where people can appear and where art can be created and judged according to the performance. The critic has an interest in defending the aesthetic ground of theater because he or she judges an event according to select criteria, among the most important of which must necessarily be its beauty.

Tellingly, another kind of reporter that possesses both a material and an aesthetic interest (if not a moral interest) in his or her field is the political reporter. For if politics does not exist the political reporter is out of a job. But, more importantly, however cynical the reporter is, however chary of their morality that reporter becomes after interviewing politicians and documenting their actions, that reporter must ultimately recognize the activity of politics as, in some sense, just and beautiful. They must defend their profession on grounds of political freedom, and in doing so, they have, like the theater critic, defended a realm of human action essential for human appearance. Moreover, the more theatrical the politics the more reporters seem to enjoy covering events. At the very least, events are springs from which stories flow; the more theatrical those events, the more stories reporters have to tell.[42]

The Spectator

As the name implies, the theater critic differs from a reporter; he or she is a critic. The critic is a spectator, but an interested spectator—one concerned not only with the event itself but in the aesthetic and moral purposes behind the event. The critic does not merely report, the critic judges. The reporter writes primarily for those who did not witness an event but who nonetheless have an interest in it. The actors in the event may be interested to read the accounts of the witnesses, if, for instance, a politician wishes to gauge public opinion on his actions. But the independent reporter does not write *for* the politician (though the op-ed writer might). The theater critic customarily writes for both those who did and did not witness the drama and those who acted in it as well.

The critic has an interest in attracting different types of readers. Some readers who did not attend the performance may still attend, so the critic provides a guide for them. The theater critic pays special attention to accurately recounting the story and giving a reasoned judgment on the material and aesthetic worth of the play. Those who have already attended the play want another interpretation of the play in order to understand moments they may not have understood while in attendance and to consider or re-consider their judgments about the drama as a whole. The actors (and anyone associated with the production) want to know how successful their interpretation was, and any constructive criticism serves to improve it. Such improvement is also part of the critic's aesthetic interest in drama. Finally, for those who did not attend and had no intention of ever attending (presumably most readers), the critic's review helps determine their final vision (from the Greek *thea*) and judgment of the event. The critic serves here as the model citizen in Arendt's terms.

The critic does not, however, write from an Archimedean point, because the critic understands well that his or her task is inseparable from the event itself. He or she has, as I have noted, interests in the event, and the consequences of his or her review affects the event itself. A bad review can close the play, certain comments can improve the acting or staging of the play, and any judgment colors the way some future audience members might view the play themselves. The critic also writes from the position of the "conscious pariah" (Ring 1991; Disch 1994, 173-185), because he or she is well aware of his or her "special" status vis-à-vis both the audience and the actors. The critic must pay more attention to the drama than the typical audience member, and the critic is also conscious that actors might play to the critic,[43] and not to the audience. But ultimately the critic is aware that he or she is part of the theater of performance, in the way audience members were aware of participating in the Theater of Dionysos.

As an interested spectator, the theater critic shares in a kind of philosophical thinking Arendt describes in *The Life of the Mind* (Arendt 1978, 92-98) and

Lectures on Kant's Political Philosophy (Arendt 1982, 55-65). Philosophical thought takes place in solitude, where one is deserted by others, but never by oneself (Arendt 1978, 185). One thinks consciously with oneself (*consciousness*: "to know with myself"). To achieve this state one must withdraw from the world of activity, from doing. To think, one does not act, one takes the position of the spectator. But the spectator is not always the eyewitness or even the first-hand storyteller (e.g., the poet or the historian). The general reporter can be a witness or the teller of facts and stories, though not always a spectator (because the reporter is by definition not by or with himself, in solitude, and because the task of the reporter is not always thinking or judgment). However, the theater critic, as a kind of reporter, is a professional spectator, but one who at times must withdraw from the site of the performance itself in order to reflect on his or her experiences there. So he or she is a member of the theatrical community but one who is not *performing* continuously, either as an actor or a member of the audience.

Thinking demands "the peculiar *quiet*, absence of any doing or disturbances, the withdrawal from involvement and from the partiality of immediate interests that in one way or another make me part of the real world, a withdrawal . . . as the condition prerequisite for all judgment" (92, see also 76). This sort of withdrawal originated in the discovery "that only the *spectator*, never the actor, can know and understand whatever offers itself as spectacle" (92). This was elaborated in *schole*—"the deliberate act of abstaining, of holding oneself back (*schein*) from the ordinary activities determined by our daily wants (*he ton anagkaion schole*), in order to act out leisure (*scholen agein*), which in turn was the true goal of all other activities" (92-93). The scholar, then, is literally one who withdraws from the action and observes the protagonists as spectators (*theatai*), and so views life "like a festival," Arendt notes in a parable of Pythagoras to that effect. The scholar understands by theory not a formal system derived from the Archimedean standpoint, but "looking upon something from the outside, from a position implying a view that is hidden from those who take part in the spectacle and actualize it" (93). The critic occupies a position sufficiently distant from the action to see the whole play in such a manner. Furthermore, the actor is concerned with *doxa*, or public opinion, but not the critic, who does not care how he or she appears to others.[44]

Nevertheless, the critic is not the philosopher. The philosopher, Arendt remarks, leaves the world of appearances to think. The spectator who judges (i.e., the critic) "does not leave the world of appearances, but retires from active involvement in it to a privileged position in order to contemplate the whole" (94). The critic attends the performance in the company of his or her fellow citizens. Thus the spectator-critic's opinion is not independent of the views of others—indeed the critic might note the reaction of his or her fellow audience members—but one who must think from what Kant called an "enlarged mentality" (94). The spectator is disengaged, but is not self-sufficient or solitary, and for this reason he or she is the model, not of philosophical thought, but of judgment.

Thus an Arendtian method in political science can be one that cultivates judgment, not pure thinking. This is not surprising because the science of politics takes as its subject matter the polis and its constituent parts, the most important of which are its citizen-actors. The citizen is not the philosopher—the philosopher must withdraw from civic activities to think—but rather the political actor and judge of political action. As spectator the citizen has the right to judge and render the final verdict on events "on no other grounds than his 'wishful participation bordering on enthusiasm,' his sharing in the 'exaltation of the uninvolved public,' his basing himself, in other words, on the judgment of his fellow-spectators, who also had not 'the least intention of assisting' in the events" (95). Those who sit in judgment, claims Arendt, following Kant, should have the last word on the event. Those professionals who sit in judgment, such as the theater critic, help guide the "wishful participants" and contribute more than most to the judgment of their fellow spectators. Is this not the goal of political science?

Only spectators hold the clues to the meaning of the whole; so spectatorship is a plural enterprise.[45] Thus it is vital to the meaning of the play that there exist more than one critic, and more than one audience. This is possible for the historian and poet as storytellers, because with each new generation there are new audiences who find fresh truths in the play no matter how many times it is performed, no matter what "tradition" has dictated about that play. So with each event there will be a multiplicity of reports and a multiplicity of original judgments rendered about it, and from them citizens will re-learn the art of political judgment. This will also contribute to public deliberation by introducing an opinion about the spectacle to the public upon which learned debate can be engaged.

Rendering Judgment

As we know from Arendt's Kant lectures (Arendt 1982), political judgment derives from taste, an aesthetic sensibility. Thus, it would seem logical that Arendt's citizen-judge is analogous to the theater critic. However, the citizen is usually engaged in action—even citizen-spectators are called upon to vote or engage in public political discourse in one way or another. The citizen does not, cannot, withdraw from the world, in the way that a critic withdraws from a performance in order to do his or her job. So I am not making such a broad analogy here. I am suggesting that the political scientist—as a citizen specially interested in the political spectacle, as an influential guide to civic judgment, and as a person concerned about the appearance of the world but one who disappears from it in order to think about it—is the appropriate analogue to the theater critic.

In modeling political inquiry along these lines, I am arguing that political science can re-create the *sensus communis* Arendt highlights from Kant's Third Critique.[46] Remember, this is the same common sense that she argues is missing in the practice of the modern scientific enterprise. I have already mentioned that she is wrong in her assessment, but I believe that her argument lends weight to social scientists who seek to model politics along non-empirical and non-formal lines. Arendt notes that the eighteenth-century aesthetic project, of which Kant was a central part, was "enormously" interested in "art and *art criticism*, the goal of which was to lay down rules for taste, to establish standards in the arts" (32). Arendt emphasized the critical project of the enlightenment because the term "critique" opposed both dogmatic metaphysics and skepticism, and this is precisely the position of many social scientists today. How does one develop a method of inquiry that does not hold positivist or empiricist truths to be self-evident and yet does not succumb to radical skepticism or even anti-foundationalism? Arendt's arguments offer a possible way around these alternatives.

Both Socrates and Kant made public, through discourse, the thinking process (37ff)—they politicized thought in a sense. Socrates did this in the marketplace, Kant as a scholar before the reading public. Though Arendt admits that the scholar is not the citizen, she recognizes that Kant believed that thinking itself depends on its public use (40), thus truth must be communicated or the philosopher will lose the faculty of thinking. So there are political purposes to philosophical thought, for truth must be communicated. This, I would argue, places political scientists in a special position, because they are professional thinkers concerned with the public realm and so are caught between the world and the study. As philosophers, Socrates and Kant recognized the need for solitude to think, but *like theater critics*, Socrates and Kant recognized the need to communicate thinking to citizens, not only to save their own faculty of thought, but to help citizens *as spectators* render good judgment.

Just as the pure spectator cannot account for the world (53), the detached political scientist in search of the Archimedean point cannot communicate easily truths about the world in a common language meaningful to the public. This is ironic because the political scientist is a thinker theoretically concerned not only about, but for, the world, by virtue of his or her subject matter. It is also ironic because most political scientists are *teachers*, and are thus concerned, in theory, with communicating their ideas to students.

Arendt seems to prefer the Greek spectator who "looks at and judges (finds the truth of) the cosmos of the particular event in its own terms" to the Kantian spectator who judges the importance of an event "not at its end but in its opening up new horizons for the future" (56). If I have read Arendt correctly, it is precisely this Greek spectator—in the theater of Dionysos, as an active critic, and as a witness to the event—that she deems crucial to the public realm. I would argue that in the modern world, the social scientist can potentially play this role, where that social scientist learns to judge events on their own terms, and does not try to impose meaning on them from abstract theories. The Kantian social scientist concerns him or herself with whether progress is being made; the Arendtian social scientist simply tries to find meaning the event itself. Both sorts of social scientist concern themselves with communicating ideas to the public and to students and so engage in research for pedagogical reasons.

The Kantian spectator is one who, as we have seen, demands that thought become public. This public is the reading public, "and it is the weight of their opinion he is appealing to, not the weight of their votes" (60).[47] Indeed, during Kant's day, this *was* the public, there was no other because either court politics rendered decisions in a secret or conspiratorial manner or the general public was constituted by subjects, not citizens, and so were, by definition, excluded from the public realm. He noted that what made the French Revolution an unforgettable event was that it was acclaimed by a reading public who were not actors, but spectators who had no intention of participating in the action itself.

I have already suggested that this describes the theater critic who addresses the readership of his or her newspaper or periodical. Consequently, it describes the condition of the political or social scientist. For these "public scholars," to use an oxymoron, speak not to the general public, but to an educated reading public. If they deploy very specialized jargon they lose this public and address only individual researchers working in particular areas. They also lose their younger students as a public in trying to teach them their ideas framed in obscure language or technical jargon. But when they employ a common language they appeal to all educated individuals, including their own students, who look to them for information with which to judge events in the world.

According to Kant, genius is the faculty of mind that creates art, but taste is that faculty which judges the art created (62).[48] Genius must communicate itself, and taste guides this process: "the judgment of the spectator creates the space without which no such objects could appear at all," or in Kantian terms, "the very originality of the artist (or the very novelty of the actor) depends on his making himself understood by those who are not artists (or actors)" (63). The political scientist, as a kind of theater critic, offers the literate public certain aesthetic criteria by which they can judge the "genius" of political action. Arendt here seems to suggest that it is the spectator himself—in my example, the political scientist—that creates the space for politics to appear. This seems to contradict Arendt's argument in *The Human Condition* that only actors make political space appear. But, as I have tried to argue in chapter 2, if one analogizes politics to classical Greek theater, space can appear in a kind of dialogue between actor, chorus, and spectator. The political scientist is situated at this nexus, seated between the *skene* and the *theatron*.[49]

The problem with taste is that it is, with smell, the most private of the senses, and as such is not communicable. "There can be no dispute about matters of taste" (66), and this is a problem for our political scientist because it would seem to be an obstacle to his public responsibilities and importance. Arendt suggests that this problem is solved by Kant in two ways—by positing the faculties of imagination and common sense (66-67). Imagination makes present what is absent and so permits us to represent events to ourselves (79-85). In doing so the imagination helps us conceptualize concrete activities and objects. It is also vital in grounding memory, and so is the faculty necessary for historical understanding. Imagination permits us to communicate concepts because we can devise "schemas" in the back of our minds which are also found in the backs of the minds of others. This common mental structure, Kant argues, helps taste become publicly communicable. Conceived in this way, the imagination itself assists political scientists in their work, by presupposing that common understanding is possible in the reading public. It also opens the door for political psychology to understand better this common background.[50]

The faculty of common sense, which sparks reflection, brings us back to where we started at the beginning of the chapter—into a realm where understanding with others is crucial to our taste, for it confirms our own taste. Where others agree with us we believe our taste to be good, where they disagree we might learn to refine our tastes.[51] This is a message delivered by the theater critic, and it is one experienced by any literate person who puts his or her ideas out in public (take, for example, the graduate student defending his or her dissertation in front of a committee or the intellectual who publishes rejoinders after a public exchange in a journal or periodical). To Arendt, it is nothing more than reflection upon the perspectives of others which one then compares and contrasts with one's own position so that one achieves an "enlarged mentality." It is the imagination "going visiting" (see Disch 1994, 157-163), a capacity I would argue crucial for the political scientist to possess if he or she has any hope to communicate his or her ideas to either the literate public or his or her own students.

Following Arendt (1982, who follows Kant), I would argue that the political scientist can offer examples by which the public judges the reasonableness of his or her argument (76-77, 84-85; see also Bernstein 1986, 235). In presenting examples the social scientist offers the reader a communicable object for their understanding. From the example the reader imagines the best possible object and takes this object as the example of how objects of this sort ought to be. "The exemplar is and remains a particular that in its very particularity reveals the generality that otherwise could not be defined" (77, see also 84). In the case of political science this would mean offering the "truth" of a principle in the form of an exemplary event, or person, or fact. In the well-chosen presentation of an exemplar the thought of the political scientist can remain communicable. If the example is not well-chosen, or if abstractions are presented, communication breaks down, and the political scientist loses his or her seat between theatron and skene. He or she either takes to the stage, or, more likely, ends up talking in an obscure section of the theater.

In the next few chapters I hope to offer examples that validate my argument here, and in these chapters my success as a critic can best be judged. I look first at instances of an Arendtian method of political research. In chapter 4, I analyze one research project in which Arendt herself engaged—the trial of Adolf Eichmann. I contend that *Eichmann in Jerusalem* was itself an exemplar of a nascent method of political research. In chapter 6, I describe and analyze the founding of the European Community as an example of the theory of revolution Arendt posits in *On Revolution*. In so doing I suggest the importance of exemplary validity in comparative politics and the possibility of fostering political judgment in the process of academic research. In chapters 7 and 8, I examine the teaching and service practices of institutions of higher education as means by which universities and colleges may teach judgment. In none of these examples do I attempt to seek an Archimedean point, for I recognize the importance of other viewpoints as I develop my argument.

Notes

1.   She is not unequivocal in her criticism of science, for she recognizes that it does reveal truth in many human endeavors. Note, for example, her high regard for biological discoveries, and their application to the human mind, in the early chapters of "Thinking" from *The Life of the Mind* (Arendt 1978). She is rather charitable toward the scientific enterprise (55).

2.   Martin Jay (Jay and Botstein 1978) argues that this connection emerges from her *Existenz* philosophy (364). Robert Pirro (1996) roots it in a tradition of German panhellenism (36).

3.   Jay (Jay and Botstein 1978), though excoriating Arendt, recognizes her importance to future scholars on methodological grounds (366).

4.   In a moment of speculative history, Arendt (1958b) recognizes the collective nature of the scientific enterprise. She suggests that objectivity was born with the founding of the Royal Society, whose members agreed to take no part in political or religious matters. Thus the origin of the ideal might be political and not scientific. She continues by noting that the Royal Society signified a political organization of science and that "no scientific teamwork is pure science" (367). But to say this is still not to recognize that an *aim* of science is to create common (scientific) sense.

5.   Dagmar Barnouw (1990) comments that her prologue to *The Human Condition* "should not be misunderstood as a critique of modern science and technology," because Arendt recognized the importance of specialized language in making scientific achievement possible. "Rather, Arendt wished to stress the implications of scientific and technological mastery for political speech and action" (196-197). This latter point is well-taken, but it is also clear that Arendt believed the scientist's quest for an Archimedean point was misguided. This argument, and not those on language, I have taken to be the central message of the prologue.

6.   See, for instance, some of the essays collected in *Essays in Understanding* (1994); for instance, "A Reply to Eric Voegelin" (401-408), "On the Nature of Totalitarianism: An Essay in Understanding" (339), and "Religion and Politics" (374-379).

7.   She elaborates this critique in "Thinking" in *The Life of the Mind* (1978), 27ff.

8.   In *On Violence* (Arendt 1970), she offers two other instances of social scientists failing to uncover truth in their attempt to model theories on the natural sciences. Sociologists need not look to "zoology" to understand the nature of human aggression, but rather to poverty in cities (59), and psychologists cannot use biological data to measure human behavior because research from animals cannot be measured against what might be required for human beings to behave in such manner (61). Psychologists and sociologists are either unclear about the difference between animals and humans, or mistakenly believe that it is merely reason that constitutes it (62). Peter Fuss (1979) clarifies Arendt's observation: "Our inability to name, that is, to fix in words the distinctive essence of the person as it manifests itself in the living flow of action and speech appears to be closely interrelated with the fact that we cannot handle the realm of human affairs (in which after all we exist primarily as actors and speakers) in the way we

can handle those things whose nature is so much at our disposal—just because we are able to name (to specify, to classify, in the end to have done with) them" (161-162).

9. Social scientists do not make distinctions between central concepts, such as power, force, authority, and violence either, and so cannot help us understand the meaning of the terms (Arendt 1970, 43). Paul Ricoeur emphasizes this point in his essay "Pouvoir et Violence" (Abensour et al. 1996, 159).

10. This explains her observation that ideologies "are known for their scientific character" (Arendt 1973, 468). She roots social science in the works of Marx (1994, 374-379), a founder of modern ideological thinking. She also suggests that its methods and worldview apply well to the development of ideology, because an ideology is "the logic of an idea" that connotes "the unfolding of a process which is in constant change" (Arendt 1973, 469), and thus one which understands itself as scientific. In response to the "tyranny of logicality" which springs from the fear of contradicting ourselves, Arendt seeks an understanding of the world marked by "freedom as an inner capacity of man that is identical with the capacity to begin" (473).

The sentiment expressed in the quote noted in the text also marks her well-known antipathy to psychoanalysis. The science of psychology disturbs her for one of the same reasons she laments the rise of Cartesianism—it effaces distinctions between people.

11. Elsewhere Arendt hints that social scientists might be guilty of philistinism, when she defines a philistine as one unable "to think and to judge a thing apart from its function or utility" (Arendt 1961, 215).

12. Such behavior is measured by statistics, but "statistical uniformity is by no means a harmless scientific ideal; it is the no longer secret political ideal of a society which, entirely submerged in the routine of everyday living [i.e., the social realm], is at peace with the scientific outlook inherent in its very existence" (Arendt 1958b, 40). She concludes that the behavioral sciences thus "aim to reduce man as a whole, in all his activities, to the level of a conditioned and behaving animal" (41). This permits the rise of bureaucracy and the administrative state, thus violating the very premises of their own objectivity. The behavioral sciences abet the victory of the social over the political, and so cannot remain neutral.

13. In contrast to science, Arendt posits a narrative method in the closing pages of *The Human Condition*: "The action of the scientists, since it acts into nature from the standpoint of the universe and not into the web of human relationships, lacks the revelatory character of action as well as the ability to produce stories and become historical, which together form the very source from which meaningfulness springs into and illuminates human existence" (Arendt 1958b, 296-297).

14. Claude Lefort (1988) argues that Arendt does not look for models of politics "but for a reference to politics in certain privileged moments when its features are most clearly discernible" (50).

15. Karl Jaspers praised the reports she was constantly sending him on her various travels (Kohler and Saner 1992, 436), and even noted that her descriptions and analysis of the Eichmann trial in her letters were the source of everything essential to the trial (434). Sylvie Courtine-Denamy (1997) notes that "all of her life...Arendt remained a passionate observer of American political life, an 'enlightened' citizen, never missing the great moments of history [in the world]" (41).

16. George Kateb (1977) remarks that "the self-knowledge that comes to us from the observation of others is superior to the self-knowledge we gain by introspection" (149). His comment highlights both Arendt's antipathy to psychological explanation and

the virtue of those who observe others, such as reporters. Though Arendt may not have agreed with the importance of this point, another advantage of reportage is the greater understanding we will have of ourselves in the process.

17. "The meaningfulness of everyday relationships is disclosed not in everyday life but in rare deeds, just as the significance of a historical period shows itself only in the few events that illuminate it" (Arendt 1958b, 39). In *The Human Condition* Arendt argues that modern social sciences, such as economics or sociology, build theories upon the very commonness of individual experience. This permits such "sciences" to employ statistical analysis (39-41).

18. Arendt referred to the founding of the United States Constitution and the French Revolution as the two single greatest "events" in modern political history (Arendt 1957, 27).

19. Consequently, I do not interpret Arendt's concept of political action as a space, strictly conceived as a gap (Honig 1995, 146). On the contrary, spaces are those places where actors engage in the event. The "agonistic disruption of the ordinary sequence of things that makes way for novelty and distinction" is a substantive event itself, it is not a(n empty) mark or site of conflict. As I also argue in the Appendix, it is not an empty space (at least as Arendt conceives it—Dietz 1996), but one cohabited by communication and agonal display.

20. I will argue below that this differs substantively from the role of the theater critic who is also a reporter and also reports the facts—of the play—but whose role it is to start the process of communication by registering at least one opinion—namely the critic's own.

21. Note, for instance, her observation concerning the role of the *New York Times* in revealing facts hidden by the Soviets during the Hungarian Revolution (Arendt 1958a, 22).

22. The degree to which she associates reportage with fact finding and telling can best be seen in her review of Rolf Hochhuth's, *The Deputy*. She admires the play because it is factual—"the play might as well be called the most factual literary work of this generation . . . [it] is almost a report, closely documented on all sides, using actual events and real people" (Arendt 1964a, 86).

23. The image of a reporter as "awash" in reading material and references is reinforced in her complaints to McCarthy about composing *Eichmann in Jerusalem*. She was drained by the amount of material she was assimilating, but she admitted that she loved what she was doing at the same time (Brightman 1995, 131, 135).

24. As an example, note the picture she paints of Zivia Lubetkin Zuckerman, a Holocaust survivor about 40 year old—"still very beautiful, completely free of sentimentality or self-indulgence, her facts well-organized, and always quite sure of the point she wished to make" (Arendt 1964b, 121). She contrasted this survivor with others who she could not take as seriously because they did not stick to the matter at hand. They did not, in short, report the facts of the case as the demands of a trial ought to have required that they do. Note also her unflattering "portraits" of, for instance, Dr. Servatius or Gideon Hausner. Finally, Arendt was not averse to presented, with a kind of "macabre humor," the portrait of Eichmann as a buffoon. This, as is well-known, caused quite a controversy among the international Jewish community.

25. Appearances demand spectators as a condition for their appearance (Arendt 1978, 46, 92-98), and reporters are among the most ubiquitous of spectators.

26. For an elaboration of her argument see "The Public Realm and the Private Realm" in *The Human Condition* (Arendt 1958b).

27. Arendt actually makes this claim concerning *all* truths—political, scientific, or otherwise—but for the purposes of my argument here I need only refer to political truths (Arendt 1978, 61).

28. This may be captured in "the phenomenon of language, for in it the past is contained ineradicably, thwarting all attempts to get rid of it once and for all" (Arendt 1968b, 204). Arendt examines the etymologies of words as a reporter might approach facts; indeed the word is the linguistic fact of the concept or object it represents.

29. This is just as true for so-called "democratic" governments as it is for tyrannical ones. Arendt notes a modern form of lying—political image-making. She recognizes that "an image, unlike an old-fashioned portrait, is supposed not to flatter reality but to offer a full-fledged substitute for it. And this substitute, because of modern techniques and the mass media is, of course, much more in the public eye than the original ever was" (Arendt 1968c, 252). This suggests that her representation of the reporter-as-portrait-artist signifies that the reporter is not out to lie, but to illustrate (or flatter) the truth.

30. That is, they exist in the world. She is not recommending a conservative acquiescence to the status quo.

31. Seyla Benhabib (1988) notes that enlarged mentality "does not mean assuming or accepting the point of view of the other. It means merely making present to oneself what the perspective of others involves or could be, and whether I can 'woo their consent' in acting the way I do" (43-44). She articulates the ethical and political consequences of this stance: "the creation of institutions and practices whereby the voice and the perspective of others, often unknown to us, can become expressed in their own right" (47). If this is correct (whatever it may mean), then reportage becomes essential in creating such institutions.

32. Taylor elsewhere refers to this as a "language of qualitative contrast" (Taylor 1985b, 236-244). Both Taylor and Arendt observe that Montesquieu exemplified this sort of thinking in trying to understand the distinction between a monarchy and a republic. Both, following Kant, place this language "in the aesthetic domain," and both recognize that such a manner of thinking, or a language of expression, is not neutral, in the positivist sense of the term.

33. Hinchman and Hinchman (1994) argue that this reflects Arendt's *Existenz* philosophy. For the constituent parts of this philosophy see this essay, as well as Martin Jay (Jay and Botstein 1978), 350-351.

34. Note Benhabib (1988) on "enlarged mentality": "we must think of such enlarged thought as a condition of actual or simulated dialogue. To 'think from the perspective of everyone else' is to know 'how to listen' to what the other is saying, or when the voices of others are absent, to imagine to oneself a conversation with the other as my dialogue partner" (44). Who understands this better than the reporter?

35. The consequence of this was articulated brilliantly by the international war correspondent for Cable News Network, Christiane Amanpour, during an interview on the Charlie Rose program on the Public Broadcasting System, November 26, 1997. She defined objectivity in journalism as giving an equal hearing to all sides of a conflict, not in treating all sides equally. For instance, in the Bosnian war, where rape, murder, and genocide have been commonplace, if the reporter treats all sides equally he or she is merely a neutral observer, and thus an accomplice, to war crimes and atrocities. The objective journalist is the one who uses his or her judgment to present facts to an uninformed world public, and this is very much a political task.

36. This, of course, is an idealized account of the reporter. While many so-called reporters emphasize sensational stories or care little about the meaning of the event, some reporters investigate the world to bring truth to the public.

37. Arendt (1978) recounts a poem of Pindar that describes the marriage feast of Zeus, at which the assembled gods asked Zeus to create a new divine being who could beautify his works "with words and music." Pindar suggests that these new beings were the poets and bards who helped men gain immortality. The bards "straightened the story" to charm people. In Arendt's words, "they did not merely report, the also set it right" (132). For Arendt, those who tell stories do more than simply report action, they contribute toward the public's judgment of that action. I elaborate this point below.

38. So they represent the storyteller who cannot withdraw from action, and lives, according to Disch (1994) "on the margins" of the public realm (155). Here I would also note Peter Fuss' observation (Fuss 1979, 165) that within each civic observer sits the actor and the witness (though I suspect this represents Arendt's early conception of the relation between the actor and the spectator, one she had modified by the writing of *The Life of the Mind*).

39. An additional virtue of journalism as a model of political understanding comes from Benjamin Franklin. In raising a call for republican schools, Franklin lauded "journalistic rhetoric" and the newspaper *The Spectator*. Studying journalistic reports cultivated a "vivid oral reading voice among boys" and so equipped future citizens with the power of the written word (quoted in Pangle 1992, 170). In newspapers students are exposed to the give-and-take of public argument, and this helps cultivate the virtues of open-mindedness and public concern necessary for republican citizenship. This reading of Franklin is consistent with Arendt's interpretation of the founding of America in *On Revolution* (Arendt 1965). By clearly articulating the issues of the day journalists foster political freedom, and students can be trained to be as clear in publicizing what they know and what they opine by vocalizing the journal article.

40. The theater critic might be analogous to what Arendt called, in "The Crisis of Culture," the humanist. The humanist "is not a specialist, exerts a faculty of judgment and taste which is beyond the coercion which each specialty imposes upon us," and so humanists "rise above specialization and philistinism" (Arendt 1961, 225).

41. He or she is also a specific type of critic—that is to say, not a food, film, or TV critic—for none of these critics cover events that Arendt would analogize to politics, as I pointed out in an earlier chapter. Though the theater critic and the music critic (live music, not recorded music) may have much in common.

42. Even a superficial familiarity with Louisiana politics renders this truth something other than a mere tale.

43. As Sandra Hinchman (1984) recognizes: "Arendt argues that the fact that they are watched while acting (*spectemur agendo*) disinclines actors to do beastly things. The audience does not simply witness action but contributes layers of judgment, meaning, and interpretation to each act. These latter, in turn, affect the self-understanding and hence the future actions of the performer, but without jeopardizing choice or freedom. Emulation at one and the same time ratifies the *Existenz* of actors and serves as a check on their tyrannical tendencies" (333). I would argue that the presence in the audience of the critic further checks such tendencies because actors have at least a material, and probably an aesthetic, interest in the success of their performance. The individual critic plays a necessary, if not sufficient, role in determining the success of most plays.

44. For this reason, Arendt argues in the Kant lectures, "the actor is dependent on the opinion of the spectator, he is not autonomous" (Arendt 1982, 55). But note Richard

Sennett's observation that in the nineteenth century the spectator depended on the actor for cues as to how his emotional life should be fulfilled (Sennett 1974). So Arendt's claim is historically contingent—though she would respond that our emotional life would not enter into the public realm in the way she describes it. I agree with Sennett that our emotions constitute part of our aesthetic understanding of the public realm, because they constitute a part of our experience of the world.

45. "Only where things can be seen by many in a variety of aspects without changing their identity, so that those who are gathered around them know they see sameness in utter diversity, can worldly reality truly and reliably appear" (Arendt 1958b, 52-53).

46. I would also suggest that political science requires a kind of flexibility inherent in the position of the critic. Arendt defines criticism as "always taking sides for the world's sake, understanding and judging everything in terms of its position in the world at any given time. Such a mentality can never give rise to a definite world view which, once adopted, is immune to further experiences in the world because it has hitched itself firmly to one perspective" (Arendt 1968b, 7-8).

47. In *The Human Condition*, Arendt states that a public need not inhabit a common physical space: "action and speech create a space between participants which can find its proper location almost any time and anywhere" (Arendt 1958b, 177).

48. See also Arendt 1961, 219, 222; and Bernstein 1986, 229.

49. Thomas Jefferson expressed this well by arguing for political science education in order to prevent tyranny. This sort of education was essential to give "knowledge of the past...that...[young citizens] may be enabled to know ambition under all its shapes, and prompt to exert their natural powers to defeat its purposes" (quoted by Pangle 1992, 173).

50. Note the Kantian roots to the recently developed schema theory as currently practiced by some political psychologists. This theory is one whose proponents argue is post-positivist, and it can serve as one example of an interpretive social science method that bears some relation to taste.

51. In Arendt's terms, "the it-pleases-or-displeases-me, which as a feeling seems to utterly private and noncommunicative, is actually rooted in this community sense and is therefore open to communication once it has been transformed by reflection, which takes all others and their feelings into account" (Arendt 1982, 72).

Chapter 4

Making an Example Out of Eichmann

Captain Avner Less: Wisliceny was further asked whether at the time you had said anything more about the number of Jews killed. He answered: "Eichmann put it in a particularly cynical way. He said that the knowledge of having five million Jews on his conscience gave him such extraordinary satisfaction that he would jump into his grave laughing."

Adolf Eichmann: That is . . . theater, theater! That is . . . I can't think of anything else to call it but theater. . . . Because that was my . . . my . . . summation in the . . . in the . . . how shall I put it . . . in this apocalyptic situation . . . which, which for a few days threw me into a state of shock not nervous shock, but . . . moral shock: The Reich is kaput, it's all been a waste, it's all been for nothing, the whole war has been for nothing. That's what I said, that's what I told you. But this is theater! I never said it, never said it, Herr Hauptmann. The grave, yes, that's the only part that's right. The grave is right, I did say that . . .

von Lang and Sibyll (1983, 164)

To say that Hannah Arendt possessed a nascent theory of reportage or theatrical criticism is not to say that it serves as the only method political scientists can learn from her. But, for reasons I gave in the previous chapter, it is probably most relevant within the framework of traditional social science. Her historical, philosophical, and literary methods, though valuable, do not speak to issues that concern most political and social researchers: namely, how one gets at the truth, presents facts, and understands social and political features of our complex world.

To clarify her method of reportage I will examine in more detail the best example extant of this method, *Eichmann in Jerusalem*.[1] She wrote this book as a report, and she acknowledges repeatedly, both in the book itself and in replies to her critics, the importance of this *form* of presentation. I contend that her method here is not strictly, or should I say conventionally, reportage, but rather a report from one who views the trial from the position of a member of an audience. That she attended the trial is decisive for my analysis and critique of her position, because her position was a "privileged" one. As part of the press corps she had access to people and facts (events) that her readers did not, and she was one of the very few who was present at the proceedings. Some "world-citizens" watched the affair on television, but this, I argue, was a categorically different kind of experience. As a reporter, Arendt discovered a method of truth-telling, as a critic at the "performance," she analyzed the event distinctively, and the combination of both roles suggests the beginnings of a method of political inquiry.[2]

I will support my claims with comparisons to *On Revolution*, a book she researched and wrote before the Eichmann trial, but one she edited while writing her report on that trial. There are elements of reportage and theatrical criticism in this work as well, which has been traditionally viewed as an historical exercise for Arendt. In this text, she blends historical concerns with a vision of the American and French Revolutions as events in the form of plays whose plots unfolded in front of contemporary spectators. As she reconstructs the history of these events the plot unfolds anew in front of her eyes, eyes that are even further removed from the action.[3] Consequently both the Eichmann and revolution books exemplify, in part, one version of what an Arendtian social science appears to be.[4]

The Court Is in Session!

With these words, members of the audience at the trial of Adolf Eichmann, the prosecution, the defendant and his attorney, all came to order. It would be a collective experience unforgettable to anyone present and depicted in minute detail by a veritable army of press reporters and television cameras surrounding the courtroom. But it would also be a collective experience that, despite the presence of television, would be one shared only by those present.

Arendt believed that an unmediated experience of this event was significant for both her life and her work.[5] I would suggest that her presence at the trial permitted her understanding of the facts that would have been unavailable to someone who was watching the proceedings on television. This medium of communication is not neutral, and following a trial at home is not the same as observing it in the courtroom. Alain Finkielkraut explains:

> In the courtroom, you can't telephone or do busy work or flop down or help your children with their homework—or even munch an apple. 'Court is in session!': bodily functions have to be brought under control, the drone of

daily life has to be suspended so that the judicial ceremony can unfold. The same principle holds true, in fact, for justice as for religion, for theater or for the act of teaching—it can be done anywhere (a table suffices), but only by isolating the time and the space of those interactions from their secular settings. . . . Television presents the sacred as food for the secular, and puts the outside world at the mercy of the private world. Under the guise of having the world enter the home, television allows the home to impose itself on the world. No work is admirable enough, no catastrophe terrible enough, no word edifying enough to make us stop eating our apple or talking back to the screen. With television, the drone of life triumphs over every interruption—*life is never silent*. It is no longer man who must step outside the eternal round of needs and satisfactions and tear himself from his life (biological, private, day-to-day) in order to make himself available to the world's humanity; the human world is delivered to his home, and is put at the disposal of life, just like the apple. . . . Such a reversal implies, more generally, the disappearance of everything that transcends the maintenance or reproduction of daily life (Finkielkraut 1992, 70-71).

Television brings the world of action, of politics, into the private realm, the world of necessity. The viewer appropriates the televised image and assimilates it into his or her daily routine. In other words, television does not normally require that the viewer *stop* and think, and so the person viewing need not distance him or herself from his or her *own* life while watching television. The television viewer is not the Arendtian spectator, and so cannot adequately appreciate events in order to render judgment about them. Thus the televised spectacle does not always have the same impact as seeing the performance in the theater (Kirchheimer 1961, 117, 422-423, 430), and this was indeed the case with the Eichmann trial itself (Rogat 1961, 14; Glock et al. 1966, 168).

"The court is in session!"—after hearing these words with her own ears, Hannah Arendt was afforded the opportunity to stop and think. She began looking at the man who would become the center of her analysis and to think about ways of presenting her experience to a reading public. Her public was to be the educated readership of *The New Yorker*, the kind of public Kant might have called world-citizens, or spectators to political truth. She chose to report the trial as a play (Young-Bruehl 1982, 340), despite denying the theatrical quality of the proceedings at one point (Arendt 1964b, 9). Arendt went to Jerusalem as a journalist, and though she wrote the postscript after receiving criticism of her book, from it we can understand how she approached her task.

This book contains a trial report, and its main source is the transcript of the trial proceedings which was distributed to the press in Jerusalem. . . . The report of a trial can discuss only the matters which were treated in the course of the trial, or which in the interests of justice should have been treated (280, 285).

In this latter clause, we begin to see Arendt break from a traditional reporter's view of journalism, for she wants to *also* consider matters which for reasons of justice ought to be treated by the press. So there is critique inherent in her method of reportage, and she attempted to color her observations with pointed commentary concerning anything relevant to the application of justice against Eichmann.

Against Eichmann—herein lies the key to Arendt's reportage, for she focused on the person and his deeds, the proper scope of her task.

> The focus of every trial is upon the person of the defendant, a man of flesh and blood with an individual history, with an always unique set of qualities, particularities, behavior patterns, and circumstances. . . . All the things that the defendant did not come into contact with, or that did not influence him, must be omitted from the proceedings of the trial and consequently from the report on it (285-286).

She consistently raises this point against her critics—she was there to cover a trial and its central protagonist, the defendant, and information extraneous to the trial would be superfluous for her purposes. In the interests of reportage, that is, in the interests of who she imagined her readers to be, she refused to turn the book into a philosophical or historical treatise. We know very well that the trial triggered an ongoing concern with judgment in the future life of her own mind, but she was not writing here simply for herself, but for a world which needed to be presented with facts, with the events themselves, with the truth.

How then did the facts present themselves to her? Which facts would she present herself "in the interest of justice"? *Eichmann in Jerusalem* is an exercise in writing—she blends facts learned at the trial and in reading the proceedings, with historical ones taught by Hilberg's *The Destruction of the European Jews* and other references. She is presented with stories of the Jews' destruction and she re-presents these stories in the form of a trial report. In short, she functions as a drama critic might, and so we ought to examine the performance in front of which she held a privileged seat.

Production and Staging

In "The House of Justice" Arendt sets the stage.[6] She contends that the Israeli government produced the spectacle, and called David Ben-Gurion "The invisible stage manager of the proceedings" (5; see also Rogat 1961, 18). She argues that if the trial never fully took on the characteristics of a drama, it certainly became a show-piece for the Prime Minister, and through him, the State of Israel. She criticized the Ben-Gurion government repeatedly for using the trial for their own narrow political purposes (265-266),[7] and for departing from the charges aimed directly at Eichmann himself.

But she recognizes the state of Israel as a legitimate political space, and states her point in terms reminiscent of *The Human Condition*. Israel

> relates not so much, and not primarily, to a piece of land as to the space between individuals in a group whose members are bound to, and at the same

time separated and protected from, each other by all kinds of relationships, based on a common language, religion, a common history, customs, and laws. Such relationships become spatially manifest insofar as they themselves constitute the space wherein the different members of a group relate to and have intercourse with each other. No State of Israel would ever have come into being if the Jewish people had not created and maintained its own specific in-between space throughout the long centuries of dispersion, that is, prior to the seizure of its old territory (262-263).

Jewish civilization, in the sense of a common civility, created the space that is now Israel. Arendt situates the trial within a political territory that has the marks of a space of appearance, thus the reader is presented with a play within a play, or a story within a story. But she argues in the postscript that the crimes of which Eichmann stood accused were crimes against humanity, so the setting itself was inappropriate for justice to be realized.[8]

(In like fashion, the American people set the stage for revolution in France. In deciphering "the meaning of revolution" Arendt argues that revolution was prepared by Locke, Smith, and the social conditions extant in the colonies before 1776. America, as a stage, was the symbol of a society without poverty. More than this, it was a visual fact that there were alternatives to poverty. "Not the American Revolution, but the existence of conditions in America that had been established and were well known in Europe long before the Declaration of Independence, nourished the revolutionary *élan* in Europe" (Arendt 1965, 24). In this sense, the French revolutionaries looked to the American scene and saw it as a possibility for their own country, even if they did not copy the American Revolution itself. The Americans had created an economic space that gave the *appearance* of relative wealth, and so Arendt notes the existence of a play within a play. Without such an appearance, the "social question" would not have taken on the importance that it did, and this story of the French Revolution might have ended differently.)

At the trial itself, she carefully paints a portrait of the courtroom Eichmann's glass booth is quite the spectacle (5, 90), as it was intended to be. She observes that the judges do not conduct themselves theatrically (4), yet notes that they are seated "at the top of the raised platform, facing the audience as from the stage in a play" (6). She contends that the Ben-Gurion government designed the "theater" so that the audience would "represent the whole world" (6), and so that the world could learn lessons from the proceedings. But the "reality [fell] short of expectations and purposes" (8). For within only a few days, the audience itself began to change—some journalists left, and native Israelis were rarely in attendance. Instead the audience consisted of survivors— individuals "who were in no mood to learn any lessons and certainly did not need this trial to draw their own conclusions" (8). Arendt identifies herself with this audience, and calls the survivors people "like myself." Arendt's perspective then, is not a solitary one, but one in dialogue with other audience members, an experience one could liken to sitting in the theater of ancient Greece.[9]

Because the audience changed, the trial itself lost its dramatic qualities. As the government continued to hear the stories of survivors, as the survivors continued to take the available seats, and as they listened to stories they could not have borne in private, "it was precisely the play aspect of the trial that collapsed[.]" Over the course of the proceedings, the protagonist in the drama— Eichmann—was no longer the central character. The new protagonists were the survivors themselves (8-9). For the sake of the reading audience, then, Arendt would attempt to re-write the drama in accordance with justice. To do this she not only recounted some of those stories that took center stage in the Israeli court, but also returned Eichmann to his position as protagonist. In this sense, Arendt portrays a critic who criticizes indirectly by re-articulating the way the drama should have gone, *if it were to have remained a drama.*

The Protagonist

Adolf Eichmann and Hannah Arendt possessed opinions about theater that were diametrically opposed. For Eichmann, the epithet "theater" signified the lie, while Arendt viewed theater as the means by which truth appears. The question that arises when viewing Eichmann's "performance" at his trial is who holds the correct interpretation. Were the spectators witnessing the truth or a lie? Arendt could not be more clear about the answer to this question.

Chapters 2 through 8 constitute the "portrait of Adolf Eichmann" (Brightman 1995, 135). These chapters are, of course, much more, but Arendt portrays Eichmann as a sort of "hero" here, obviously not in a moral sense, but according to the structural requirements of theater. In these chapters Arendt recounts various stories—of his life, of Nazi atrocities, of the bureaucracy of the Nazi party and state, and of the "policies" leading to the Holocaust. She weaves these stories within the context of the trial, always carefully returning to Eichmann's own words.

Eichmann's words become the central "fact" of the trial for her, and her presentation of them would become one of the controversies surrounding the publication. Arendt continually took Eichmann's words at face value (Young-Bruehl 1982, 342), a position that mystified her friends, energized her critics, and angered the Jewish reading public. She castigates the prosecution and the judges for not believing Eichmann when he made statements and for people generally for thinking he was pathological liar. In doing so, she argues, the judges (and indeed all observers), "missed the greatest moral and even legal challenge of the whole case" (26).[10]

I believe that one reason Arendt assumes that Eichmann is not lying is because she conceives the trial in classical dramatic terms. I have already described classical drama as one whose conditions of performance include actors that do not hide their emotions. At the theater of Dionysos they could not do so because the audience would not understand the play. Actors in classical drama hide themselves behind masks, not to hide who they truly are, but rather to exaggerate features to make what they represent obvious to a distant public. If actors were to truly hide who they were they would be, in the modern sense, hypocrites. But as Arendt illustrates in *On Revolution*, hypocrites are individuals who ultimately lie to themselves (Arendt 1965, 103).[11] Lying to oneself requires a moral sense, which itself is constituted by such things as the capacity to live with oneself as a friend. Lying cannot be maintained by "normal" citizens for very long because they could not live with themselves after a time. This did not appear to be a difficulty for Eichmann, so Arendt concludes that he is not lying.

On the contrary, Arendt portrays Eichmann *as he appears to her*. A banal, evil man, Adolf Eichmann hides nothing, lacks conscience (in the sense of being able to think, and live, with himself), and represents himself the way he is. Even though he is a character the ancient Greeks could have never appreciated, Arendt sees him playing his role truthfully[12] and recounts his life and his testimony as inviolably part of his character. In the process she describes Eichmann as déclassé, boastful,[13] inarticulate, cliché-ridden, forgetful (i.e., lacking memory sufficient for judgment),[14] lacking initiative, and ultimately comedic,[15] in a pathetic[16] sort of way. As she reminds us elsewhere, pathos means re-suffering the past (Arendt 1968b, 20), and pathetic actors move audiences (Arendt 1965, 34). Eichmann certainly re-suffered his past at his trial, and the audience was moved by his testimony, though they did not pity him.

Eichmann lacked judgment because he could not permit his imagination to go visiting. He was completely unable to look at events from the viewpoints of others, and he was incapable of uttering independent thoughts. He could speak only in cliché and "officialese" (48, 53, 145, 252). In terms of classical drama, he was wholly and inescapably an actor; so much so, that he apparently never took the position of spectator as Arendt describes it. As we know, this was tied into his (in)ability to think and to judge (49). She notes that the problem for the Israeli government was that his persona might be perceived as that, not of a monster, but as a clown (54). Arendt's own imagination goes visiting in these pages, as she seeks an adequate representation of Eichmann's persona. She sees how Eichmann represents himself, and how Israel wants him represented. In presenting both versions, Arendt offers the reader different viewpoints from which he or she (though absent) can view the proceedings.[17] In this way, she leaves the traditional role of the reporter, and takes on the characteristics of a critic, among whose tasks is teaching the reader aesthetic judgment.

Eichmann lacked a *persona*, to use her term in *On Revolution*. There she describes the etymology of the term as a mask that replaced the actor's own face and countenance, but in a way that made it possible for his voice to sound through. In Roman times, the persona was vital to the legal protection of the citizen, for "the law had affixed to him the part he was expected to play on the public scene, with the provision, however, that his own voice would be able to sound through" (Arendt 1965, 107). Politics demands a persona. Eichmann abandoned any possible persona—he preferred to be assigned his place in the public sphere, and he willingly ceded the right to have his own voice heard. This is quite the opposite of Jews and others who had their personae stripped from them.

When one unmasks the persona from a person one reveals a natural human being. When one unmasks the hypocrite one leaves nothing behind the mask—"because the hypocrite is the actor himself in so far as he wears no mask" (107). This permits the hypocrite to assume any mask, any identity, and he uses this mask as a means of deception.[18] Eichmann presented Arendt with the case of an individual who neither was a hypocrite nor possessed a persona. He was, truly, a character which demanded a fundamentally new interpretation.[19] Here was a man who was truly thoughtless, one who was incapable of making the sorts of distinctions necessary to even understand what purposes a mask served.[20] Because Eichmann was incapable of possessing an enlarged mentality, he was also ignorant of the importance of masks to the *dramatis personae*. So Arendt cannot help but take him at face value.

Rewriting the Plot

I have already suggested that Arendt reaches beyond the traditional boundaries of reportage into theatrical criticism. She also pushes theatrical criticism to its limit, by re-writing the plot, in the interests of justice. Justice motivates her to re-tell the story of the Holocaust when it is ignored and the story of the trial when it is forgotten. She describes the first, second, and final solutions in suggestive detail because she wants to pay "attention to certain facts that are well enough known but that Dr. Servatius chose to ignore" (56). Thus Arendt inserts extended historical narrative into the drama.

Both the story of the Holocaust and Arendt's version of it are well-known,[21] so I would simply like to highlight aspects relevant to the theme of the chapter. First, in recounting history Arendt shifts the scene to any number of locations—among them, Eichmann's office(s), Heydrich's office, the Wannsee Conference, the deportation and killing centers, and, of course, the courtroom itself. Weaving the trial in between these other sites, Arendt moves the stage for the reader, and in doing so leaves the facts of the trial in the memories of only those who attended it. In transporting the reader to different scenes she not only illustrates testimony and documentation from the trial, she sends the reader's imagination visiting. Those who were at the trial, or who watched it on television might have been capable of imagining many of these places as well, but those readers (especially in future generations) who were not there may not have the same ability to do so. As a critic, Arendt understands that it is her responsibility to her reading public to re-write the scenario.

Second, Arendt appropriates phrases, gestures, and general speech from the trial itself to make her presentation both more colorful and more "authentic" to the reader. She takes special pleasure in mocking Eichmann's speech and mimics it as another means by which she can bring the reader to the trial itself. Note the way she satirizes Eichmann's responses on, for example, page 82. Her presentation is sarcastic, to be sure, but she builds upon the original text from both the interrogation and the trial, and it serves to emphasize Eichmann's failure of speech and thought.[22] It is also a way in which she can take Eichmann at face value and register outrage at the same time.

Third, she is careful not to present a story of hopelessness. Throughout her report, she tells stories of heroism, sacrifice, and community in order to both provide balance and give the sense that individuals still acted politically during this horrific time. She recounts stories of heroic German resisters (110-111), welcomes the presence of Jewish resistance fighters (123), admires the strength and resolve of the Danes (171-175) and Italians (179) in combating anti-Jewish policies, and isolates Sergeant Anton Schmidt as proof positive that "the holes of oblivion do not exist . . . under conditions of terror most people will comply, but *some people will not*" (232). She inserts these stories because, as a reporter she has the responsibility to present the balanced, factual truth to the reader, but as a critic she wants to suggest, and even teach, judgment to her public.[23]

Fourth, Arendt seemed to believe that dramatic moments waxed and waned throughout the trial. I have already noted her comment that "the play aspect to the trial collapsed under the weight of the hair-raising atrocities" (8). Moreover, she criticizes the prosecution for bringing irrelevant witnesses in part because they made sitting in the courtroom insufferable. But she also indicates "dramatic moments" when they arise (though she may be taking some artistic license with some of these). For instance, while Abba Kovner, a survivor, described the help he received from a German army officer,

> a hush settled over the courtroom. . . . And in those two minutes, which were like a sudden burst of light in the midst of impenetrable, unfathomable darkness, a single thought stood out clearly, irrefutably, beyond question— how utterly different everything would be today in this courtroom, in Israel, in Germany, in all of Europe, and perhaps in all countries of the world, if only more such stories could have been told (231).

In passages such as these, she conflates reportage, theatrical criticism and play-writing. Arendt is not recording simply her own thoughts because of the "irrefutable" nature of the collective thought. Note as well Eichmann's death scene—she describes how he went to the gallows "with great dignity" and gives a detailed description of his last words and the hanging itself, as if she had been there. "He was in complete command of himself, nay he was more; he was completely himself" (252). Is she reporting the scene or (re)writing it? One need not deconstruct her text in detail to recognize that Arendt was not only recording truth, but she was sometimes inventing it. Though in accordance with her own purposes, she dramatizes a moment so that the reader can participate indirectly as a member of the audience, in order to better render judgment.

Finally, there is some evidence in the text that Arendt herself learned the importance, and difficulty, of telling stories. In witnessing witnesses tell stories, she judges most of them to be irrelevant to the proceedings and long-winded as well. Some witnesses, she notes, told worthwhile stories—Mr. Aharon Hoter-

Yishai, Mrs. Zivia Lubetkin Zuckerman, and especially Mr. Zindel Grynszpan. The good storytellers had a number of things in common: they answered questions put to them by the prosecution and used relatively few words in doing so (228). In the seemingly endless sessions through which all audience members had to sit, Arendt realized "how difficult it was to tell a story, that—at least outside the transforming realm of poetry—it needed a purity of soul, an unmirrored, unreflected innocence of heart and mind that only the righteous possess" (229). Thus the trial itself gave Arendt pause to reflect on the very process of writing in which she would present her own story to a reading public.

Taste

Her final chapters ("Epilogue" and "Postscript") begin the story of the thought with which she ends her life—her analysis of judgment. It begins with reflections on the judgment of the Court itself, though she also makes judgments that transcend the boundaries of the story.[24] In her "judgment" of the Court, Arendt deploys certain literary techniques. After recounting the Court's decision and explaining why it was a bad one,[25] she offers an alternative argument as to why retributive justice against Eichmann was necessary (277-279). In doing so she offers her own "address to the defendant." With this, Arendt becomes an actor in her own review. She imagines (and writes) her own speech regarding what she would say to Eichmann if given the chance, and does so by writing the words the judges should have spoken to him.

In her "speech," she acknowledges Eichmann's own story—"You told your story in terms of a hard-luck story"—and concludes (while "looking at" Eichmann) that "no member of the human race can be expected to want to share the earth with you. This is the reason, and the only reason, you must hang." Note Arendt's clever response, for she turns Eichmann's own arguments, about why the Jews "had" to die, back on him. Eichmann had said that no German should have to share the earth with a Jew. In composing the speech, Arendt's imagination goes visiting—to the world of the judges and to Eichmann's own world so that she can come back to her own world with an enlarged mentality. She can then present her own judgment to the public and in a language of "perspicuous contrast," to use Taylor's term (Taylor 1985b, 123-30). In short, Arendt offers examples of her method in the text itself.

Ironically, the publication of *Eichmann in Jerusalem* thrust Arendt onto center stage in a play she wanted no part in performing.[26] The controversy surrounding it transformed Arendt from an understudy (with an active imagination) in one drama to a performer in another. She assesses *that* performance in the postscript to the book and in "Truth and Politics" (Arendt 1968a). She judges herself to be merely the reporter of events (Arendt 1964b, 285-287) and criticizes those who did not want to confront facts.

But in reflecting on her own participation in the Eichmann affair, she ponders the problem of human judgment more generally. Her thought in the postscript can be read not merely as a critique of Eichmann's inability to think and judge, but, following the controversy surrounding her book, of her own reading public and its ability to make judgments.[27] With the collapse of religious standards, men and women were thrown back on themselves to find guidance. People had to judge "each instance as it arose, because no rules existed for the unprecedented," thus judgment is rendered in the particularity of each case (295). But these words are not addressed to a public that judges Eichmann, but one that ought to judge itself—"How troubled men of our time are by this question . . . has emerged in the controversy over the present book" and over Hochhuth's *The Deputy* (295).[28] In the postscript, then, Arendt does not criticize Eichmann's judgment as much as she does her readers. This serves as the beginning of her sustained reflection on the process of, among other things,[29] reportage and criticism, itself.

She thus considers the theatrical question, who controls the drama—the actors themselves, the director, or the audience?[30] I have tried to argue in chapter 2 and in this chapter that, to a great degree, the audience sets the terms under which the drama is staged. Though I have also recognized that the producers of the drama do their utmost to influence that audience into accepting this or that character or plot. Initially it surprised me that Arendt became as exasperated as she did (or that she became exasperated at all) over the controversy surrounding her book, given what she must surely have understood about audiences.

However, on further reflection, and in taking the position of Arendt in the matter, I realized that it was probably difficult to distinguish between the producers of the drama and the audience, for to a great degree, they were one and the same. Her audience—an enlightened, educated, maybe even largely Jewish, public—was not prepared to hear certain things about Eichmann and about the Jews' own participation in the Holocaust. In response, some members of that audience produced a response—theater meant to subvert Arendt's subversive text. In the end, so to speak, the critic must recognize that the actors themselves present the facts, and the reporter merely diffuses them. Thus, Arendt welcomed an end to the whole affair.

This has implications for the political scientist. We need to teach our students that when we publish and put ideas on the public stage we become actors. The critic takes the stage in some instances, so we must prepare our students to *take the part* of the theater critic. The political scientist becomes citizen—not simply one who reflects, but one who acts by making public statements, taking stands, and teaching others. We act this way in addition to taking on the role of learner.

The Arendt controversy within the Eichmann drama ended (except for the very few academic specialists still interested in the characters).[31] But political action in general never ends; the historian brings episodes to a close by writing their finales. Each ending brings about a new beginning. In closing the narrative of Arendt's story of Eichmann I want to begin examining its relevance to "our" human condition—the condition of individuals concerned about the public community known as the university.

With chapter 5 I initiate a review and analysis of the three pillars upon which the contemporary American university rests—research, teaching, and service. I will argue that the central political justification for higher education is to interest students in politics and provide examples by which they can judge, with other citizens, political action. This justification means recognizing the political purposes of research, teaching, and service, and in chapters 6 through 8 I consider how each of these academic areas can be transformed to generate interest and cultivate judgment on the part of students.

In chapter 6, I play the part of an historian and circumscribe a story in order to make sense out of a particular set of facts. I employ "enlarged mentality," and develop a language of perspicuous contrast, in seeking truth to an "event"—the founding of the European Community (EC)—through the eyes of different political organizations proposing European political unity. In examining the founding of the EC through the lens of Arendt's theory of revolution, I reconstruct that theory. I argue that her notion of conciliar democracy excludes the possibility for action among elite politicians, and that the "lost treasures" of which she speaks so eloquently in *On Revolution*—political councils—contribute to their own failure. Consequently, the example validates, and advances, Arendt's theory.

In doing so, I seek to understand the event from competing perspectives—elite politicians concerned with "building Europe" in the face of the Soviet military threat and the American cultural threat, and European "revolutionaries" convinced that federation is the only way to maintain the "space of appearance" in the European theater of politics. As the characters in the drama confront each other, the plot resolves itself tragically, as Arendt herself might have characterized it. For in "building" Europe, the public space is lost, and the possibility of a European *politics* (in Arendt's sense of the term) is abandoned. In its place lies the administration of European things.

Chapter 6 not only provides an alternative reading of events well-known to comparative political scientists and international relations experts, it also exemplifies an Arendtian research strategy for political science. But, as I will argue in chapters 7 and 8, it can do so only in the context of a reassessment of the general purposes of higher education. I am not trying to offer a research methodology based on Arendt's principles—first because I do not think there is one single method to be found, second because Arendt herself denied the relevance of her ideas to such a positivist notion, and third because that would not fit into the general argument of this book. I contend that universities are, or ought to be, primarily teaching institutions, and any reference to a research methodology must be placed within a pedagogical agenda.

In this light I discuss, in chapter 7, ways in which Arendt's notions of political theater, the space of appearance, and judgment can influence curriculum development and change at institutions of higher learning. I continue this line of argument in chapter 8, by extending these pedagogical tasks to the area of community service. There I suggest that a university, conceived theatrically as a space of appearance, is one which encourages service, not for the sake of participation or traditional notions of citizenship, but for the sake of political judgment. In chapters 7 and 8 (and by extension chapter 6), I maintain that the public, civic responsibility of universities and colleges is to cultivate taste and discernment in the minds, not only of students, but of faculty and administrators as well. This is a radically different way of understanding both the civic purposes of universities and the idea of democracy in higher education. It is remembering that citizens are not only actors, but spectators as well, and this differs from the ideal of citizenship conceived traditionally as active participation.

Notes

1.   Her biographer, Elisabeth Young-Bruehl (1982), claims that the trial changed her methodological concerns, and she admired reporters who "stood guard over facts" (263). Let me add that she understands the "genre" of the report a bit differently than Erving Goffman (1959). Goffman, I emphasized in chapter 1, viewed his own work as a report, though he also perceived it as a framework around which the world can be understood, and in this way, as a means of representing the world. Arendt remains faithful to the idea that reporters present the world, and so does not claim to consider questions of theory or structure. Nevertheless, both consider their tasks to be observation and judgment, and so I think it is fair to characterize Goffman's work as, in some sense, an exercise in theatrical criticism.

2.   Arendt self-consciously played the part of theater critic rarely in her own life. The one memory we have of her as a theater critic is in her piece "The Deputy: Guilt or Silence?" (Arendt 1964a), a review of Rolf Hochhuth's controversial drama about the role the Catholic Church played in the Holocaust. She presumably saw this play performed because she remarks in a letter that she believed it to work better as factual reportage than as drama. And her analysis of the play in the essay reflects her concern with its content more than its form, or than the performance of it. She recognizes that the controversy surrounding it is like that surrounding *Eichmann in Jerusalem*, published at about the same time (1964b, 295ff).

3.   There are a number of reasons to consider *On Revolution* an exercise in theatrical criticism: (1) She tells a story, or rather she tells three of them—those of the American Revolution, the French Revolution, and conciliar democracy, (2) in so doing, she presents dramatis personae and a plot, (3) she argues that the French revolutionaries looked to America as a stage (to visualize a world without a social question), and the American revolutionaries looked to France as a stage (to make corrections or addenda to the constitution), (4) she argues that the revolutions, though they began as restorations, opened themselves up to radically new stories, thus they were dramas in their own right, and (5) she moves back and forth between the different plot lines (i.e., the American and French Revolutions) throughout the book in order to understand the totality of the events, as a good theater critic necessarily does. Having said all this, *On Revolution* is not structured in precisely the same way as *Eichmann in Jerusalem*, but there are enough similarities to warrant a comparison between the two.

4.   No scholar or commentator of whom I am aware has noticed many, if any, connections between these two books. Indeed many have tried to explain *On Revolution* as a development of themes extensively articulated in *The Human Condition*. Others have connected *Eichmann in Jerusalem* to her later concern with judgment in *The Life of the*

Mind (which she herself does at the beginning of the latter). Still others have tried to find common themes running throughout all of her works (e.g., her concern for the public realm, her intellectual relationship to Jaspers and Heidegger, her German-Jewish identity, her critique of totalitarianism and/or modernity). But no one has sought to associate these two books together and separate from her other writings. This has always puzzled me, considering that she wrote or edited both simultaneously, and that both were published in the same year. I believe that the two works have a methodological concern in common with each other that we do not find in the same fashion elsewhere in her *oeuvre*.

5. "To attend this trial is somehow, I feel, an obligation I owe to my past" (quoted in Young-Bruehl 1982, 329). In order to do so, she rescheduled classes she was supposed to teach and even the terms of a Rockefeller Foundation grant.

6. In truth, she does so even before the first chapter by quoting an epigram from the German dramatist, Bertolt Brecht. Was this another indication of the degree to which she was prepared to see the event as theater? It is also curious, and telling, that immediately after completing both *Eichmann in Jerusalem* and *On Revolution*, she writes a piece on Bertolt Brecht (collected in Arendt 1968b).

7. Beyond partisan political purposes, the Ben-Gurion government also used the trial to educate the world about the plight of the Jews (Glock et al. 1966, 1; Rogat 1961, 4). According to at least one study, it did not succeed in educating the public well (Glock, et al. 1966, 136, 68-75, 165), which, the authors of this study argue, may have been a blessing in disguise (175).

8. She notes the irony resulting from Eichmann's trial in Jerusalem: "it was Eichmann's de facto statelessness, and nothing else, that enabled the Jerusalem court to sit in judgment on him. Eichmann, though no legal expert, should have been able to appreciate that, for he knew from his own career that one could do as one pleased only with stateless people" (Arendt 1964b, 240)

9. Arendt was not the only observer to see the trial as theater. Note the comments of Yosal Rogat: "The trial took place in a room that was literally a theatre; the staging was that of an *avant-garde* play. Not only the moral issues but the sets were stark black and white. They contrasted the sombre, weighty dress of the judges and the Orthodox Jews, covering up individual frailty with solemnity and tradition, to the unreal modernity of Eichmann's glass showcase, exposing completely" (Rogat 1961, 14n). The reporter for *The New York Times*, Homer Bigart, likened the trial to a folk opera—"with poets and lecturers fainting, and with much time devoted to painting the lurid background of the holocaust" (cited in Rogat 1961, 39).

10. Specific examples of this include accepting Eichmann's explanations: (1) on why he was cooperating with the Israeli authorities (241), (2) of his own guilt, and (3) on why he took the Madagascar Project seriously (76).

11. "The hypocrite . . . when he falsely pretends to virtue plays a role as consistently as the actor in the play who must also identify himself with his role for the purpose of play-acting; there is no *alter ego* before whom he might appear in his true shape, at least not as long as he remains in the act. His duplicity, therefore, boomerangs back on himself, and he is no less a victim of his mendacity than those whom he set out to deceive" (Arendt 1965, 103). The hypocrite wants to appear virtuous to others and to himself as well, and in doing so he bears false witness against himself. What Arendt had discovered in Eichmann was a man incapable of bearing false witness against himself, because he was incapable of conversing with himself. He lacked the two-in-one necessary for thought, and therefore judgment, to occur.

12. Many, if not most, readers of her report found her representation of Eichmann incredible. After reading excerpts from the trial, and seeing parts of it on videotape, I question Arendt's portrait here. On tape, Eichmann's nervous demeanor suggests that he lied while responding to questions from the prosecution. And as Avner Less, the officer who interviewed Eichmann for the Israeli police, observed, Eichmann's lies were easily identifiable by his manner of speaking (von Lang and Sibyll 1983). That is, his *appearance* changed when confronted with a lie, so even in Arendt's terms, there ought to have been room to recognize deceit. This may reflect the difference between observing Eichmann face-to-face and seeing him behind a glass box in a courtroom, but other "reporters" also judged him to be lying quite often.

13. Arendt records Eichmann's "problem" with bragging at many points in the text. I have noted in chapter 2 that exaggeration was a necessary component of classical theater—something the actor needed to do to get his point across. Thus Eichmann was truly an actor and (as we shall see presently) possessed very few capacities of a spectator.

14. In forgetting, Eichmann demonstrated an inability to remember or tell stories, part of the capacity for making independent and moral judgments.

15. Young-Bruehl (1982) believes that her husband, Heinrich Blucher, convinced Arendt to view Eichmann as a clown (331).

16. See, for instance Arendt 1964b, 145.

17. Arendt employs this sort of method on many occasions, and in different ways, in the text. For instance, she uses the parenthetical aside repeatedly, as if to check what she has just reported with an alternative perspective. She offers these alternatives, as she writes the story, to exemplify ways that the reader can cultivate judgment. For instances of parenthetical asides see pages 56-58, but they occur throughout the text as well. Another example occurs on page 105, where Arendt describes not only Himmler's slogans (e.g., My Honor is My Loyalty), but how different participants in the trial were interpreting it: "catch phrases which Eichmann called 'winged words' and the judges 'empty talk'." So Arendt again presents different perspectives, a phenomenology of public, plural judgment, which accepts each perspective *as it appears* in the public realm. After considering each side, Arendt generally renders her own judgment. But it is her method of both presenting the truth and in assessing the justice of a particular event. A final example of this method is reflected in the survivor stories Arendt chooses to present to the reader (e.g., the stories regarding the role of the *Judenrate*, 117-126). She does not present all stories, though, for she believed most of them to be superfluous to the trial. She presented only those she deemed relevant to the facts of the case and the judgment on Eichmann. She uses the same method in *On Revolution*, for instance, in describing certain failures of the French Revolution (Arendt 1965, 74ff). There and elsewhere she presents competing perspectives of the revolution—e.g., alternately, that of the revolutionaries, the people (the interested spectators), and outside observers, in order to permit the reader to acquire an enlarged mentality concerning these events.

18. George Kateb (1977) describes the hypocrite as "a compulsive role-player, changing from one role to another, able to feign even naturalness, and finally succumbing perhaps to self-deception, to being an actor without knowing it, paradoxically filling himself with emptiness" (151). Eichmann feigned naturalness and succumbed to self-deception, but he realized that he was an actor in a drama (von Lang and Sibyll 1983), and who, for whatever reason, never chose to leave the stage. This may explain his desire to give interviews to journalists while living in Argentina, and his tireless justifications of his actions, in interviews conducted in both Argentina and Israel.

19. Berel Lang characterizes Eichmann as a superfluous human being, "retaining the appearance of a person, but lacking the capacity for freedom and reason that were, for Arendt, essential to the definition of any such being" (Lang 1994, 51). Eichmann was a new kind of evil-doer.

20. Eichmann could not judge because he could not think, and he could not think because he never stopped to think—he just kept doing. Thinking is aporetic—it demands that one stop to reflect; something, apparently, Eichmann never did. See Beatty 1994 on Arendt's observations about thinking and judging.

21. For a summary of Arendt's account of the Holocaust in *Eichmann in Jerusalem*, see Young-Bruehl (1982), Courtine-Denamy (1997), and Elon (1997).

22. This may be what Young-Bruehl (1982) means by her "ironic" tone in the book (338). Amos Elon (1997) also notes that her sarcastic tone contributed to the multiple misunderstandings of, and attacks on, her book (28).

23. She treats the American and French revolutionaries with a mixture of criticism and praise and concludes *On Revolution* with a similar optimistic nod. She raises hopes that "lost treasure" such as ward systems or conciliar democracy can be reclaimed in the modern world and reminds her reader, through the words of Sophocles, that the polis permits one to live life with splendor (Arendt 1965, 281).

24. For instance, "it is in the very nature of things human that every act that has made its appearance and has been recorded in the history of mankind stays with mankind as a potentiality long after its actuality has become a thing of the past...[T]he unprecedented, once it has appeared, may become a precedent for the future...all trials touching upon 'crimes against humanity' must be judged according to a standard that is today still an 'ideal.' If genocide is an actual possibility of the future, then no people on earth...can feel reasonably sure of its continued existence without the help and protection of international law" (273).

25. She also judged the Israeli Court as inappropriate to conduct this sort of case, an opinion she shared with many scholars of international law (Rogat 1961, 32-43; Woetzel 1962, 245-72).

26. For a summary of the controversy surrounding *Eichmann in Jerusalem* see Elon 1997.

27. For example, Arendt believed Michael Musmanno's review of her book (*The New York Times Book Review*, 19 May 1963) was typical of those who sought to disparage her. A review of his review suggests that at least in this case Arendt was correct, because it is clearly biased. It distorts the "facts" of her book by presenting, in exaggerated form, only those elements that some might find objectionable and by taking phrases out of context for polemical purposes. Most importantly, Musmanno mistakes the central theme of the book as an exploration of Eichmann's conscience. By virtue of Arendt's "method" this could never be a theme because the conscience is not something that appears.

28. In *On Revolution* note her opinion of nineteenth century revolutionaries as she draws lessons from the French Revolution: "There is some grand ludicrousness in the spectacle of these men—who had dared to defy all powers that be and to challenge all authorities on earth, whose courage was beyond a shadow of a doubt—submitting, often from one day to the other, humbly and without so much as a cry of outrage, to the call of historical necessity, no matter how foolish the outward appearance of this necessity must have appeared to them" (58). Here she goes beyond the "facts" of the case (the event itself) to pass judgment on spectators of that event. She critiques their ability to judge—

their ability to see cases in their particularity and the desire of actors, such as Lenin, to generalize events into theories of historical necessity.

29. For example, storytelling, history, poetry.

30. I do not include the playwright here because the playwright is not part of the performance of the play. Though contributing to the staging of the play, he or she cannot be in control of the action, because the playwright is not present in the theater, as these others are. Or more correctly, the playwright may be in the theater as the action unfolds, but only as an actor, director, or audience member.

31. Academic specialists are not the reading public Arendt had in mind in describing Kantian spectators, probably because the academic specialist withdraws too deeply from the public. Thus, his or her thought does not reflect the activity of a public intellectual, or often even of public concern.

Chapter 5

The University As a Theater of Politics

The Argument So Far

In chapter 1, I established the importance of a dramaturgical theory of action and its contribution to the methodology and pedagogy of social science. I analyzed different dramaturgical theories of action and concluded that all shared certain premises: political action is based upon performance (of roles); in acting politically the citizen masks him or herself to hide his or her private self and to present his or her political self to the world; acting effectively requires practice and training; political acts ultimately depend upon the presence of spectators; and spectators in some fashion determine truth in political action and regulate in some way the standards of that action. I found these theories wanting because they did not acknowledge the extent to which politics depends on citizens capable of judging action intelligently. I also raised questions about the role of the political and social sciences in both civic training and in higher education and argued that political science professors ought to help their students practice civic judgment. I suggested that Hannah Arendt's concept of the space of appearance can help us understand dramaturgically the nature of political action and the role of judgment in politics.

In chapter 2, I contended that Arendt's conception of the space of appearance originated in her understanding of classical Greek theater. Spaces of appearance, we will recall, are characterized by human action and permit human beings, as citizens, to present and represent themselves to others and to participate in the creation of human immortality. They are spaces where humans can be free existentially in place, as well as in time. The Dionysian conception of political theater gives a significant role to spectators as observers who can at times participate in the theater and at other times give meaning to the action unfolding.

Building on the importance of the spectator to political action, in chapter 3 I discussed professional spectatorship in politics. I reconstructed a nascent theory of reportage from different sources in her work and from her understanding of the importance of factuality. In her Kant lectures she recommends an "enlarged mentality" and I argued that political analysis can cultivate this if we imagine the analyst as a kind of theater critic. Out of the ideals of a good theater critic— one who reports what one sees, one who situates the drama historically, one who adeptly recounts narrative, and one who makes astute judgments about the performance—Arendt offers us a model of political research that both lends itself "to normal speech and thought" and helps the analyst appreciate the political world from the perspective of other individuals. This, I argued, is one means by which teachers can help transmit to their students skills useful to making informed political judgments.

In the previous chapter, I exemplified this method by studying Hannah Arendt studying Eichmann. I maintained that her method was not strictly, or should I say conventionally, reportage, but rather a report from one who views the trial from the position of a member of an audience. As a reporter for the *New Yorker* magazine, she held a privileged position, because she had access to people and facts (events) that her readers did not, and she was one of the very few who was present at the proceedings. Some world-citizens watched the affair on television, but this, I argued, was a categorically different kind of experience from the one that she enjoyed. As a reporter, Arendt discovered a method of truth-telling, as a critic at the performance, she analyzed the event distinctively, and the combination of both roles suggests the beginnings of a method of political inquiry.

With this chapter I begin to analyze the relevance of Arendt's ideas to higher education. What can Arendt teach us about how to analyze political action, how to communicate ideas to students, and how to govern ourselves in universities and colleges? I will focus on social science education and argue that professors ought to, as the first purpose of these disciplines, teach political judgment (and by extension social and economic judgment), to their undergraduates. I will also argue that graduate education ought also to involve the teaching of such judgment, though it may not be the first purpose of such an education. By teaching judgment I do not mean to suggest that professors can actually instill or inculcate judgment into passively receptive students. I mean that professors can create conditions under which students can learn to enlarge their mentality. They can do so by approaching their subject matters theatrically in the manner of the ancient Greeks and by creating spaces of appearance within the university. These spaces become examples to the students, and they can learn politics by experiencing political discourse and action in their everyday lives as students. In this sense, the spaces of appearance at the university themselves serve as exemplars through which citizens can make valid judgments. In sum, social science education can be about teaching judgment, through an understanding of the "enlarged mentality," which itself results from approaching politics theatrically, in the manner of the ancient Greeks.

Before describing how this can be done, though, I need to give reasons why teaching political judgment is the first purpose of the social science disciplines. I examine other arguments that the first purpose of social science is enculturation (both the classical tradition and arguments for multiculturalism), utility (professional and vocational training), pragmatic social practice (teaching what the university knows), civic education (community services and service-learning), and character development. While all of these are important ends in higher education, they all presume both interest in the part of the student to want to achieve these objectives and judgment on his or her part about how best to achieve them. However, we cannot presume that students come to universities interested in the subject matter or able to judge the actions of individuals in the world. The task for departments of social and political science is thus to teach interest and judgment about politics.

In the third section of the chapter I begin to examine what it would mean for the university to become a theater of politics. As theater the university can help generate interest and teach judgment about politics on the part of both students and faculty. Universities can generate interest in politics by revealing dramas within the university itself, reinforcing a visual culture, using narrative to grip its audience, releasing childhood desire to play, and involving students (and faculty) as both actors and spectators in the performance. The university can help individuals understand the important role of the spectator in the performance of the university and its governance. Universities can foster political judgment on the part of both students and faculty by enlarging the mentality of its members, by encouraging students to witness events and teaching them how to examine what they have just witnessed, by inculcating skills of critical thinking and analysis, and by offering opportunities for public deliberation on the part of all students and faculty.

This must all be translated into practice, however, and that involves thinking about the relevance of this to the three pillars of the theater in question: research, teaching, and service. We might view these as three stages which all members of the theater view and act in simultaneously. In the last section of the chapter I suggest that the difference between actors and spectators at universities ought not to be as cut-and-dried as it is often presented. I will argue that through these three stages, our students can learn to become the next generation of jurists—interested spectators who as citizens collectively judge the public world. This chapter will lead into more detailed discussion (in chapters 6, 7, and 8) of the practical means by which political and social science teachers cultivate judgment through research, teaching, and service.

The Purposes of Higher Education in the Social Sciences

There are many reasons to attend university and major in a social science discipline. Social scientists enculturate students into a civilization; they train students for professions; they inculcate civic values into developing citizens; they cultivate the moral sense in individuals; and they teach the public what they know about the world. But I will argue that the most important political purposes of the social scientist are to generate interest in the events of the day and stimulate the capacity of students to make informed and reasoned judgments about those events. Social and political scientists can generate student interest by making politics theatrical and can help students make informed judgments by engaging their ability to think, speak, and write critically. In so doing students can also become more civilized, better professionals, informed and active citizens, and future educators.

Civilization and Culture

The first argument for higher education in general, and political and social science in particular, is enculturation. Universities expose students to a culture or cultures, most typically "western," in order to teach the student the traditions of that culture. Students learn not only the intellectual and moral legacies of their cultures but the sorts of ideas that ought to be understood and accepted in order to be considered for adult membership in that culture.

Allan Bloom popularized a debate over this argument after the publication of his *Closing of the American Mind* (Bloom 1987). In it he castigates the American university for not promoting western ideals or teaching the Great Books, and instead pandering to the narrow interests of particular groups within the academy. Bloom, and other conservative critics such as Dinesh D'Souza, Lynne Cheney, Athanasios Moulakis (Moulakis 1994), and Thomas Pangle (Pangle 1992), criticize both traditional disciplines and interdisciplinary studies for contributing to the moral decline of Americans and recommend that they radically reconsider their educational purposes, methods, and curricula. They claim that professors politicize the university and divert students' attention away from learning about their culture in the process.[1]

Pangle charges political science with special responsibilities. First, it must question the positivist nature of modern political and social science. Second, it must introduce the Great Books into the training of every student in political science. Finally, it must balance empirical and normative theory in they way it trains students of politics (Pangle 1992, 201-208). Pangle offers Aristotle's *Politics*, Alexis de Tocqueville's *Democracy in America*, and W.E.B. DuBois' *The Souls of Black Folk* as examples of studies that avoid positivist fallacies and derive their methods from the lived experiences of persons. In studying texts such as these, students can learn from thinkers who have connected their own theories with the practices of the "commonfolk," something that many contemporary scholars neglect to do (181).

The second form of this argument comes in the guise of multiculturalism. Here culture is not necessarily a common one, or specifically the preserve of a set of individuals based on their class, race, gender, or religion. On the contrary, America is a diverse set of cultures, and the American university ought to reflect this fact by promoting area, regional, gender, ethnic, religious, and sexuality studies as means by which all Americans can come to appreciate and defend publicly the different cultures to which they belong. The goal is still to enculturate students, but the means are not the same. Where intellectual traditionalists recommend a common set of readings, such as the Great Books, multiculturalists complain that this would pervert the meaning of American culture because it ignores many other intellectual contributions to the American tradition. Instead multiculturalists emphasize readings neglected previously by the western tradition, readings that offer students a variety of perspectives on their culture so that they can come to a reasoned decision about what it means to be an American and how they can best contribute to the common culture, however they ultimately define it.

Multicultural studies have also been defended according to the classical tradition. Martha Nussbaum supports interdisciplinary programs, service learning, and post-modern analytic methods through essentially Socratic and Stoic argument (Nussbaum 1997, 20-35). She uses classical reasoning and textual support to critique both the Great Books approach and an antipolitical postmodern approach. Indeed she shares a fundamental curricular goal with the intellectual traditionalists—introduce philosophy to students early in their academic careers. This will permit them to possess the tools necessary to examine their own lives and ideas. Making students fit for freedom, liberal education enables students to critique the practices around them, readies them for their civic obligations, and develops their "narrative imagination."

The special responsibility of the social sciences in multicultural education is to inform students and train them methodically in the diverse ways people live. Social and political scientists ought to offer new topics for study that emphasize diversity and train students to appreciate a variety of methodological approaches to these topics. Thus social scientists ought to become involved in interdisciplinary studies and should promote investigative techniques corresponding to the multifarious ways of knowing the world. This is an essentially political critique of traditional areas of, and methods in, the social and political sciences.

While both intellectual conservatives and multiculturalists recognize the importance of enculturation to the training of the undergraduate student, we ought to acknowledge the central role critical thinking and judgment play in enculturating students. Both sets of scholars present curricula whose purpose is to have the student think critically and prudentially about the world in which they find themselves. On the one hand, the Great Books are so because they have required students to think deeply and critically about central questions of humanity. On the other hand, multiculturalism is another means by which students can discern truth or meaning in the world by reflecting on and analyzing what might seem to be common ideals. But often these ideals are, on second glance, a cover for political or ideological interests that distort the plural nature of the human condition. On both sides, higher education is a set of practices aimed at cultivating students' capacity to judge the world by critically reflecting on the ideas and practices constitutive of some culture or cultures. If the purpose of university and social science education is to develop judgment in individuals, then the focus of the debate shifts. The question then becomes which sort of training helps students reflect critically, and thus cultivate better judgment.

Following Arendt, the answer is whichever cultivates the enlarged mentality, and a good case can be, and has been, made for either program (see, for instance, Honig 1995). Multicultural studies expose students to a wide variety of experiences or they deepen the understanding students have of their own experiences by having them read and discuss others who have thought through their cultures more deeply. But Great Books can do the same thing, especially when students read critical theorists such as Kant or Marx, who can teach them the virtue of reflection and argument.

Neither a Great Books program nor a multicultural curriculum can guarantee that students will become interested in the issues set forth by either one. In fact it is quite possible that students can go through an entire year of either sort of program without feeling captivated by the learning of, and intellectual challenges presented by, the culture or cultures to which they are exposed. Poor grades and high attrition rates after the first year of college are sometimes indications of this failure to captivate the attention of students. Before considering what will be taught, it may be prudent on the part of educators to consider how whatever is taught can be done so that students will pay attention. This is where politics as theater can make its mark, because viewed in this way politics can become something visually and aurally stirring to students. It can spark an interest and concern for politics that might not naturally be there (even among political science majors). It can also challenge students to enter into debates over curricula—over whether it is more appropriate to their own education to learn the Great Books or to be exposed to multicultural experiences and opinions. Politics as theater can assimilate students into a culture of learning.

Professional Training

The university is also responsible for preparing students for the workforce—a central political task because this practice sustains and reproduces the material foundation of the community. Academics defend liberal arts training because it readies students for the challenge of the capitalist economy. First, it transmits the knowledge and methodological skills students will need to thrive in their chosen profession. Economics majors are prepared to accept positions in finance, accounting, and marketing because they have the background requisite for making prudent decisions that will enhance the profit of their employers. Advertisers and newspapers hire communications students because they have received practical training in making copy. Political science students often choose the legal profession because they have been exposed to the law in public law classes and have learned constitutional history in American government. Sociology undergraduates often train for careers in social work and move into positions in the social service sector.

Second, social science undergraduates are prepared to think clearly about problems, and their problem-solving capabilities make them attractive employees to many sorts of companies, governmental agencies, and non-governmental organizations. Systematic training in research methodology prepares students for handling a variety of research and policy problems that arise in both the private and the public sectors. Moreover, the information absorbed by the students provides a background essential to understand the purposes and long-term interests of employers. Employers are attracted to liberal arts graduates (as opposed to, say, graduates of a business program) because many of them come to work prepared with the background knowledge of American and world society, politics, and economics, that permits them to put into perspective the goals of the organization in which they work. This helps them recommend policies to their employers that makes those employers wealthier or more powerful or both.

Finally, social science majors are trained to think not only clearly and systematically about problems, but also critically about the world. Employers recognize that these critical abilities give such students an edge because they can recognize problems to be solved more quickly. Instead of being handed a problem to be solved, the social sciences require students to find the problems they want to solve. They suggest to students that there may be multiple ways of discovering these problems, that they can use multiple "methodologies." A business student will approach the capitalist economy economistically—that is as a series of discrete events and potential problems that can be revealed and solved by starting with certain utilitarian premises about human nature and society. A social science student is challenged to think about the capitalist economy in terms other than economic ones—culture, psychology, social policy, and political theory all come into play in understanding the nature of the economy. Instead of case studies meant to train students in a disciplined approach to certain economic problems, a comprehensive social science curriculum asks the student to decide for him or herself how best to understand the economy and what resources to bring to bear on problems in that economy. The intellectual independence cultivated by these means appeal to many employers who want to hire individuals with creativity and initiative.

All of this is very practical and good for the economic interests of the nation, employers, and of course the students themselves. We often judge the strength of college and university programs on the basis of how well they have placed their graduates in professions. But critics since Socrates have argued that this cannot and should not be the ultimate purpose of education. We are not training our students to be economically useful, they charge, we are training them to be good practitioners of their art. This good practice is not useful for some other purpose, but a good for its own sake (Anderson 1993). Indeed, how do we know what constitutes a good economy in the first place, or what good professional practice is, or what sorts of challenges employers can expect from the economy in the future? It is only by training students to evaluate perspectives and to criticize economies that they can develop the sort of independence of mind useful to employers. This might instigate sustained critique on the institutions who will ultimately hire them or on the government that protects the economy into which they will ultimately find their place.

So the usefulness of social science rests in its ability to generate the critical thinking abilities of students. Though this may not be useful at all times to the economy, or potential employers, it is so to students—not to find work, but to be able to reason about the world and articulate clearly its problems. It deepens their understandings about that world and themselves and helps them think critically about the usefulness of their potential employers and the economy itself. This helps them understand their own self-interests more profoundly, which is crucial to any graduate searching for a job. They have learned to judge themselves and their economy from a variety of perspectives learned in their social science classes, thus enlarging their mentality.

Certainly students have material interests into which this sort of justification taps. Many, if not most, students are interested in their subjects because they are interested in how training in those areas can help them find employment in work that is materially, intellectually, or psychologically rewarding. Too often, though, students are not aware of what their interests are, or are mistaken about those interests—those students who change majors (maybe more than once) or who seem directionless upon graduation reflect this fact. Of course, some uncertainty is normal and healthy, but social science can help students clarify their interests in order that they are able to begin to make choices about their futures.

Viewing the world dramaturgically can help students become more interested in politics and clarify what the benefits are in becoming politically interested. In presenting a variety of events to students in a dramatic fashion, political scientists can generate excitement in students and give them reasons to engage themselves politically in the world. Professors challenge students to perform and indicate to them how good performance is in their own interest. They help define for the student the very concept of "interest" and teach them the benefits of clarifying their own interests. This develops the individual personally, morally, and intellectually, and furthers his or her own economic interests.

Civic Virtue

A third purpose of a university and social science education is to inculcate civic values into students. Pangle (1992) notes that this goal has been pursued by the American founders and cites Benjamin Franklin, Thomas Jefferson, Noah Webster, and Benjamin Rush to support his claim. American political science was founded on this very proposition, and early leaders in the discipline such as Charles Merriam were concerned for the health of American democracy. Such concern was revived after World War II as the social sciences fought Nazism and Communism and the political and psychological characteristics that scholars believed contributed to their ideological successes.[2]

The legacy has been assumed by proponents of service-learning who claim that the social science curriculum can be transformed to reflect new ways of learning. Either in conjunction with already existing courses or as separate programs, service-learning classes ask students to volunteer their time and energy by contributing in some way to their communities. But service-learning also incorporates a reflective component to the volunteer work—either a seminar, or a learning journal, or term paper that requires students to think through their experiences and discuss them with others. Consequently, students must analyze the problems they encountered as part of their work and situate that work within the political history of the agency and the social theory that justifies or explains it. Service-learning programs are being used extensively throughout the country and have generally succeeded in inculcating a sense of community and civic responsibility among students.[3]

But is citizenship education a central purpose of social science education? What constitutes the focus of civic education? Is it to teach students how to make choices in a liberal culture? Is it to cultivate their communication skills and tighten the bonds of their communities? If it is to tighten the bonds of community, how do we identify what those communities are? Is it to train students in republican virtue? If so, what are the virtues to which republicans adhere, and how do we determine these choices? Clearly all of these questions imply that students must understand how to judge which virtues are important to sustain the polities to which they belong. We cannot expect our students to act civically without first being able to critically assess the nature of citizenship. Consequently, though it may be a goal of university education, it cannot be a primary one.

Furthermore, in citizenship education the distinction between political or social science and politics itself becomes effaced. Social science education demands detachment from political action; learning about politics transcends the activity. Such learning must be good for its own sake, because civic loyalties are themselves transitory characteristics. Being a good citizen of this or that polity, or supporting this or that administration or party, ultimately depends on where and when the citizen lives. Yet students can learn about politics regardless of these conditions in their lives.

Encouraging volunteerism may be better left to politicians than political scientists. Should political scientists be involved in the active process of socializing students and promoting particular habits, dispositions, and attitudes toward the state? Certainly professors play a role, as teachers and citizens, in sharing their political and social concerns with students—because they too are responsible for the nurturance and transformation of community life. But this is not the central purpose of academic life. Ultimately a tension remains between socializing students into a certain type of citizenship and developing their ability to make choices for themselves.[4]

A virtue of service-learning may be that it can generate interest in politics on the part of students. Many students respond well to out-of-class experiences. But that only supports the claim that social science classes can benefit from a variety of teaching methods, not that citizenship education is the central purpose to higher education or even that service-learning should be a required part of the curriculum. Where service-learning contributes to political interest and judgment on the part of students it will contribute to a greater sense of citizenship on their part.

The benefit of service-learning comes from its capacity to engage individuals in critical thinking (Gorham 1992, 181-191). In critically thinking about politics, and in making political choices, students have an opportunity to exercise good judgment in their future experiences. So the pursuit of civic virtue depends initially on the capacity of students to think logically and judiciously about politics. Indeed we cannot teach citizenship so much as we can expose our students to exemplars of civic life. Students can then reason for themselves why civic life is worth nurturing.

Teaching Useful Ways of Thinking

Charles Anderson (1993) argues that there is an intrinsic purpose to higher education—to teach students the collective knowledge and understanding of the university. More specifically, it is to teach students useful ways of thinking. "The task of the university is to find out what can be done with the powers of reason. . . . The basic work of the university is to create systems of reason, practices of inquiry" (56-57). Education should help students "evaluate perspectives and diverse bodies of knowledge" and "apply thought or reason to the discrete elements of knowledge they have learned" (76). Teaching practical reason involves learning in a logical progression (100). Initially students must master the material studied, then learn how to employ critical reason. From there students can learn the art of judgment and become creative and innovative in the way they investigate intellectual problems. Finally, students can transcend their own education by asking the "big questions"—e.g., what is the mind supposed to be doing in this world?

Anderson recommends a core curriculum directed toward the teaching and learning of civilization, science, the social sciences, and the humanities. Introductory courses in these disciplines lay the groundwork for the more difficult tasks of practical study and applying what the student has learned to his or her profession and the business of living. Practical reason becomes the ultimate justification of a university education as graduates can serve the world through good practice. At universities citizens learn what good practice is, in their professions and in their political experiences.

What does the university know, though? How do we know what the university knows? In other words, who is to judge and how is one to make that judgment? In exposing students to subject material we not only inform them of particular facts or ideas, but we exemplify important facts or ideas. Students then learn to judge particular facts or ideas as important; they receive this education at the same time that they increase their base of knowledge about the world. For instance, teaching students about the constitutional convention or separation of powers in an introductory American government exposes them to the constitutional debates and *The Federalist Papers*. It also exemplifies what the professor thinks is important to know about the founding of American government. Students then are exposed to an exercise of judgment (on the part of the professor teaching the course). If the professor articulates his or her reasons for choosing the events or texts that he or she has, then the student can learn why reading these texts or about these events is important.

Of course, to appreciate good practices one must be both interested in them and able to judge their importance and usefulness. This holds as well for mastering material and employing critical reason. In order to hold the attention of students long enough for them to master academic subjects the professor or the material itself captures their interest. Though some students may arrive at campuses prepared to think politically, others do not, and this includes political science majors. Their very existence indicates that political interest is not something given to students, even those who declare formally that they are willing to dedicate two or more years to its study.

Nor will students employ critical reason unless motivated to do so. Motivation here means being interested enough to want to critique rationally the object of study. It also means being interested in pursuing critical reason for its own sake—being motivated to explore the power of reason and in deploying it systematically in the pursuit of truth and meaning. I argue below that students can learn critical reason through the development of critical thinking skills but that these skills ought to be taught primarily to generate interest and foster judgment.

The Special Responsibility of Political Science

In 1989, the American Political Science Association organized a Task Force on the Political Science Major to assess the goals, purposes, and methods of the major (Wahlke 1991). It concluded that the political science major should "maximize students' capacity to analyze and interpret the significance and dynamics of political events and governmental processes" (49). It should be neither a pre-professional program to train political scientists nor a program to produce "good citizens." It should aim at turning politically interested and concerned students, whatever their career plans or their other interests, into politically literate college graduates (50). The Task Force recommended a series of "core" topics and a learning sequence to ensure that majors become "politically literate."

But it assumed that majors arrive at universities interested in politics and did not acknowledge the essential role of judgment in creating political literacy. We cannot expect first-year university students to be uniformly interested in politics, nor can we assume political science students to be interested in politics.

Students often choose the major for some utilitarian reason, e.g., as a conduit to law school. For such students the major is merely an instrument to another end, and many graduate in the major without participating in politics or thinking systematically and consistently about its problems. Throughout chapters 6, 7, and 8 I will offer specific examples of how universities can generate political interest and judgment among students, but let me explain in general terms here what it means for interest and judgment to be generated.

Interest

Arendt (1958b) defines the term interest as something "which lies between people and therefore can relate and bind them together" (162). Analytic political theorists might define it as a policy that one prefers or one that can maximize the advantages or minimize the disadvantages to oneself. To have an interest in something means to find it curious or worth considering. Regardless of definition of the term, or the conception of the self that it reflects, the political task of the university can be to make students interested in both the term itself and their own interests. They can help students recognize what binds them to their communities and to each other, and they can help students explore their own political preferences as adults. In the process they can catalyze the curiosity of students about politics in general and at the university.

Universities can make politics relevant to the daily lives of their students. They can help students recognize that their positions as students are political ones, that they are members of very specific communities, that there are material and economic concerns apposite to their educational careers, and that in understanding all of this they can articulate their preferences more prudently, judiciously, and effectively. In short, universities can make students aware of the in-between space that relates them to others.

First, universities can be sites of drama. Students can come to recognize their own educational experiences as both constructed and staged. Rather than accepting their daily lives as part of a natural order to things (e.g., as a collection of activities that they ought to do without considering the reasons for doing them), students can realize the political nature of their status in the university community. They commonly recognize their political science courses as particular subjects that impart knowledge and information about the field of politics. But they do not always comprehend the sorts of choices that go into creating a course or organizing a major. I will suggest in chapter 7 ways in which professors can denaturalize courses and give students the sense that political science results from human decisions. The politics of the classroom can serve as an exemplar for the world. The world thus comes home to the student, and he or she begins to share more deeply in that in-between of which Arendt speaks.

Second, universities can make politics more interesting to students by employing new methods of instruction. Modern technology permits teachers to reinforce a visual and aural culture. The Internet, interactive learning journals, videos, even recorded music can reach students who have grown up in a television culture. But they also appeal to young people used to hearing stories, and to being entertained, by their elders. Technology does not "work" simply because we live in a post-industrial age, but because it offers other means by which we can captivate our audiences as we spin political tales. However, universities can only do so with integrity if they explain that the technology they use has a politics itself. For instance, political science instructors might exemplify the relationship between technology and politics by recounting the political and economic decisions made to "wire" their campus. Students can then learn which sorts of struggles were undertaken to do so, who was awarded contracts to build the system and for which reasons, and whether the Internet benefits certain groups on campus rather than others. In the process of learning about technology and politics, then, students also learn about the constructed (and staged) nature of their campus.

Third, university professors can use narrative to grip their audiences. Martha Nussbaum (1997) charges students with developing a "narrative imagination" while in school (85-112). Telling stories cultivates fancy and wonder at the world and compassion for others. It also helps students appreciate the literary work as a sort of friend, and this is a political concern. While reading, the author and student engage in a dialogue, and the student learns to think in community with the work. There is a sort of literary friendship that arises, one that helps students communicate and articulate their thoughts. The friendship can be dramatized in classes where the professor (or a student) reads a text out loud in order to stimulate discussion about that text.

Story-telling also cultivates the enlarged mentality as I have argued in previous chapters. This not only fosters the skills of judgment, but it also makes the lives of other individuals more interesting to the student. Often students of political theory are intimidated by the ideas of philosophers and they find the "material" both difficult and boring. But when students hear about the life of Marx, or Mill, or Burke, or Augustine, otherwise abstract and complex thinkers become characters in a story to them. They pay more attention to details, and then it is the responsibility of the lecturer to explain their ideas as they describe their lives. Simply knowing that Augustine was a troubled teenager, or that he partied too much in Carthage as a student, can help convey his doctrine of the free will, or the libido dominandum, much more easily to students who might otherwise wonder what the point of his ideas are (or were). Even reading Marx's love letters to his wife shows students a passionate man, rather than cold-hearted ideologue. In telling stories, the professor reinforces the staged nature of the course and subject field.

Narrative can also make research more interesting. In chapter 6, I will tell the story of how the European Community (now Union) came to think of itself as a democracy. I do so to illustrate how a series of political choices led the nations of Europe down a particular political path. I also introduce a series of characters each of whom has a different role to play in the drama. This offers a number of different actors the opportunity to speak, and the reader can then learn to appreciate those perspectives in making his or her judgment about the success or failure of democracy in the European Union. But the reader can also recognize that history is often written by the actions and speeches of politically passionate individuals. Ultimately, the narrative form of the chapter permits me to introduce more abstract ideas, such as democracy and freedom, to the reader without overwhelming him or her in technical language.

In the end, I gather lessons from my own research about the practicality and relevance of committee work to democratic politics. I will apply these lessons in chapter 8, as I argue for community service at universities that create spaces of appearance. Research conducted in Italy and France is thus valuable to me for the lessons it provides at home. Whether or not the European Union is, or will ever be, democratic, is less important than how my findings can help me democratize the conditions of the workplace. So the chapter exemplifies not necessarily how one should write a research chapter, but how one can explore the ways in which research has tangible meaning in the everyday activities of the scholar. In theory, this sort of connection is made regularly only by professors of education whose research specialty is that of higher education.

In chapters 6 and 8 I suggest that this is also the responsibility of other academics as well. This is what it means to politicize research, and this is how to help future professional researchers connect theory and practice. Often young researchers will try to live their theory in practice by joining particular organizations or fighting for causes, and this is important for their political lives. But they can also be made aware that the practice of doing research has consequences at the institutions for which they do that research. It is another way of making students more aware that they help construct the stage upon which ideas and information are conveyed to future audiences.

Fourth, universities can stir the desire to play by getting their students involved in political activities. By engaging them as citizens, universities convey the world to students. They help students realize the dramatic nature of the community beyond the university and engage them in activities that may go beyond their immediate needs or interests. They help the student appreciate his or her longer-term interests and give them a sense that the good of the community corresponds to their own personal or political goals.

Finally, universities involve students and faculty as spectators to the comedy and tragedy of academic life. Students do not always have an interest in engaging actively in their classes, in clubs or associations, in community service, or in student government. Or they engage too actively in them to enjoy their studies or take an interest in ideas. Universities require students to stop-and-think and so afford them the time to cultivate interests in subject areas (in this case politics). As members of audiences—in the classroom or as observers watching some confrontation on campus—students can have a respite so that they can appreciate their temporary world. I have already suggested that this cultivates judgment, but I also think that it nurtures a particular kind of interest. Student-spectators come to appreciate the university as a whole—as a set of interlocking relationships and institutions and as a place of work for hundreds and even thousands of individuals. Students see the university as something in which they enroll to achieve some other end, and I have been (and will be) suggesting that universities can overcome this sense. But this sense of detachment is not all bad, and students sometimes reasonably believe that they do little more than pay tuition and take classes.

Undergraduates possess a unique vantage point as members of the university community who are for the most part not responsible for the successes or failures of the institution. They are young, without economic or political power, and most of them spend between four and five years at a university or college. As first-year students their interests in the university are minimal at best, and even by the time they graduate they have not invested the time, energy, or money at the institution that administrators or professors have. Moreover, they have not used their education for other ends, as the alumni have, so they have not reaped the full material benefits of their university education. Students, then, are the members of the university *community* that can assess the university in the manner most detached from their economic interests. While students may have *potential* interests in the university, they have not been realized while they are still at school. Thus they, more than the faculty, administration, or staff, have less at stake in being actors at the university and correspondingly more as spectators. It is often in their interests for students to observe the politics of the community passively—in order to learn, pass judgment on their professors, and enjoy the experience of being a student.

Judgment

Following Arendt, judgment is a capacity based on taste and the enlarged mentality of the person judging. The student ought to be exposed to a variety of political and moral perspectives by individuals or authors who exemplify different stands. Students learn to judge politically by first being able to envision a situation from different points of view. From there they learn to critically assess those points of view and determine the truth or meaning of the situation. The meaning with which they imbue the situation and the lessons they learn from it are enhanced because they arm themselves with not simply more information, but knowledge from a variety of sources. While none of these perspectives can tell the student what or how to believe, the student garners knowledge sufficient to appreciate the force of argument from others. In learning from example, they can then determine for themselves the justice of that situation.

Universities can encourage students to witness events and teach them how to examine what they have just witnessed. In bearing witness, students actively and immediately gaze upon events. In the chapters to follow, I will suggest ways in which universities can encourage students to be witnesses, but witnessing can come in a variety of forms. It can be part of any course. First, students can witness the politics of the classroom itself. Where the classroom and department are dramatically revealed, students appreciate the immediacy of their own situation. Students can also be assigned projects requiring them to be a witness at events external to the university. I regularly assign students the task of interviewing individuals for term papers or class projects. This forces students outside of the university and challenges them to consider the arguments and ideas of individuals unfamiliar to them. Invariably they return to the classroom enriched with perspectives about which they would have otherwise remained ignorant, and they teach those perspectives to others in the class during oral presentations.

Students can also witness the activity of research and scholarship. A number of educational theorists have lauded the use of student learning journals (Brookfield 1995) around which students learn to learn. In making students conscious of their own learning styles, and the techniques used to teach them, students bear witness to the process of education. It dramatizes scholarship and makes them more conscious of learning as an activity. Undergraduates who realize how they learn best sometimes come to this knowledge as a revelation. But even graduate students, engaged in systematic, sustained research papers, theses, and dissertations, can learn to appreciate better the activity of scholarship. This helps the student judge not only the topic at hand, but the enterprise of research in general. I offer an example of the pedagogical activity of research in the next chapter.

Beyond bearing witness to events and their own actions, students ought to practice skills of critical thinking and analysis in order to better learn political judgment. Teaching critical thinking has proved to be very effective in helping students understand and assess material in the social sciences. Professor James Hoefler employs optical illusions at the beginning of his international relations, judicial process, and legislative process classes in order to teach students that there might be more than one way to look at an issue and that they must appreciate the context of an issue before rendering judgment on it.[5] Professor Mel Cohen encourages logical analysis and "strong sense" critical thinking by asking students not only to think critically about issues such as the right to burn the American flag, but also to examine which character traits permit them to engage in critical thinking in the first place.[6] Some professors distribute questions in anticipation of a future examination or class and encourage students to think through problems before they are called on to defend them.[7] Even these simple innovations encourage students to think about thinking. Critical thinking affords students the opportunity to bear witness to their own reasoning processes.

The process of critical thinking ultimately depends on whether students deliberate on issues, and this is where political science takes on a special responsibility in the university curriculum. Democratic politics is defined by the capacity of the public to deliberate on issues of common concern. By analogy, class participation is an essentially democratic activity. In order for students to transform critical thinking activities into exercises that cultivate judgment they need the chance to discuss issues with others. In exposing them to the reasoning of others students enlarge their mentality (both individually and collectively). A fairly common practice among political science professors is to use a public issues agenda, such as commonly provided by the Carnegie Endowment, Pew Trust, or the Kettering Foundation.[8] To dramatize the impact of these programs even further professors ought to consider placing on the agenda the politics of corporate foundation giving on higher education. But even without being self-conscious of the process, public issues agendas prompt students to talk about public concerns with others. This can only help students become more aware of the activity of deliberation itself, and professors can publicly recognize the activity to students while they engage in it. I discuss the political act of teaching political and social science more systematically in chapter 7.

Actors and Spectators

The theater of the university is built upon three pillars—research, teaching, and service. Though I employ this tripartite description in the next few chapters, it is misleading. Higher education depends ultimately on *learning*, and both students and teachers engage themselves and each other in this common exercise. In examining the political nature of research, teaching, and service I will emphasize how universities can create spaces of appearance and how they can help students understand the facts that constitute their world.

The university nurtures scholars, and scholars act as spectators. I have been arguing that the spectatorial role of the scholar is both essential in charging actions with meaning and in recognizing actions as essentially political. The crafts of research and teaching rest on creating not simply interested and just actors, but also individuals willing to distance themselves from action in order to render informed and prudent judgment. Rendering judgment represents a political act, so individuals who appear distanced from political action are sometimes themselves acting politically.

In the remainder of the book I discuss ways in which universities and colleges can cultivate spectatorial action. I have already outlined the importance of criticism to spectatorial action, and as critics citizens learn to judge the political world. But mastering judgment does not make them magistrates, because they cannot judge alone. Critics engage themselves with the theater, and just as theater critics learn from other critics, the actors, and the audience, so citizens learn from other citizens. In this sense the citizen is not the sitting judge of action, but rather the interested juror.

Ideally, jurors are those citizens who collectively sit in judgment of criminal or civil actors. They are equal to each other, formally anonymous, interested in the proceedings, at attention all the time, aware that they are in the presence of live actors, and curious to arrive at the truth of the crime or civil complaint. Of course, very few juries live up to this ideal, but at least jurors become more involved in the issues than other citizens without an immediate interest in the ruling. In ancient Greece jurors related to principals in the case as the critic in the audience relates to actors on stage. Sophocles glorified the trial in *Antigone*, as did Plato in *The Apology*, and both dialogues point up the critical role jurors play as a collection of citizens. Two millennia later, Tocqueville, in *Democracy in America*, contends that the jury system in the United States buttresses the republic. In all these cases, the ideal jury is such not only for the characteristics I have just mentioned, but because jurors learn from taking part in the activity.

Indeed, learning is the central activity of being a juror. Under most circumstances, jurors cannot leave the courtroom. Nor can they speak. Their central tasks are to listen carefully to the proceedings, deliberate with each other outside the courtroom, and then return to the courtroom with a judgment that is read by the foreperson or the presiding judge. At no time in public can they verbalize their presence; thus they lose the capacity to act in any substantive manner. They lose the capacity to act in a theatrical manner, where they can make their presence known to others, as others make their presence known to them. In the courtroom, jurors act by observing, and by observing they learn. But they learn within the theater of justice, they are not removed from it. Were they to be removed from the courtroom they would immediately lose interest in the proceedings and lose interest in learning about the action in them.[9]

This is the difficult task of universities—how to sustain the desire to learn about the world by teaching the art of spectating. I make the analogy to juries because, like jurors, students learn to think collectively about certain subjects by introducing them into different spaces in the world where political and social actors appear. The challenge for universities and colleges is to maintain their interest in the world even after they leave the juror's box. After graduating students can choose to think systematically and maturely about politics or not, and the social sciences play a large role in encouraging them to consider all the world a stage. Social scientists cannot force students to sit in the critic's/juror's box for the rest of their lives, but we can persuade them that the action on stage or in the courtroom is sufficiently interesting and important to stay there and learn more about it. We can also teach them skills of reportage defining their capacity to observe events.

Research, teaching, and service can all make spectators more interested in the action. They provide exemplars for spectators who want to learn how to make informed and reasoned judgments about that action. This is the first purpose of a social science education at universities. In permitting potential jurors to learn about the world universities not only teach about political action, but they teach political action. Students learn, as jurors, to deliberate collectively, and learn the critical importance of an active and informed audience.[10] They may not have the background or intellectual sophistication of the magistrate, but neither are they indifferent to the proceedings as those who do not care to observe. They also learn balance in a way that the interested parties in the courtroom cannot be prepared to accept. Most importantly students understand that to learn about politics and society one must be prepared to learn with others. Solitary learning remains a contradiction in terms here. Consequently, students learn politics in the original sense of the term—as a study in the ways in which people live with each other.

In his study of the American jury system, Jeffrey Abramson (1994) recommends that jurors move "from passive spectator to active participant" (254). He lists policies that would initiate this change—permitting jurors to ask questions and take notes, allowing jurors to discuss the evidence during the trial, giving pre-instructions to juries, and making those instructions comprehensible and written. In most cases, students ask questions and take notes in class, and they can discuss what they have learned during the semester. But I will make policy recommendations to encourage both students and faculty to learn about the world, and from each other, in order to make their experience as political spectators active ones.

In the next chapter I take what is in many ways the consummate spectatorial activity—academic research—and activate it. I politicize the activity by recognizing its consequences for my actions as a university professor and in my capacities as a teacher, advisor, and administrator. Rather than arguing for politically inspired research into politics, following Arendt's argument in her lectures on Kant I have chosen to exemplify the practice. My example, democratic ideas in the founding of the European Community, is not arbitrary, because I employ its conclusions in chapters 7 and 8. Through the study of institutions such as the European Coal and Steel Community and various cultural foundations and congresses in the 1940s and 1950s I have learned better how to judge both politics in general and the politics of universities. Politicians and intellectuals active during this period taught me different ways of understanding democracy, and in considering their ideas on the matter (in enlarging my mentality, so to speak), I have then been able to judge the relevance of democracy to the European Union. I have also been able to judge the relevance of European Community democracy to democratic practices in the university. Clearly there are many other research topics and research techniques that can also contribute to the learning of judgment. I encourage scholars to pursue them, if not for themselves, then for their students.

Notes

1. See Bloom (1987) 313-382. The argument can be distorted, however. For instance, Athanasios Moulakis (1994) recommends that professors eschew passionate political exchanges in the classroom because "they induce the participants to defend their convictions rather than discuss their ideas" (134). Moulakis offers no evidence that this actually occurs in classrooms. Furthermore, this conviction makes little historical sense. Karl Marx or John Stuart Mill (or even Plato) wrote great books because they were exposed to controversial issues. Their philosophical writings engaged the political ideas of the day passionately, and they are judged classics presumably because their messages transcend the historical context of their day and speak to controversial issues of ours.

2. For a history of the civic mission of political science see David M. Ricci, *The Tragedy of Political Science: Politics, Scholarship, and Democracy* (New Haven: Yale University Press, 1984).

3. For examples in political science see: Robert Koulish, "Citizenship Service Learning: Becoming Citizens by Assisting Immigrants," *PS: Political Science and*

Politics, September 1998, 562-567; James D. Chesney and Otto Feinstein, "Making Political Activity a Requirement in Introductory Political Science Courses," *PS: Political Science and Politics*, September 1993, 535-538; Glenn Beamer, "Service Learning: What's a Political Scientist Doing in Yonkers?" *PS: Political Science and Politics*, September 1998, 557-561; Vincent L. Marando and Mary Beth Melchior, "On Site, Not Out of Mind: The Role of Experiential Learning in the Political Science Doctoral Program," *PS: Political Science and Politics*, December 1997, 723-728; Benjamin R. Barber and Richard Battistoni, "A Season of Service: Introducing Service Learning into the Liberal Arts Curriculum," *PS: Political Science and Politics*, June 1993, 235-240; and Harry C. Boyte, "Civic Education as Public Leadership Development," *PS: Political Science and Politics*, December 1993, 763-769. For university-wide programs see George D. Kuh, John H. Schuh, Elizabeth J. Whitt and Associates, *Involving Colleges: Successful Approaches to Fostering Student Learning and Development Outside the Classroom*, San Francisco: Jossey Bass, 1991; and Richard Guarasci, Grant H. Cornwell, and Associates, *Democratic Education in an Age of Difference: Redefining Citizenship in Higher Education*, San Francisco: Jossey Bass, 1997.

4. Mark Weaver, "Weber's Critique of Advocacy in the Classroom: Critical Thinking and Civic Education," *PS: Political Science and Politics*, December 1998, 801.

5. James M. Hoefler, "Critical Thinking and the Use of Optical Illusions," *PS: Political Science and Politics*, September 1994, 538-545.

6. Mel Cohen, "Making Critical Thinking a Classroom Reality," *PS: Political Science and Politics*, June 1993, 241-244.

7. Andrew Green and William Rose, "The Professor's Dream: Getting Students to Talk and Read Intelligently," *PS: Political Science and Politics*, December 1996, 687-690; John L. Seitz, "Mission Impossible? Making a Political Science Final Exam That's Fun to Grade," *PS: Political Science and Politics*, September 1996, 525-526.

8. Daniel W. O'Connell and Robert H. McKenzie, "Teaching the Art of Public Deliberation—National Issues Forums in the Classroom," *PS: Political Science and Politics*, June 1995, 230-232; Elizabeth T. Smith and Mark A. Boyer, "Designing In-Class Simulations," *PS: Political Science and Politics*, December 1996, 690-694.

9. In discussing the formation of local juries in the United States, Jeffrey Abramson (1994) raises the interesting point that jurors at the founding were both spectators and actors simultaneously. Local juries grew directly from colonial experience in using juries to resist the crown, and the trials of John Hancock and John Peter Zenger reflect the revolutionary purposes of the local jury (23-24). On the issue of jury nullification, colonists rallied for the "right of juries to decide questions of law" and in the colonies they "turned local juries in times of crisis into centers of resistance to parliamentary law" (68). Only after the constitutional convention did the concept of an impartial juror emerge, and eventually the right of jury nullification evaporated. In Arendt's terms, and consistent with her argument in the final chapter of *On Revolution*, the American citizen lost a space in which he or she could appear because the citizens lost their right to nullify laws.

10. Abramson (1994) argues for unanimity as a decision rule among jurors. "[T]he requirement of unanimity necessitates that jurors conduct extensive deliberations out of which collective wisdom flows. Each must consider the case from everybody else's point of view in search of the conscience of the community. Each must persuade or be persuaded in return" (183). Abramson's phenomenological point exemplifies Arendt's argument that judgment requires an enlarged mentality. (He concludes that "the search for common justice starts with the different experiences attached to identity in

America"— 246.) Though we cannot require unanimity on anything in the classroom or in life, the point is well-taken that students should be prepared to both argue their positions thoroughly and to listen with an open mind to those who disagree with them. At the very least, the jury system is one where jurors can deliberate face-to-face, and in the absence of unanimity, this personal characteristic of the practice forces them to put their opinions at risk. So the analogy to jurors suggests that students ought to learn to take stands in public and that taking stands are courageous acts.

Chapter 6

Action and the Founding of the European Community

"From a man I have turned into a function, and a not very interesting function at that."

Robert Marjolin (1953, 246)

Through the years there have been a host of academic theories employed to make sense of the growth and development of the European Community (now Union), including realism, federalism and functionalism (and their neo-variants), intergovernmentalism, concordance theory, regulatory regime theory, and so on. Each has represented not only a different perspective on the problem of European integration, but a veritable research program and strategy that has involved tremendous time, money, and effort on the parts of the participating researchers and their organizations.

In this chapter, I do not offer another research strategy, agenda, or program, one based on Arendtian ideas. Rather, I suggest how researchers can incorporate political judgment into the practice of academic teaching and service by applying Arendt's ideas about conciliar democracy and the space of appearance. I have chosen this subject matter because I render judgment over the practice of committee deliberation and decision-making that will be relevant to my discussion of university administration in chapter 8. I realize that my approach in this chapter is unorthodox, but I employ it in conjunction with arguments in chapters 7 and 8, and I contend that in speaking about an Arendtian method in the social sciences, I am speaking not simply of research, but also of teaching and administration.

Lost Treasures

The project of European unification is, to say the least, enormous. So enormous, in fact, that one can only marvel at how rapidly both the idea of Europe and the fact of its increasing organization are establishing themselves. Within a few short years freedom of movement, goods, services, and labor have increased dramatically, and soon there is to be a political status apposite to these "new" freedoms—the citizen of Europe. With this status comes a new political condition: the European public space. Since World War II this public space has gone by various names—the European Coal and Steel Community, the European Economic Community, the Common Market, and now, the European Union. These names have reflected the essentially economic nature of "Europe," but it has also existed politically in both theory and practice. From the dreams of the resistance during the war, through the occasional successes of the European Parliament, up to the creation of European legal citizenship status today, a number of Europeans have treated the Community, now Union, as a political entity, with a defined space for political action.

Yet what do we imagine when we think of a European public space? Is such a space even imaginable? Can there be something that goes by the name "European public"? Is there a European theater of politics? How would such a space be framed institutionally? Who would be citizens within this public space? These are questions that many have asked of the European Community, especially in the years immediately following World War II, when the ideology of Europeanism was at its strongest.

Arendt's theories of revolution and political action apply well to this subject matter, and we can view the years immediately following the war as a time of great potential for the European movement, but one that also lost "treasures" of a European revolution. I will also contend that her theory fails to account for the difficulty, if not the very impossibility, of creating stable, free, democratic spaces of appearance in the modern world, because revolutionary spaces can sow the seeds of their own destruction.

In the terms I have been using here, the contemporary theater of pan-European politics is represented as a spectacle that does not permit audiences to engage in the performance. Moreover, such a theater was constructed in the years 1945 to 1955, by both the actors on the stage and individuals who purported to be members of the audience themselves. I will judge their performances as a critic, by piecing together reports of their actions, and in doing so I play the role not simply of a reporter, but of a historian. As a critic, I will separate myself to a certain extent from the theater of my research—namely both the historical events themselves and Arendt's theory with which I analyze those events—in order to suggest a nuance in Arendt's theory of revolutionary conciliar democracy that I believe she herself did not recognize. In this way I not only critique the founders' project of unification, but also the social scientific theory I employ in interpreting that project. So I am observing not only the events themselves, but the theory that reconstructs a coherent narrative of those events. Consequently, I offer this chapter as an example of how one judges the results of the activity of research itself.

In *On Revolution* (1965), Arendt compares the French and American revolutions with a number of purposes in mind: (1) to understand the means and goals of the revolutionaries themselves, (2) to explain how these revolutions succeeded and how they failed, and how the success and failure of the revolutionaries were inextricably intertwined, (3) to indicate ways in which the eighteenth-century revolutions (especially the French) influenced revolutions in the nineteenth and twentieth centuries, and (4) to introduce political terms and actions (e.g., freedom, power, authority, space of appearance, and conciliar democracy), emerging from these revolutions, that point toward political justice and ways to "endow life with splendor." In this chapter I would like to describe the ways in which the "revolutionists" and "founders" of the European community succeeded and failed in establishing a public space where freedom can dwell. I contend that the goal of political freedom for European citizens was incompatible with at least one of the means by which it was to be achieved—a public space of discussion known as the conference. I present a reason for the failure of revolutionary conciliar democracy that even Arendt did not recognize.

She begins the book by suggesting that the "interrelationship of war and revolution . . . has steadily grown . . . [and that] it has become almost a matter of course that the end of war is revolution, and that the only cause which possibly could justify it is the revolutionary cause of freedom" (17). I will treat the end of World War II as an attempt by revolutionaries to create a European public space based on political freedom. By freedom, Arendt meant direct and ongoing political action by citizens that permits their collective self-determination within certain spatial limitations.

> This is especially clear for the greatest and most elementary of all negative liberties, the freedom of movement; the borders of national territory or the walls of the city-state comprehended and protected a space in which men could move freely . . . What is true for freedom of movement is, to a large extent, valid for freedom in general. Freedom in a positive sense is possible only among equals, and equality itself is by no means a universally valid principle but, again, applicable only with limitations and even within spatial limits (275).

Freedom is thus circumscribed by a physical space in which citizens possess not only civil but (and especially) political rights. Through their political participation they actually create this space where they can determine the character of their own lives, what I have termed the "space of appearance." Within the space of appearance citizens empower themselves and each other. Thus Arendt, following Montesquieu, characterizes freedom as power, and vice versa (150).[1]

The space of freedom and civic power has taken different forms throughout history. I noted that Arendt, in *The Human Condition* (1958b), saw the polis as the first, and probably most successful, public space of freedom. Here citizens lived together, equally, under conditions of isonomy, or no-rule. In *On Revolution* she explains that in the late eighteenth century, these free spaces emerged in the forms of revolutionary councils. The American and French Revolutions created institutional arrangements for empowering citizens to experience political freedom, direct and ongoing political action, within spatial limits. In the French Revolution municipal councils and *sociétés populaires* emerged (239ff), and the American Revolution bred the Jeffersonian idea of the ward system (248-255). In the nineteenth and twentieth centuries we have seen similar examples of conciliar democracy in the Paris Commune of 1871, in the original soviets of the Russian revolutions, in the short-lived Hungarian uprising of 1956 (266-267; see also Arendt 1958a and Kohler and Saner 1992, 306), and in the student movement of the 1960s. Arendt believed that these popular spaces would be the means by which the citizens of a revolution could found freedom and citizens after the revolution could renew the original revolutionary experience of foundation.[2]

These councils possessed a number of characteristics in common: (1) they arose spontaneously out of the conditions of revolution itself, (2) they were organs of order as well as of action, along lines modeled by Madison in Federalist #10 (Sitton 1994), (3) they crossed all party lines (thus members of all parties sat in them together, and more importantly, party membership played no role whatsoever), (4) they were territorially, and not functionally, based, (5) they empowered a political elite based solely on political criteria—"those who cared and those who took the initiative . . . those who had committed themselves to, and now were engaged in, a joint enterprise" (Arendt 1965, 262-264, 278), and (6) their authority was based not on coercion or persuasion but on mutual respect and mutual recognition of the importance of deliberation. Councils provided an alternative to a representative party system, a system that could not for various reasons reconcile problems of power, authority, freedom, and equality.[3] The council system was a way to solve the problem of how to reconcile equality and authority, and this was done in a federated conciliar hierarchy where authority "would have been generated neither at the top nor at the bottom," but on each layer in a federated, pyramidal structure. Councils, then, were spaces of appearance in the truest sense of the term—places where equal citizens empowered themselves in creating political freedom.[4]

Yet the spaces created by the modern revolutionaries were not sustained. They failed, Arendt argued, for a few reasons. In the broadest terms, the leaders of the revolutions, especially the French, were overwhelmed by "the social question"—the appeal to solve the problem of poverty, the demands of the emotion of compassion and the sentiment of pity, and the tyrannical actions resulting from the active pursuit of these ends (59-114). Such social concerns overdetermined the possibility for councils to play a continuing significant role in founding public institutions. Moreover, professional revolutionaries assumed leadership of later revolutions. These professionals were influenced by the messages of historical necessity sent by Hegel in his philosophy of history, Marx in his theory of political economy, and Lenin in his method of political organization—"with the obvious and paradoxical result that instead of freedom necessity became the chief category of political and revolutionary thought" (53). Consequently, forms of hierarchical political organization, such as parties and interest groups, emerged as (the most efficient) means by which individuals secured their private and social needs.

The councils were overcome by parties and party systems which had emerged during this time period. Parties and councils came into conflict during revolutions, with councils losing each time, because parties were far more successful at answering "the social question" that arose during the revolution. Parties were designed for representation of interests, not of opinion or action, and while this made them less democratic, and even "political" in Arendt's sense of the term, it rendered them far better administrators of private needs. For those previously out of power who demand, not political freedom, but food, clothing, and shelter, the party was a much more efficient means by which to distribute these necessities. Finally, councils themselves failed to distinguish between action and administration. For example, factory councils repeatedly assumed the management of factories, efforts which always ended in failure (273-274).[5] Consequently, both partisans and councilors effaced the differences between the realms of freedom and necessity.

In examining the early efforts to create a European public space, we can identify another reason for the failure of free spaces to appear in the modern world, a reason that Arendt herself did not recognize (or rather could not for the sake of her theory). The practice of discussion, and communication, held to be the *sine qua non* for free public spaces to emerge, can contribute to the demise of such spaces. More specifically, I argue that particular forms of discussion transform free spaces into bureaucratic ones, so the very success of the space of appearance—its capacity to permit citizens to talk—engenders its own failure to be sustained.

Throughout this chapter, I will try to show how the political elite concerned with building Europe believed their task to be unprecedented and necessary. The particularly revolutionary-minded elite envisioned the birth of Europe to be a violent process, one that would have to continue well beyond the end of the war itself. In other words, there was room for militancy in the building of Europe, and militants saw their window of opportunity shrink as the 1950s waned. This window of opportunity became smaller only in part because professional politicians overwhelmed the citizen-actor. I will argue that within the domain of professional politicians themselves there were those who tried to create spaces of appearance (which I call "elite" spaces of appearance). So professional politicians were not constitutionally opposed to the public space upon which freedom can be found. Moreover, the popular movement for European unity transformed itself, and became more bureaucratic in the process. Most importantly, the very practice of public discussion generated and promoted by these movements destroyed the spaces of freedom that, according to Arendt, they would have normally created.

Arendt's democratic message has been discovered recently by a number of political theorists who see great possibilities and hope in the council system (Isaac 1994, Passerin d'Entreves 1994, Canovan 1992, Ring 1991, Sitton 1994). Citing contemporary political history, these theorists claim that Arendt's theory of action is exemplified in conciliar politics, and that conciliar politics is an effective way to give as many citizens as possible the opportunity to act publicly. Arendt's theories of revolution and action, then, are seen as foundational for a participatory politics.[6] For example, Jeffrey Isaac (1994) maintains that Arendt "supported a kind of insurgent politics, rooted in civil society, that would invigorate rather than replace mass democratic politics" (156, see also the Appendix).

Others see Arendt's democratic theory as a springboard for a more practically minded politics (Dietz 1994, Bernstein 1986). For instance, Mary Dietz argues that Arendt's theory of action ought to be supplemented by Simone Weil's concept of work as methodical thinking—a "liberatory form of instrumentality." In privileging action over work, Arendt "reduces work to an object orientation that prohibits genuine relations with others . . . [and] she reduces teamwork to routinized performance of motions that prohibits speech and deliberation"(878). Politics becomes theatrical and loses a "dimension of substantive purposefulness that finds positive expression in the vocabulary of 'problem,' 'solution,' 'means,' 'end,' and 'method'" (879). Dietz suggests that Arendt's theory ought to be supplemented by Weil's notion of "methodical politics" for a number of reasons. It identifies problems and determines a "means-end sequel, or method, directed toward a political aim. It reaches its full realization in the actual undertaking of the plan of action, or method itself" (880). It permits a substantive political order to be built upon the creative, natal, theatrical politics that Arendt identifies so well in revolutionary and immediately post-revolutionary times. Thus Arendtian citizens can "search for the best specification of the problem before them [and] pursue solutions to the problem once it is identified" (881-2). It is a practical approach to the problems of mass, technological society and serves to identify and correct the very problems Arendt identifies as endemic to modern society. Both participatory and pragmatic theorists, however, agree that Arendt's theory can be a valuable check on mass democracy, and the institutions she admires (e.g., workers' councils, elementary republics) can teach citizens to make already democratic polities more just and more participatory.

In retracing the early history of the European Community I will argue that its founding signals neither a realistic possibility of democratic participation nor a groundwork for methodical politics. Rather the very early history of a European politics—during and immediately after World War II—presents a futile exercise in the constitution of freedom. Freedom and action, in Arendt's senses, were impossible to constitute, even granting the possibility that the founders of the EC did not want to construct a democratic system. Political freedom could not have been constituted by the European founders, even had they established conciliar politics or elementary republics, because the logic of

Arendt's argument would have precluded that. In making this case I build on ideas first presented by Alan Keenan (1994), who argues that "the political realm and the freedom it houses can only be found by accepting their inevitable 'loss'" (299).[7] In my terms, the theater of politics constructs and protects freedom of performance as it precludes participation by potential actors in the audience. We move away from politics as a Dionysian theater of performance, and toward politics as bureaucratic imperative. I detail this argument in the last section of the chapter.

In the next two sections, though, I argue that the early history of the EC reflects the failure of the revolutionary impulse to recreate and maintain itself. The institutionalization of the politico-cultural European space destroyed a nascent public space and resulted in a performance restricted to the stage itself. Two elite groups created their own spaces of appearance and helped, ironically, to destroy the public space: a traditional political elite—"mainstream" politicians and policy managers such as Churchill, Adenauer, Schumann, Kennan, Monnet, and Spaak—*and* a popular, "revolutionary," elite—Spinelli, Rossi, even (curiously, given his class background) Coudenhove-Kalergi. The professional elite diverted the revolutionary momentum for a people's Europe. But the revolutionaries themselves also failed to found a European public space. Thus, the European stage was not to be modeled on the theater of Dionysos, and a potential elementary republic sowed the seeds of its own destruction.

While their intentions might have been "pure," the revolutionaries were presented with an uphill battle in this regard for a few reasons. First, it is difficult (to say the least) to sustain a revolutionary, theatrical impulse beyond a short period of time (as Arendt recognizes). Second, the forms of organization promoted and deployed by these European revolutionaries also worked against the maintenance of an ongoing European public space. The definition of that space in these early years contravened the possibility of popular participation. Europe gave birth to rival spaces of appearance—an elite and a "popular" space—suggesting that popular participation does not always create the only true public space. Furthermore, the popular space contributed to its own demise, as the attempt to found and augment the popular, revolutionary impulse foundered and destroyed itself. While the elite and popular movements for European unity worked at cross-purposes, they shared a kind of organizational logic that subverted the maintenance of (an) elementary European republic(s). Organizational forms such as conferences, congresses, committees, study groups, working groups, and cultural agencies were part of both elite and popular spaces of appearance, and such forms both facilitated and constricted the possibilities for public participation during the immediate post-war years.

By the time public participation was turned into reality—as we begin to see toward the end of this period in the form of a European Assembly—it was already too late. The forces of bureaucracy, technocracy, and systematization had established themselves, and a European assembly was to become only a shell of what Arendt might have hoped it would become. Militancy had declined, Europe was a market (and was marketed as such), political education was becoming formalized, and federalism was now formulated as a *realpolitik* solution to a foreign policy problem, the Soviet threat. In short, Europe was becoming organized, and this organization quashed any nascent potential for sustained public participation.

Staging the European Revolution

"I cling fanatically to hope for a united Europe, and I'm totally convinced that one single correct move could stave off the worst and give us time."

Hannah Arendt, in a letter to Karl Jaspers
4 March 1951 (Kohler and Saner 1992, 168)

I have already noted that Arendt saw a close connection between war and revolution, and this seems to have been relevant to the period during and immediately after World War II. Certainly there were no revolutions in the Western European countries in the manner of, say, Russia during World War I. But the political, economic, and social crises created by the Nazi aggression catalyzed a dormant movement for European unification. This movement emerged not only from a traditional elite who saw both political and economic advantages of unity, but also from resistance movements that bred both political leaders and a popular will to eliminate war and suffering forever. Even Arendt herself, during this time period, viewed European unification as politically significant, holding out great hope for the "new Europeans" immediately after the war, but holding no illusions about their ultimate failure by the early 1950s.[8]

The crisis of Europe, in the eyes of the European revolutionaries, was fourfold—political, economic, social, and cultural. Politically, the rise of fascism demonstrated the pathological consequences of nationalism and the growth of the nation-state. This had been noted by radicals in the early part of the century, but no one then was prepared for totalitarianism and the Holocaust. Economically, the war had decimated Europe, and there were enormous problems of reconstruction. Many Europeans were grateful to the United States for providing assistance, but they were wary as well that the Marshall Plan might afford the United States too much influence on the domestic economies of European countries. Jean Monnet (1978) saw the unity movement as a natural response to economic crisis (65-66). In connection with this economic crisis, opinion creators noted the collapse of civil society. Dispossession and homelessness were rampant, and millions were dependent upon public assistance in some form or another to survive immediately after the war. Political leaders saw the danger that Communism might take hold of the dispossessed in these countries. Directors such as Roberto Rossellini, Vittorio De Sica, and Federico Fellini represented social breakdown in films like *The Bicycle Thief*, *Open City*, and *I Vitelloni*. For many the crisis went beyond political, economic, or social upheaval. The post-war era was to test the strength of European civilization itself.

The idea of a European civilization or culture has persisted over the centuries. Denys Hay (1957) has traced a "sentimental attachment" to the word Europe to the thirteenth and fourteenth centuries. After this period Europe comes to be identified with Christendom, and after the fifteenth century the word "European" was used interchangeably with that of "Christian." These linguistic practices were reinforced by the advent of *portolani*, the traveler's maps used by scholars for study. By the eighteenth century, Europe was fully entrenched as an idea in the minds of scholars and intellectuals, and this Europe included lands east to the Ural mountains. Derek Urwin (1991) has outlined "the persisting idea of Europe" up through World War II, and others, most notably Denis de Rougemont (1965), have recounted the various schemes of European unity of Sully, Saint Simon, Abbe St. Pierre, Hugo, and others. In one sense, then, there has been a long tradition of Europeanists, at least among scholars, intellectuals, and members of the political elite.[9]

But Europe as an idea is not translated into a social movement until the twentieth century. For it is at the beginning of the century that a "revolutionary" tradition that the movement for European unity begins. Corrado Malandrino (1988) traces this history from 1913 to 1920 and roots the revolutionary post-World War II drive for European unity in this period. Malandrino has connected European federalism with socialism during these years and has traced this history of various leagues that connected the two movements—the European Unity League, the Lega dei Paesi Neutri—and the establishment of a journal—*Cœnobium*—in conjunction with them. Such movements "created from such origins the drive for a new Europe, capable of resolving in a positive way a crisis of civilization" (490). They were engaged in cultural battle for they were presenting a new order as "a defense of the European people from 'a new resumption of barbarity'" (490). The ideals of Woodrow Wilson influenced European federalists after 1917 because "the President offered the suitable political occasion to create a new terrain for pacifist and internationalist action for the masses" (495) Wilson's idealistic liberalism, then, was influential in Europe as an ideology to mobilize "the masses" for Europe. Malandrino traces the effect of Wilsonianism on the Euro-socialist writings of a number of political activists and concludes that "the debate on European and internationalist themes was by now exhausted" (509). Europe had become an idea that was to be left to others to use as an ideology to combat "counterrevolutionary" forces. Consequently, it came to be deployed in revolutionary fashion.

By the early 1930s the idea of Europe was being (re)created within two political spaces an elite group of politicians who saw unity as a rational method of organizing the continent and a popular movement led ironically by aristocrats, most notably Count Richard Coudenhove-Kalergi and Count Carlo Sforza. Both groups, however, conceived of European unity as a political device to mobilize the masses.

The two most celebrated political leaders pressing for European unity at this time were Aristide Briand and Edouard Herriot. In a 1926 speech describing the Anglo-French-German negotiations of 1925, Briand declared that "we spoke

European; it is a new language that we will have to learn," which he re-stated at a League of Nations meeting in 1929 (quoted in Carter 1966, 20). A Swiss delegate to the League of Nations, Professor William Rappard, declared that nationalism was antithetical to the "progress of civilization" which demands "more and closer intercourse between individuals and collectivities" (Rappard 1930, 3-4, see also 261, 301). Briand reasserted these principles in 1930 in a "Memorandum on European Union" (Zurcher 1958, 7). Herriot (1930) maintained that Europe was facing "decadence and grandeur" and declared that "what we need to organize is not a struggle, but an equilibrium. We are preparing to discipline a continent which in the course of centuries has disrupted a large part of its vital energies in wars which really amounted to civil wars" (12). Europe was not a political space, but a society that needed to be organized on scientific principles. Indeed, Herriot suggested that the organization of a European federation should be studied following "the precepts laid down in the *Discourse on Method*" (57). The act of federation requires "great minds to show (Europe) her common interest and duty" (235). These minds will help rationalize Europe not only politically, but culturally to fight the degenerate cultural effects of, for instance, Hollywood (245). In short, Europeans need to develop and protect their "language" and culture in the face of "external" forces, but Europe ought to be organized by an elite scientifically trained for the effort.

A simultaneous movement for European unity was being promoted by Count Richard Coudenhove-Kalergi. Coudenhove-Kalergi (1926) founded the Pan European Union in the 1920s and envisioned it as a youth movement. Declaring that "the only force that can realize Pan-Europe is the will of the Europeans," he maintained that Europe's youth must exert the energy necessary to realize the collective "will" of Europe (xi). Fearing that Europe was "growing poorer, weaker, and more barbarous,"[10] Coudenhove-Kalergi called for young people to blend "Hellenic individualism" and "Christian Socialism," to forge a European ideology (29), "open up its African colonial empire," to produce "all the raw materials and foodstuffs it requires" (34), and federate politically. He believed Europe's culture to be "that of the White Race" (29), but also asserted that "all the peoples of Europe are mixed peoples: mixtures of Nordic, Alpine, and Mediterranean strains, of Aryan immigrant and Mongoloid autochthonous blood; of fair and dark, on long-skulled and short-skulled, races" (152). These racial remarks functioned as an ideological justification for European nationalism. Coudenhove-Kalergi recognized the effectiveness of nationalism for mobilizing the public and deployed this sort of rhetoric for the purposes of mobilizing individuals toward European union. He reinforced this strategy by stating that the greatest enemies of pan-Europe would be "protected industries" and powerful capitalists (187-190). The movement for pan-Europe was interrupted by fascism and World War II. Coudenhove-Kalergi himself sought exile in New York, but he remained a somewhat influential (if marginal) elder "statesman" of the populist movement for European unity (Zurcher 1958). His class status would give him access to political leaders, and he proved to be an effective conduit between European militants and the political elite in Europe and the United States.

Other popular movements for European and Atlantic unity arose in the 1930s, most notably Clarence Streit's Federal Union in the United States, the European Political Union, and the Federal Union of the United Kingdom. All of these movements attempted to mobilize individual citizens for the European cause, and many of them tied their schemes into particular economic programs. Some conservatives called Coudenhove-Kalergi's plans "socialist," and attempted to document all such movements as a socialist movement for the United States of Europe (Sennholz 1955, 64-69, 85-106). The philosopher Eugen Rosenstock-Huessy (1969) argued that European unity was real despite of the plurality of states and nations that constitute Europe. He contended that what unified European civilization was its political forms and popular revolutionary tradition (454). But despite their efforts, the popular movement for European unity remained unorganized and politically powerless. In fact, the historian Alan Milward has remarked that federalism was a weak doctrine in the 1930s because the popular leaders failed to mobilize enough support for the movement among common citizens (Milward 1992).

The movement existed as a "lost treasure" in Arendt's terms, waiting to be rediscovered and reissued. The revival came after the initial shock of the beginning of World War II, and it came from the resistance to fascism. The historical evidence is replete with examples of resistance fighters clinging to pan-European ideology. Indeed, Walter Lipgens (1982) cites the resistance movement as one of three sources of the re-emergence of an integration movement (along with a growing sense of unity to European civilization and the immediate post-war economic crisis). Lipgens argues that Europeanism during and immediately after the war was anti-statist, anti-bureaucratic, and appealed to resistance leaders for a number of reasons. First, it represented a stand against the state and nationalism and one that would prevent future wars. Second, it would solve both the "German problem" and the problem of economic necessity. Finally, resistance leaders themselves recognized a need to "maintain European civilization" (44-62). There is also the sense that a European integration movement could perpetuate a space of appearance. "The Resistance dream was that wartime camaraderie would persist into the post-war world to encompass the whole of society" (Urwin 1991, 8).[11] In fact, the earliest international documents for European union originated in a meeting between the resistance leaders of different countries on May 20, 1944.

The resistance movements bred a self-consciously radical form of European federalism called "integral federalism": "To speak of federalism means giving a concrete expression to the clear sentiment . . . of the radical solidarity and interdependence among all men to each nation, people, or race to which they belong."[12] It was a federalism that meant not simply uniting disparate political units, but fighting those industrial monopolies that would inevitably seek to control a federated Europe. A federated Europe meant a socialist or social democratic Europe to these resistance fighters, and this meant the creation of a "new political class" that could maintain such a fight.[13] As one participant recalled: "We had felt the European idea not only as a unifying solution for the European peoples, but as a way to realize a new type of society; it was not only Europe, it was a new European society."[14] It was a European movement based on resistance to fascism and nationalism, but also to industrial capitalism. This required political action on the part of the people.

More specifically, out of the resistance movements emerged what can be called Euro-militancy—organized, popular, militant action for European unity. Such militancy was borne out of manifest action and suggests an empirical account of what Arendt describes as "natality"—the human capacity for creativity and initiative. The birth certificate, so to speak, was the Ventotene Manifesto, written by two resisters being held by the Mussolini regime on the island of Ventotene—Altiero Spinelli and Ernesto Rossi (Spinelli and Rossi 1988).[15] Taking cues from Hegel, Marx, and Lenin, Spinelli and Rossi set out the "basic principles of a free European Federation" including "direct representation [sic] of citizens on federal assemblies" (15). They judged the state to be the "master of vassals bound into servitude" (20), and complained that "men are no longer free citizens who can use the State to achieve collective goals" (23). Fascism has created a "revolutionary situation." But, they add, "at the very moment when the greatest decisiveness and boldness is needed, democrats lose their way, not having the backing of spontaneous popular approval, but rather a gloomy tumult of passions" (28). They ask what is to be done and proceed to map out a revolutionary strategy for mobilizing European citizens against the state and for an international federation. In their vision, "citizens will be independent, and will be sufficiently informed as to be able to exert continuous and effective control over the ruling class" (37). In Leninist fashion, they perceive the masses as "waiting to be guided," and see as their task the creation of the social and political "discipline" necessary to accomplish this goal (40). They conclude with a "foundational" thesis for the Movimento dei Federalisti Europei (MFE):

> We are in fact convinced that a federal structure is a necessary condition for the development of free political life. Only through such revolution can the problems of each country be solved in such a way as to make use of all the forces which together maintain the essential values of our civilization (49).

Spinelli and Rossi have in mind a popular political movement guided by those "forces" that can "together" maintain the values of European civilization.

Note all that is expressed in the Ventotene Manifesto. It is a declaration of action in the name of citizenship. Spinelli and Rossi claim that the state is an inadequate public space for the free exercise of civic rights, and that another, larger space is needed—the space of Europe. To achieve this action demands revolution, but one guided by those who can provide discipline. In its very birth, then, the popular movement for European unity contained within it the ideological seeds that might sow the destruction of spaces of appearance.

Spinelli and Rossi declare the need for such a space (one that the state has failed to provide), but they also claim that such a space needs to be "disciplined" and remain skeptical of the possibility for practical democratic action. They fear the "gloomy tumult of passions," and thus suggest that a European federation include, not popular assemblies, but direct *representation* of citizens on those assemblies. Finally, the institutions of a European federation are a precondition for the creation of a European civic "spirit," not vice versa.[16]

The Manifesto gave birth to a European citizen's movement (not party)— the MFE. At least initially, the MFE organized itself as a militant organization. Composed of divisions, sectors, and hierarchically federated local councils, the MFE itself took on the characteristics of a Leninist party. The militant him or herself was not a "simple citizen," however, but was rather part of national cadres that were disciplined and demanding of their political and economic rights. "The militants must meet their needs and the citizens must help them for one must have the courage not only to demand a voice, but also to demand money."[17] Militancy, however, meant not simply a form of organization for political power, it meant organization for knowledge (about Europe) as well. In one of the earlier editions of its journal, *Europa Federata*, the editors write about "readings for Militants" and suggest not only books to read, but revolutionary methods of reading. Militants, the author "Publius" (probably Spinelli) writes, ought to choose and read books "in common," and notes that reading will help militants "to visualize Europe."[18] By the mid-1950s, *Europa Federata* was publishing manifestoes to the "fellow-citizens of Europe," criticizing the political elite of Europe for not possessing "the European will" or even "a good European will."[19] In short, one could not be a militant European "if we cannot change our method of thinking."[20]

This militant aspect to the MFE helped ensure that it remained a movement, not a party, as one of its leaders, Mario Albertini, mentioned at the Fifth Assembly of Militants of the Congress of the European People.

> We were not a party; a party is made by conquering the power in order to realize some objectives that it judges necessary for the well-being of the citizens; in our case [the movement] acted not to take government from the nation-state, it did not act to create a state. A party is made to divide while we did it to unite.[21]

Jean Monnet (1978) recognized the sincerity of the militants in his memoirs, but argued that organizations like the MFE remained essentially powerless because they could not organize themselves into parties. Consequently, he added, they were useless to him and his "action committee" in the 1950s (406). As a broadly based social movement, Spinelli and others envisioned European unity as requiring more than just political organization, but military organization as well. The MFE called for a European army composed of "citizen-soldiers." But this citizen's army would be "a strong instrument of European education and civics."[22] This institution would serve to change the interests, sentiments, passions, and thoughts, "of every single European citizen."[23] The citizen-soldiers, along with the militants, were to be the organized popular arm(ie)s of the European movement.

The movement transformed itself over time[24] and did so through the various public spaces of appearance it created. I will be arguing that one form of public space in particular—the Congress or conference—contributed mightily to this transformation. By the middle of the 1950s the MFE and the Union of European Federalists (UEF) might have called themselves movements, but they looked more like parties. They published journals with "official" lines, governed themselves through central committees, distributed propagandistic texts on topics such as "how to speak to workers," and developed a charismatic group of leaders.[25] Moreover, the federalist "movement" was developing an organized body of writing, a doctrine. Many of the intellectuals supporting the movement claimed that the idea of Europe itself was a "movement of ideas."[26] These ideas were to secure for Europeans "a supremacy of civilization, according to the European tradition."[27]

I would like to suggest that within this public movement, this space of appearance, this "lost treasure," there was a political argument for a different kind of Europe—another lost treasure buried within a lost treasure. This was the movement for European unity based on regionalism. A few individuals, including on at least one occasion Spinelli himself,[28] began to argue that Europe only made sense if regional powers were built into a federated European space. The most articulate opponent of European "unity" and proponent of European regionalism was Leopold Kohr (1978). In *The Breakdown of Nations*, a book originating from a famous article published in 1941, "Disunion Now,"[29] Kohr argued that greater physical size would lead to greater power and aggression and developed a "size theory of social misery" (34). He argued that to prevent war and ensure democratic politics and economic prosperity European nations needed to be divided into regions, not unified. He called for "small-cell" political unions based on the "mattress principle"—a great multitude of small independent springs, not interlocking springs (77). Kohr's arguments were for the most part ignored, by both the European political elite "designing" Europe as well as the popular movement for European unity.[30] Such an argument remained lost within the broader arguments for integration, as the popular idea of unification superseded the idea of federation. As even Kant argued in "Perpetual Peace," international federation would have to be based on elementary, separate republics. But this remained at best only a sub-text in both the elite and popular discourses on European unity. Ironically, this sub-text was the one speaking for elementary, plural spaces where citizens—as Europeans—could participate in the collective making of "the continent."

Paralleling the popular calls for European unity, a political elite began to take seriously the possibility of unification, and most histories of the integration movement focus on the role of national and "European" leaders in the creation of those institutions leading to what we now call the European Union. A space of appearance was carved out of elite politics in Europe (and the United States), one that pressed for integration in the face of attempts by national leaders to aggrandize power for the purposes of state-building. Some scholars, most notably Alan Milward and Stanley Hoffman, have argued persuasively that political leaders pressing for European union did so to enhance either their own power domestically or the power of the nation-state itself (Milward 1992, 318-344; Hoffman 1964; Costa Bona 1988). Clearly these individuals had no designs for "integral federalism" or militant political action; they were more inclined to envision Europe in manners similar to those of Briand or Herriot, as an organized political space to defend European states against (communist) aggression and to promote steady, efficient, capitalist economic growth.[31]

Despite their motivations, however, an unofficial coterie of political leaders and "opinion makers" sought to shape what they imagined to be a revolutionary space, a space circumscribed by ideals of fraternity, good will, and civility. This space would be one inhabited, not by every citizen, but by men of particular dignity, initiative, and creativity. It would be a space of appearance, then, within the larger community of political leaders. These "creative" leaders viewed themselves in regard to European unity, not as representatives of their constituents or "peoples," but as creators of the space of European appearance itself. They therefore envisioned themselves as men of action, not unlike the "founding fathers" of the United States. It was as if they had read Arendt's warnings in *On Revolution*; they modeled themselves after the American politicians who had succeeded (at least for a time) in founding a new country with stable institutions and never after the French who had failed.[32] The elite space of appearance was crafted on the basis of certain understandings political leaders had of themselves *as Europeans*. These were based on certain readings of the political context of the day—those problems of *realpolitik* and economic development that they felt certain European integration could solve, or at least ameliorate.

Regardless of national background, the "European" political elite shared characteristics, ideas, and fora for those ideas that created a realm where they could converse, and, to paraphrase Arendt, "appear to others as others appeared to them." Members of the European elite immediately after the war included Konrad Adenauer, Jean Monnet, Robert Schumann, Alcide De Gasperi, Paul-Henri Spaak, Luigi Einaudi, Paul Reynaud, Robert Marjolin, Walter Hallstein, Lord Gladwyn, Harold Macmillan, and Winston Churchill. All of these individuals were concerned with the post-war problems of Europe, as a whole, and all at one point or another, and in one form or another, advocated "European" solutions to these problems. Such an international public space included those Americans concerned with Europe-wide problems, such as George Kennan and Charles Kindleberger, as well as academics and journalists from many countries, including Richard Mayne, Howard K. Smith, Hajo Holborn, and Denis de Rougemont. While all of these individuals promoted particular policies, and often for the purposes of their own nation state (Milward 1992, Costa Bona 1988), they all helped create a public space where politicians,

European bureaucrats, and opinion leaders could, in the words of the former head of publications for the Council of Europe, "speak European" (Carter 1966).

The political leaders in this elite space of appearance shared certain principles. First, most if not all of them, tended to view post-war Europe as a civilization, and one in decline. More precisely, according to Hajo Holborn, Europe was the "center of Western civilization, the most vigorous of all historic civilizations" (Holborn 1951, 189), and one that was facing a crisis of historic, world-changing proportions.[33] This sentiment was shared by other members of the European elite (see, for instance, Chamberlin 1947, 2, 19; Smith 1950, 3, 14; Reynaud 1951; Brinkley and Hackett 1991, 53; Gladwyn 1966, viii, ix; de Rougemont 1965, 17, 20; Macmillan 1969, 151; Adenauer 1966, 248; Monnet 1978, 269, 270, 356, 357; and Spaak 1971, 252). But within this "historic" civilization, there were extraordinary individuals who could "save" Europe and maintain its traditions.[34] These were, of course, the political leaders who could "speak European" and lead the continent out of its post-war darkness. To do this required, above everything else, a "good will," in the tradition of Augustine and Catholic social thought more generally. Adenauer (1966) insisted that "all men of good will" must unify Europe (407, see also 363) and described himself as "a man of good will, a German who wanted understanding of France" and that because of this good will "Frenchmen should receive me with due respect" (340). Denis de Rougemont (1965) explained that "Europe's will to live means her *will to unite*" (63) and discussed those great individuals who have promoted European unity throughout history. Lord Gladwyn (1966) emphasized that only the "ruling few" could inaugurate Europe, not the masses (135), and urged British politicians to develop "the will" for Europe (vii). Paul-Henri Spaak (1971) described Walter Hallstein as "an ardent believer in a united Europe and whose goodwill was beyond question" (164) and praised the European elite for its "power of goodwill, born of our instinct of self-preservation" (435). Finally, Jean Monnet (1978) mentioned the need for political leaders to possess the "good will" necessary to make European unity a reality (373, 432).[35]

Beyond will, or even good will, this European elite would possess a certain civility, permitting pluralism and open discussion. These leaders would construct (or reconstruct) "a civilization of discussion and debate, where overmastering passion seems to be constantly to re-examine the natural universe and human relationships, Destiny and the meaning of life" (de Rougemont 1965, 48). A civility based on a kind of civic friendship (Monnet 1978, 76) would allow the European elite to speak with "a vocabulary of necessity" and a "sober syntax" (Fontaine, in Brinkley and Hackett 1991, 52). An extension of that nineteenth- and early twentieth-century argument that the European mind was something distinct and world-historical, some public intellectuals praised European civilization as "an open civilization" and its leaders as creating such a civilization (David Mitrany, in Grotius Seminar 1963, 44). The conclusion was often drawn that Europeans should "permeate the world with [their] political, social, and cultural outlook and experience," but always mindful that this was to be an elite, not just any European (Mitrany, 44; see also de Rougemont 1965). In the words of a 1963 secondary school history text, dedicated to teaching the "young citizens of Europe" the achievements of the founders of the European community, the European "defines mental adulthood and intellectual courage in terms of the ability to withhold judgment as against the abdication of responsibility and intellectual integrity for the sake of simplicity" (Wales 1963, 48).

All of this is not to re-hash or belabor the point that the European elite was ethnocentric, imperialist, or blind to the "minds" of those outside the continent. It is to suggest that such an elite thought itself creating a culture of discussion, intellectual inquiry, and rational analysis, and that such a space of conversation, along with the good will that brought leaders to that space, would define the space of civility. This would be a space where each leader could hold others together, and at a distance. Their common conversation and concern for Europe would bring them to this conversational community, but their respect for diversity and the integrity of each others' thinking would separate them. Such a distance was necessary to the exercise of a sort of Cartesian method of political analysis and was essential to recognize the other leaders as common citizens of the European community. It is because he has tried to understand Frenchmen, that Adenauer, for instance, can argue that he is due respect from them. It is also because they understand the plural nature of this community that Harold Macmillan (1969) can describe De Gasperi, Adenauer, and Schuman as men "truly imbued with the European spirit" (186).

What we see emerging, then, is an elite space of appearance with its particular norms (e.g., good will, civility) and its own boundaries. To be sure, it was a restricted space, but it was a policy/high politics space that, to its own collective mind, engaged in a kind of "revolutionary" thinking. Europe was something to be made through the struggles of great men, the founding fathers, and these were to be struggles against not (or not simply) the masses (whom they perceived as unconcerned with making Europe), but against a domestic national or provincial elite hostile to supranational politicians appropriating their powers. Most importantly, despite numerous proclamations that it was to be an exercise in economic cooperation, many, if not most, members of this elite clearly perceived the creation of a new politics. In the words of Walter Hallstein (1962), "the logic of economic integration not only leads on toward plurality by way of the fusion of interests; it also involves political action in itself" (65).[36] Some understood this new politics functionally (e.g., Monnet, Spaak), others federally (e.g., de Rougemont, Gladwyn), and still other confederally (e.g., Marjolin, Churchill, De Gaulle), but all envisioned a new European theater of politics, where traditional, national forms of public action would be transcended. The post-war world presented to this elite not only new actors and crew for this theater, but a transformed stage itself, a space where Europeans, and not only the French, Italians, and Germans, could appear. To the "masses" it might have been uninteresting theater; to the popular European movements it might have been a theater to which only a very few were invited. But it was politics as performance, public display, agonal struggle, and it was also politics whose purpose was the communication of ideas and opinions (see the appendix). Besides, members of the popular movements often found themselves backstage, occasionally performing with the main actors. These backstage performances took place during repeated committee meetings to unite Europe politically and culturally.

The most illustrative of these spaces was Jean Monnet's Action Committee for the United States of Europe.[37] In 1955 Monnet intended to leave the European Coal and Steel Community (ECSC) because he believed that he could press for European unification much more effectively as a citizen. He initially envisioned a Front for the United States of Europe, which, despite its revolutionary moniker, would be open to both specialized European movements and business organizations. He changed his mind, and on October 13 of that year he founded the Action Committee, whose membership he opened only to political and trade union leaders (though it was funded with help from the Agnelli family, German industry, the Ford Foundation, Shell, Unilever, British Aircraft, and British Steel). The Action Committee was not a mass organization, then, but rather an elite action group that would pressure the domestic leadership of the European states to form a federated union. The delegates to the Action Committee felt a sense of mission to the work, and all felt a strong attachment to each other and to Monnet especially. Through the Action Committee a bond of civic friendship was built between the members. The Action Committee was disbanded in 1975, but has since been revived in 1985 as "The Action Committee for Europe," though about one-tenth of its members are industrialists or bankers, and it focuses on economic and monetary issues more than political ones. Nonetheless, the Action Committee was the best example of an elite public space, engaged in political struggle (with domestic governments), and one carved out of a larger political elite. Despite its restricted membership, it functioned as a site of dissent and change within the larger theater of elite European politics.[38]

If, as I have been arguing here, the post-war European theater was (re)born of two mothers—popular movements and a political elite, and if we can document this in birth certificates such as the Ventotene Manifesto[39] or public pronouncements by political leaders as diverse as Churchill, Monnet, Adenauer, De Gasperi, Spaak, and others, then the birthmark of such a space was European citizenship. Members of both the elite and popular movements argued that a European politics demanded civic rights, duties, and responsibilities. Altiero Spinelli was clear that federalism for Europe signified "giving birth to a European citizenship."[40] At the European Cultural Conference at Lausanne in 1949, the poet W. H. Auden declared that the European civic movement was part of the "unfinished World Revolution," that the symbol for this Revolution was "a naked anonymous new-born baby," and that the very civilization of Europe was at stake.[41]

Citizenship rights were considered to be indispensable to the creation of Europe, in this early period, though there was great debate both between and within the popular and elite movements as to the nature and extent of these rights. While most civil and political rights seemed to be taken for granted, the popular movements pressed for social rights as well.[42] Moreover, there was debate over the concept and extent of human rights for European citizens.[43] Not all agreed with the federalists who proclaimed that "The Federal Union will have to be founded on a declaration of civil, political, and economic rights that guarantee the free development of the human personality[.]"[44] But citizenship rights, however defined, were considered essential to the freedom of action for Europeans, because such rights could "translate" into new political rights for citizens as members of nation-states.[45] Put in other terms, Europe could protect against the condition of statelessness that Arendt observed throughout Europe in *The Origins of Totalitarianism* (Arendt 1973, 267-302).

Beyond the protection of citizenship rights, European unity would also create a new civilization that would be good for its own sake and would further protect those aforementioned rights.[46] I have already noted a number of individuals who saw in modern Europe a decline of its civilization and who argued that European unity was its (often only) salvation ("it will be impossible to save our civilization if the United States of Europe does not happen").[47] Indeed, even an early report by technocrats on "The Economic Integration of Western Europe" noted that "the crucial and compelling reason for Western European Union" was that it provided "the main hope for a regeneration of Western European civilization and for a new period of stability and growth."[48] The responsibility of "men of action" in Western Europe, then, was to create both the political and cultural space necessary to enhance the freedoms of citizens. But what action was to be taken? There were many different schemes— some calling for economic integration, others for mere confederation, still others for complete unity. The schemes for "uniting" Europe were almost as numerous as the people advocating such a goal. But the space of politics, Arendt reminds us in *The Human Condition*, is one of plurality, and plurality depends ultimately on not only on action, but on speech. None of these advocates for European unity were at a loss for words, and I want to examine the one site of action they shared, the one place where they all made an appearance. The one public space common to all Europeans of good will, the one place they could speak out on the political and cultural crisis of Europe, was in a small theater known as the "conference."

Europe by Committee: Creating and Destroying a European Space of Appearance

Conferences, or as the French or Italians might call them, "Congresses," were by no means invented by these "good Europeans," but they were employed by both popular and elite movements as the political arena in which ideas about Europe would be presented. Indeed, Geoffrey Barraclough (1963) has noticed that the congress has been a metaphor for European unity. In the seventeenth century, for instance, "Europe was likened to a great congress; indeed it was thought that in the great peace congresses—at Nymvegen, at Utrecht, at Aix-la-Chapelle—Europe itself was acting, settling its own affairs" (29-30). In this section, I will argue that many politicians, technocrats, and academics active in the European movements (both elite and popular) shared this sentiment, and attempted to create "Europe" as a political and cultural space, from these conferences. But I will also maintain that the conference or congress as a political form excludes many from acting and constrains political action in general. In promoting or expanding freedom, the conference shaped and/or restricted the methods by which these "citizens" acted. The "congress" did foreshadow a future Europe—but it would be a routinized, bureaucratic Europe, not one that encouraged public action. Consequently, the attempt to found freedom and augment political authority, at least in this instance, was bound to fail.

In the final section of this chapter, I suggest that the conference is a form of collective action that includes both the public and the private, the political and the social. Many "revolutions" fail to sustain their participatory character because the conferences around which they organized themselves necessarily exclude many citizens from attending as they permit a few others to appear. In making these arguments, I introduce an additional reason for the failure of councils, beyond those offered by Arendt in *On Revolution*,[49] and one that challenges her understanding of public space. Furthermore, I render judgment, as a spectator interested in the performance of Arendt's ideas, on the success of the concept of the space of appearance. In so doing, I recognize its weaknesses for my own contribution to the research stage.

The effectiveness of the conference form was not lost on Jean Monnet (1978), as he reflected upon the Schuman Plan conference of 1950:

> It was still less than two months since the opening of the conference, and already the essentials of the [future ECSC], had been worked out. But what struck me most forcibly was the rapid change in the attitude of my colleagues. Day after day I could see the cohesive effect of the Community idea, which was working on men's minds long before it assumed practical form. Although all the delegates retained their well-marked national characteristics, they were now working together on the same quest. So much had their viewpoints converged during the past few weeks that they now and then asked one of their number to speak on behalf of the whole group. . . . [There] friendship grew up among the heads of delegation, who soon formed a united group. . . . Material surroundings have an effect on people's attitudes (334).

Monnet believed himself fortunate to have a private dining-room amenable to conferencing, with a table sufficient to producing harmony.[50] Indeed, he shares the table metaphor with Hannah Arendt, who also characterizes it as an object that facilitates civic relationships.[51] Toward the end of his *Memoirs*, however, Monnet has developed these observations into a theory of European conferencing:

To persuade people to talk together is the most one can do to serve the cause of peace. But for this a number of conditions must be fulfilled. One is that the talks be conducted in a spirit of equality, and that no one should come to the table with the desire to score off somebody else. That means abandoning the supposed privileges of sovereignty and the sharp weapon of the veto. The second condition is that everyone should talk about the same thing; and third, finally, is that everyone should seek the interest which is common to them all (474; see also 230, 236).

From this can come friendship, "the result of joint action rather than the reason for it" (76). This "theory" echoes points Arendt makes in her theory of action, though she would not necessarily agree that talk always serves the cause of peace. For Monnet, the "method" of conferencing is best expressed through the literary form of the memorandum (83). The ideal form of conferencing, the one upon which a future Europe would indeed model itself, was the Action Committee. "This was the new form of authority I wanted to establish in Europe: the collective authority of the whole Action Committee" (408). The Action Committee, then, was not merely an organization pressuring governments, it was the embodiment of future Europe itself, the ideal which Europe might found and augment itself. The European Community itself, Monnet concluded, was "only a stage on the way to the organized world of tomorrow" (524).

Whether or not other Europeanists shared Monnet's theory of conferencing is moot, for the practice of conferencing in the creation of a politico-cultural space of action opened up possibilities for talking about European citizenship and closed down possibilities that many citizens could actually appear in public to act and re-present themselves. In what follows I emphasize those post-war conferences designed to unite Europe in an explicitly political or cultural manner,[52] particularly those that focused on the question of European citizenship, and eschew those conferences concerned with "the social," that is technical questions of economic integration. Nor do I have the space here to detail every conference relevant to European political unity because there were so many (presented by so many different groups or organizations), so I highlight some of the most far-reaching in terms of scope and participation. These conferences brought together representatives from both elite and public movements for European unity. In the terms of Mary Dietz, these conferences both laid the groundwork for, and represented, the "methodical politics" that she argues ought to follow revolutionary, agonal struggle.

By 1943 "pan-European" conferences concerning European citizenship had become quite regular. In the spring of that year the fifth annual conference had been held at New York University, attended by exiles and presided over by Coudenhove-Kalergi. In 1944, a draft constitution for a United Europe had emerged from this conference (Zurcher 1958), while in Europe the Comité Français pour la Fédération Européenne discussed "the creation of European citizenship in addition to national citizenship."[53] It was becoming clear that political movements for European unity were focusing their efforts on this concept. One year later, this committee included in its charter the goal to push for a European government that would act directly upon the citizens of Europe.[54] September 1946 saw a conference at Hertenstein which brought together 119 leaders of the most organized federalist groups in Europe. Article six of its report requested a charter for the rights of European citizens.[55] One month later, many of these same representatives met at Luxembourg to delineate further the structures of a Federal Europe. Further conferences were held in December at Basle and Paris, and discussions turned to items as specific as a European passport, the symbol of European citizenship.

In 1947, a number of conferences were held to discuss the prospect of European union and citizenship: a Socialist conference at Montagne in June, the Union of European Federalists (UEF) conference at Montreux in August (its central committee had already met at Amsterdam the previous April), and the MFE conference in Rome in the fall. All these conferences concerned themselves with both the rights of European citizenship, as well as a cultural analysis and defense of European civic virtue. The Montreux conference labored over the practice and structural principles of federalism and developed organizational rules and principles governing these in a future European community. The French introduced ideologically radical proposals designed to shape Europe in a decentralized and "corporatist" manner. But Spinelli, who was beginning to depart from his militant ideals at Ventotene, and Henri Brugmans, politician and future author of *L'Idée Européenne*, objected to that as impractical. In 1948, at conferences at Aja in May, Interlaken in September, and Rome in November, members of the Federalist movement debated these rival positions and decided finally to support Spinelli and Brugmans. "Integral federalism" was becoming history, in favor of a moderate and constitutional approach. The popular movement was organizing itself to work with an elite movement emerging at that time.[56]

The elite began to organize itself at The Hague in May 1948. Here at the Congress of Europe, 750 representatives began deliberating about, among other things, the establishment of a cultural commission that would define Europe culturally and the virtues of the European citizen. In the plenary session, the chair, Salvador de Madariaga, encouraged the delegates to create European virtue in the hearts of citizens in order to establish European political institutions.[57] Many of the delegates spoke repeatedly of strategies to diffuse European values and civilization, and programs of civic education were considered. The best way to do this, it was agreed, was to create a European Cultural Center. The "central task" of the European Cultural Center would be to "raise the voice of Europe," which meant promoting an "awareness of European unity" and providing "a meeting-place for leaders of thought enabling them to express a genuinely European point of view." Such a "meeting-place" would involve strict government, for it would "exercise vigilant care over the word actually used in discussion and without which no pact can be concluded" while encouraging the "free circulation of ideas." The Center would ultimately plan the federation of European universities, as well as the coordination of adjunct organizations for the "mothers and teachers" and "youth." It will, the conferees noted, be important to solve "at the European level the actual problems of child-nourishment, character-forming, reforming young delinquents and the rehabilitation and adoption of war victims."[58]

This was all to be part of a broader "popular campaign plan."[59] One critical purpose of the popular campaign was to propagandize for European unity and to create in "the masses . . . an atmosphere of 'goodwill'." Beyond goodwill, the popular movement would teach the European public the "style of European thought," and "to concretize the European conscience." This meant a specialized European education and the creation of schools for European militants. "The cadres of specifically European public opinion are constituted in this way." European militants were to be organized, and documents from the Hague conference set out precisely how this was to be done: militants were to be documented, young people recruited, collectives created, a literature developed (including brochures, bulletins, and memos), a specialized secretariat established, and a manifesto propounded. In other words, popular, revolutionary European movements were to become disciplined, categorized, and placed within systematic, bureaucratic cadres. The "administrative base" was "to embody the will of the European union according to the principles defined at The Hague." The European "will" then, turned out not to be something in the hearts of Europeans, but the result of organized civic training created in committee and distilled by cadres of militant Eurocrats. The subcommittee noted the necessity to decentralize the propaganda, and this suggests the possibility for citizens to appear with others in the name of Europe. But The Hague delegates wanted Europe as well organized as their committee.

However, the conference was organized in ways not always apparent to the organizers themselves, as Harold Macmillan (1969) recalled. The conference,

> proved somewhat unwieldy. Three committees were formed—political, economic, and cultural—presided over by suitable figures of distinction, each aided by its managing bureau and attended regularly by a solid core of devotees. Others of us wandered about, like students at a university, from one classroom to another, attracted by some notable speaker or by some specially keen debate. To most of us, again like undergraduates recently released from school, the chief attraction was the opportunity for making new and renewing old friendships (161).

Macmillan's remarks suggest that the conference itself was a means to create European citizenship, where national citizens came to be schooled in the art of Aristotelian civic virtue. The conference itself was a method by which people learned not simply goodwill, but friendship associational friendship that would form the basis of civic respect. Here we have the various characteristics of Europe beginning to come together—the managing bureaus structuring the committees and subcommittees, the educational process that trains the European, the social bonds that become institutionalized through fellowship in committee.[60]

The European citizen was clearly something to be organized. In a follow up report to The Hague meeting, the Joint International Committee of the Movements for European Unity suggested what was to be done. "Our real common good lies in an idea of man and of liberty" and these conceptions are "the result of a permanent dialogue . . . carried on between several doctrines or several creeds."[61] This dialogue offers both promise and hazards to "European man" who must recognize the diversity of his civilization. The cultural committee clearly recognized the plurality inherent in European society, and praised it as a defense against totalitarianism. Plural European public opinion had to be given "a regular means of expression" (14) and this meant the creation of a European Cultural Center, conceived initially as a standing cultural committee.

The purposes of the European Cultural Center were clear: (1) to inform public opinion by means of press and radio of the purposes and aims of union, (2) to prepare collections of documents "on the agents of national culture and the cultural agreements now in force among various nations," (3) to study measures to reestablish the autonomy of universities, (4) to facilitate and intensify the exchange and circulation of ideas, books, publications, and persons, (5) to "coordinate research on the conditions of European man in the twentieth century, pedagogy, hygiene, relationship of the individual and the technical world, professional guidance within the framework of Europe as a whole, etc.," (6) to "provide a meeting place for the upholders and creators of Western culture," (7) to "exercise through the intermediary of this cultural council a kind of right of supervision and of correction in the use of key words in official documents by the other federal bodies" (15-17). The Cultural Center would "render [Europe] more conscious of itself" (18), and would serve as a "permanent Forum, an agent of intellectual and moral vigilance, an instrument of coordination and the seat of initiative" in order to "play a decisive role in the formation of a European conscience without which the union, which is recognized as necessary, would lack a firm basis and sound direction" (17).[62]

The report reflects one effect of the plurality of delegates attending the conference, namely that many different messages, not all of them compatible, came out of the conference. For instance, one sees again great hope for an institutionalized space of appearance where Europeans might celebrate their plurality. The Center would also function didactically by raising the level of "consciousness" in Europeans through cultural exchange and educational programs. On the other hand, the report also states that there is a "real danger" in the verbal confusion surrounding political words (11), and wishes to resolve this potential confusion by defining democracy, liberty, and equality once and for all (13, 14).[63] In a plural Europe, this failure to recognize these words as contestable suggests that such collective self-consciousness and conscientiousness will be something besides learning democratic deliberation. The Cultural Center is also designed to coordinate not only research on such things as the "hygiene" and "professional guidance" of Europeans, but also the cultural practices of Europeans themselves (e.g., in coordinating meetings of the "upholders and creators of Western culture"). Finally, and most ominously, the Cultural Center will "supervise" and "correct" European government discourse on key words. Free speech, and diverse viewpoints, would be permitted, except not in a future federal government of Europe. Such language on the part of conferees raises questions about the "moral vigilance" of the Center, and they might have demonstrated their commitment to democratic participation without the Orwellian language.

"Moral vigilance" was evident in the opening remarks by Madariaga at the European Cultural Conference at Lausanne in December 1949: "We have not only [a] right but [a] duty to aid in the creation of Europe by defining her culture, that is, by calling forth her awareness."[64] Speaker after speaker arose to declare, in the words of delegate Richard Livingstone, that "we must learn to think and feel as Europeans" (9 December 1949). The conference must, in the words of another, "devise ways and means of creating a European public opinion [.]"[65] Here intellectuals, politicians, and political activists met to continue mapping out precisely how this was to be done, and they were informed by treatises such as the aforementioned "Europe and the Revolutions," presented by W.H. Auden. To be sure, there was one voice of dissent, Stephen Spender, who, in a speech on December 11, criticized the sense of self-importance the delegates gave themselves and implored the delegates not to talk irresponsibly about what makes a "European." He warned them not to turn the Cultural Center into another institution of propaganda. Nevertheless, delegates pressed forward in their quest to organize European culture. Specifically, this conference enumerated and explained educational programs designed to socialize youth toward Europe. After all, they reasoned, language learning must begin when one is young.

The "Report on Education to the Lausanne Conference" carried many suggestions on how to effectuate a "thoroughgoing reorganization of the education, special and general, which is the dominant factor in the upbringing of the youth of all European countries."[66] The delegates to the Educational Committee recommended particular curricular changes, especially in the area of teacher training. But the delegates also mentioned programs to develop pedagogical materials, scholarly exchanges, graduate research bursaries, European training institutes, and other reforms at the elementary, secondary, and higher education levels. All areas of education were to be imbued with a European spirit, and a systematic, universal, organized program of European instruction would "make Europe the object of research" in order to deepen and stimulate "the European conscience."[67] "The important thing remains that the new citizen learn to recognize the [central elements] of his history and the reasons for which they are citizens of Europe." More than anything, this meant that European education should "aim at the selection of elites in all social classes for the dissemination and promotion of the European idea."[68] These elites were to be trained not only in the content of the European idea, but in its very form. Consequently, secondary school students should be "guarantee[d] a proper training in independent judgment, while safeguarding their autonomy as human beings" and should be taught history "inspired by a European spirit." Furthermore, "a considerable part of the time-table should be devoted to civic instruction on European lines." Elementary school students would receive instruction from graduates of "Elementary Training Colleges," who would use "special radiophonic broadcasts . . . organized in a European spirit."[69]

Even adult citizens would be educated with a view to "informing as many different sections of the public as possible of the problems and values of European civilization." But, given the special conditions of adult learning, study centers for workers should be established "for the discussion of social and psychological problems on a plane transcending national preoccupations." The report also recommended "inter-European occupational competitions . . . for the purpose of encouraging healthy competition and stimulating pride in good work," "international training periods . . . to enable urban and rural workers to obtain a knowledge of the most up-to-date methods of work and exchange their special knowledge," "people's holiday camps," "workshops . . . to reinforce the development of a European spirit," and "popular libraries . . . specially suited to increase international information and to develop technical knowledge and the realization of the essential values of labor and humanity."

The European citizen was to be a product of a specific, and formal, European education. The education committee's emphasis on the values of labor suggested the influence of socialism and the worker's movement, and in Arendt's terms, combined the values of the *animal laborans*, the *homo faber*, and the man of action within the single person of the citizen. Citizenship, and by extension political action, was to be the product of a disciplined, organized system of education, and was to mix both public and private concerns. In the steps toward the "methodical politics" of a European union, action would need to be supplemented by other forms of human activity. But this meant arresting the unpredictability of action and the spontaneity of plural men and training citizens systematically.[70] Citizenship, to the members of these committees, demanded first not political action, but a rigorous training in the development of a European consciousness. The first training institutes, as Macmillan had commented, were to be the committees themselves, where men of "European spirit" could meet, learn from each other, and establish European civic virtue— goodwill, civility, and friendship.[71] The *Rapport General* of the Lausanne conference described Europe as diverse and so was itself "of necessity a school of tolerance" (20). But as those same delegates insisted in that same report, "an Institute should not be termed 'European' unless its Board of Directors includes at least two persons of a nationality other than the country in which the Institute has its headquarters" (17). The Europe that must "stand for dialogue," the Europe that "must . . . become the one place is the world where a human being can make his voice heard" (20), was also to govern that dialogue and those voices, and would "of necessity" be defined through its own rules of procedure.

By 1951 the European Cultural Center was becoming active, as we see in reports from Denis de Rougemont and others.[72] It had established various study groups and commissions on a variety of cultural projects, including film, religion, popular culture, and books. It had also established exchanges of both people and resource materials. The Center planned to create radio programs and pedagogical methods to instruct the youth of Europe. De Rougemont wished to schedule a series of 25 talks on European Unity, sponsored by the Center, and such talks would form the basis for a European-centered university curriculum. This was to be part of a larger project of European seminars conducted by historians discussing all aspects of European history relevant to the creation of the European citizen. Finally, de Rougemont noted that the Center could work with the Association of European Study Institutes and mapped out the rules and regulations that would characterize these institutes as specifically European. The membership of the Center was restricted to public corporations, international organizations, national cultural institutions, and "personalities representing the European organisms." In other words, the Cultural Center itself was not to be the domain of the European citizen, but of larger institutions mediating, if not representing, the European citizen. In the end, the Cultural Center project failed to go beyond these initiatives, but it represented a coordinated, bureaucratic effort on the part of "good Europeans" to establish an institutional basis for civic virtue.

In the meantime, the Union of European Federalists began to organize a campaign to promote popular participation in European institutions. In May 1950, seeing the burgeoning success of the elite creating the Schuman Plans, the UEF formed the "European Vigilance Council" to press for popular representation and power in future European assemblies. At the Council of the Peoples of Europe conference at Strasbourg, on November 20, 1950, the Congress of the UEF adopted a resolution calling for the direct election of citizens to representative institutions of a federal Europe. There the European Vigilance Council mobilized 5000 young people to stage demonstrations in favor of this proposal. They seemed to activate public opinion in Italy, but in the other countries "the federalist movements . . . were not organizationally mature in order to face such a task" (Vercelli 1991, 71). Though the federalist movement remained the site where problems of unification were "thought through and elaborated in precise terms" (74), in most countries of Europe it could not mobilize support for direct participation by European citizens, and, as a result, Europe's "institutions" came to be designed by the elite. Eventually the result would be the European Coal and Steel Community, and later the European Community, after the Treaty of Rome in 1957.

Yet even the so-called popular movements for a federal Europe were beginning to move away from their prior "militancy." At the Paris "Ad Hoc Assembly," September 1952, of the UEF, members attempted to design political institutions—for instance, delineating a future European Political Community (EPC), a bicameral legislature, and a European civil service. Apparently, most of the motions at the Assembly were ghost written by Spinelli himself (Willis 1971, 46). A few changes had been taken in the approach by these popular movements. First, the delegates committed themselves, not only to representative institutions over participatory ones, but to a Senate. Second, the delegates proposed a European civil administration, and one that would prohibit, "in particular, active or militant political behavior."[73] Thus, not only had the federalist movement accepted a sort of "functional" administration of Europe, they disavowed servants of this administration to engage in the sort of political activity that they themselves had previously assumed to be fundamental to a European spirit. Certainly, many members of the movement were still committed to militant action, but over time this waned, and the possible space for citizens to appear began to close.[74]

After the early 1950s efforts to create and sustain a space where citizens could directly make and re-make "Europe" grew weaker, and generally focused on the creation of a European parliament or assembly. Almost all the European institutions after this time were modeled after the ECSC, that is, as functional bureaucracies designed to administer policies set by some board or committee. This became the focus of conferences at Messina (June 1955), Venice (May 1956), Brussels (June 1956), Paris (February 1957), and, finally, Rome (February 1957). The role of the "people" had been confined to occasional demands for a directly elected parliament (Scalingi 1980, Lindsay 1960). Nevertheless, these demands revealed the treasures that had been lost, and the fight for a directly elected European Parliament represented the conscience of the lost European "revolution."[75] The revolution revived itself in the early 1980s when the Crocodile Club proposed institutional reforms to the parliament in order to secure more direct representation for citizens, and more power for the European Parliament in general. But this also reflects the Arendtian limits of the revolution, because the parliament remained a representative body beholden to party interests, rather than an institution of direct popular participation. Such possible institutions such as councils of militants or popular assemblies had long been abandoned as practical political fora. They were, apparently, insufficiently European.

Was the European Theater of Politics Ever Possible?

By the early 1950s Robert Marjolin could not have been the only "good European" perceiving himself as a function. The possibility of human action had been superseded by the requirements of functional behavior, and the spontaneous freedom that was so promising (and promised by both the elite and popular movements) had failed to institutionalize itself. By the mid-1950s the revolutionary moment had passed, and with it the possibility of sustaining popular participation within the European community. The most democrats would fight for was a directly elected European parliament. Methodical politics had subsumed revolutionary politics, but as I have demonstrated, it did so without retaining characteristics of that revolutionary origin. Was this a failure of will on the part of politicians, academics, and opinion leaders? Did they make the same mistakes as the political actors in the French and American Revolutions? Did functional thinking overpower the thinking of those in favor of a political Europe? I do not see evidence for any of these claims, and I have tried to show how significant the depth of feeling was on the part of the European revolutionaries toward their supranational project.

On the contrary, I would like to suggest that the problem may lie within the logic of Arendt's argument itself. The founding of "Europe" reflects the difficulty, if not the sheer impossibility, of founding and augmenting freedom within institutions (and thus spaces of appearance). Alan Keenan (1994) makes this argument in regards to Arendt's analysis of the French and American Revolutions. He theorizes that "the political realm and the freedom it houses can only be found by accepting their inevitable 'loss'" (299). Keenan notes that freedom, as the capacity to begin, initiate, and create, is structured by Arendt as an abyss, a hole formed when one new event breaks into a continuum. This abyss is unpredictable, unimaginable, and unknowable. Yet to sustain this abyss, so to speak, political actors must create foundations that themselves are not abysses, but rather institutionalize the promise of the freedom and creativity offered during those moments of revolution. Yet, Keenan rightfully asks, "how can a political entity be brought into being in a way that *founds* a new identity and history ("re-starting time") without denying the arbitrary and contingent nature of that beginning?" (300). He maintains that this paradox is unresolved, and *not resolvable*, in Arendt's theory of revolution. Freedom exists because of the "singularity of the willing agent and the *present moment* of the willing act," and one that can sustain itself only by recognizing "the necessity of the future to the present, a recognition performed in the act of *promising*" (302, 303). It is promising, then, often in the form of a contract, that maintains the revolutionary power of freedom within institutions, "by respecting both the plurality of those who inhabit the political realm and the uncertainty introduced into political life by the future" (304). Promising holds political actors together "into the indefinite future" and "transforms freedom from the simple possibility of new beginnings into 'worldly' *political* freedom" (305). This is maintained by power, according to Arendt, but power itself is a potentiality, something that "springs up between men when they act together and vanishes the moment they disperse" (Arendt 1958b, 179). Consequently power itself is transitory, momentary, and cannot be institutionalized.

Keenan recognizes the obvious consequences of this.

> It would seem, then, that there is no plausible explanation for how the public realm, by its nature radically potential, could ever be maintained beyond the sporadic moments of its actualization because its reliance on power is in fact only a reliance on another form of potentiality. It would seem doomed to a mere chance existence (306).

Political promising is insufficient to maintain spaces of appearance. More to the point,

> to the extent that the freedom of the political realm is founded on a *specific* project, it cannot be entirely free: the "space" for action opened up by such a promise will necessarily form boundaries to and limits on the possibility of

new action . . . it is a free act that at once makes less than fully free all acts that follow its law and example (309).

Thus, for instance, the specificity of the European project precluded its potential to create and sustain free spaces of appearance. The promising inherent in documents such as the Ventotene Manifesto sowed the seeds of the project's own demise, so to speak, by positing particular political methods for uniting Europe. I have already elaborated the essentially dictatorial (or at least un-spontaneous and un-free) message in that document.

Keenan, with Arendt, separates authority from power but argues that even that concept formed the boundaries for free action by being located within texts—in the American case, the Mayflower Compact, Declaration of Independence, and Constitution. Rather, authority is another stage in the attempt to create and maintain freedom. Keenan concludes that the foundation of freedom includes four stages or moments: the space of appearance, power, promising, and authority. Ultimately the principles that sustained the foundation of America were those of "mutual promise and common deliberation" (Arendt 1965, 214).

Keenan does not appear to make the distinction between mutual promise and common deliberation and accepts both as the promising inscribed into the original texts of the founding. Thus he claims that the principle of promising possesses, "in the form of authority, a stability that promises alone have proven not to" (314). He also notes that Arendt does not account for the fact that "augmentation," the process of instantiating authority in the foundation of political space, is more conflictual and unstable than Arendt assumes.[76] As a result, Keenan maintains that the act of foundation will always bring a "constitutive threat of conflict and violence" (316). In short, "a promise, like any agreement, is at best a point of conjuncture, a site at which conflicting goals, intentions, forces, and projects find common expression or formulation but never an identity of meaning" (317). Thus promising-as-foundation "lodges within the promise a certain kind of violence" (318).

Keenan overstates his case here because he does not distinguish between the stages of promising and mutual deliberation. As Jeffrey Isaac, Mary Dietz, Margaret Canovan, and others have noted, the act of mutual deliberation is potentially an act that can found and re-found spaces of appearance. Deliberation is in fact that space that Arendt describes as one characterized by speech and distinctiveness (Arendt 1958b). Democratic deliberation, while most certainly conflictual, is not necessarily potentially violent. Certainly violence can erupt in particular situations, but deliberation is effective in building political communities because it is seen as an alternative to violence (Gundersen 1995). For instance, the European revolutionaries after World War II pursued their aims without recourse to violence. Though there were power struggles, and political conflicts, these "good Europeans" created and sustained, however temporarily, spaces of appearance that were remarkably free from force and violence. I would argue this was because they attempted to instantiate common deliberation into the process, as they moved away from a reliance on promising.

But this movement itself revealed the impossibility of augmenting that foundation of freedom, because the means they chose to deliberate mutually, while peaceful, were made routine. The choice of the conference, the congress, and the committee, as the method of sustaining the revolutionary impulse, was both necessary and self-defeating. How else could citizens have deliberated? What other "options" were open to these individuals, given that they had a specific project in mind? How can one organize a project such as this without conferences and committees? Yet the conference is a form of talk that demands, indeed sustains itself on, routine and bureaucracy. The conference (from the Latin "con" meaning "together, and intensive" and "fer-re" meaning "to bear or to bring") historically has been a kind of "bearing together," a form of action that implies tolerance and mutual support. In theory, it promotes the "bearing with strangers" Arendt suggests is indispensable for living (Hansen 1993). It also promotes the sort of Aristotelian friendship Arendt admired, one that generated respect among individuals, without animosity or violence. Such friendship constitutes "a regard for the person from a distance which the space of the world puts between us, and this regard is independent of qualities which we may admire or of achievements which we may highly esteem" (Arendt 1958b, 218). The conference institutionalizes civility.

Yet the conferences I have described in this chapter reproduced respect for people precisely because the participants admired their outcomes (e.g., goodwill, civility) or because some conferees themselves had achieved great things in their lives (e.g., Adenauer's demand for respect because he had helped the French). Moreover, I have tried to demonstrate that conferencing, rather than creating moments of mutual freedom, became a method of discourse. Conferences were planned, memos were written, seats were assigned, speeches were delivered, and most importantly, many of their participants took them to be microcosms of civilized communities.[77] The conference itself became not only *a* form, but *the* form of mutual deliberation, but it was a form designed to minimize conflict and disagreement, by placing "administrative" questions in the hands of the conference managers. Yet in attempting to minimize conflict, the conferees agreed to rules and practices that prohibited not only violence, but spontaneous, revolutionary speech and action. It was, then, *because* the practice of mutual deliberation was not "violent" that prevented it from founding freedom.

What emerged slowly from these politico-cultural conferences and committees, then, was the constitution, not of freedom, but of administration. The founding fathers of the European Community took their constitutional mission seriously as an exercise in the rational administration of things. The participants could not help but learn how to be functions, and not very interesting functions at that. To recall Edouard Herriot, they had indeed succeeded in achieving equilibrium while avoiding struggle, and they had instantiated methodical politics (to the French—the Cartesian method) within community institutions.

In turning to the teaching and service functions of universities, we must give pause to consider what my conclusions here imply for institutions of higher education. In the case of Europe at least, committee decision-making seemed to preclude a possible politics of a space of appearance. Thus, this chapter critiques the possibility of the very concept around which I have organized much of my book. But I consider that conclusion to support my general argument—after all, the stated purpose of this chapter was to offer a model of judgment for political research. In examining a particular historical example, I have been able to judge, from the perspective of a critic, the usefulness of Arendt's concept; to some extent I have thus been able to judge the theater of research in which I had worked. In so doing I recognize its limitations, and this I hope has helped me articulate both the concept and its limitations to a general reading public and to students of political science and history. Most importantly, I hope that it has helped persuade the reader of an argument of the book, namely that research ought to be placed within the broader context of learning.

In applying lessons learned from the early period of European unification to the practices of universities and colleges in the United States, we might consider seeking alternative forums of discussion and deliberation among faculty, students, and administration. In maintaining spaces of appearance in universities, we ought to try to avoid the problems experienced by even the European revolutionaries themselves and reconceptualize the pedagogical and service practices of institutions of higher education. In this sense, my research here is relevant, not for any discoveries it makes concerning the founding of the European community, but because it taught me, as a researcher, how to render judgment about certain problems with which I have been confronted in my post as a teacher and administrator. I have employed academic research as a means toward a pedagogical end—teaching and learning lessons relevant to politics of higher education and the structure of universities and colleges as teaching institutions. I have *politicized* my research in the Arendtian sense of that term.

Notes

1. Montesquieu claimed that power and freedom belonged together by rooting both in the I-can instead of the I-will. His equation goes something like this: power = I-can = I-am-free-to = I-have-power-to. Arendt claims that his influence on the Founding Fathers was significant in this respect and contributed to their profound understanding of the separation of powers.

2. She traces this original revolutionary experience on pages 141-214.

3. Arendt argued that representation was inherently inimical to political action. "[T]he whole question of representation . . . actually implies no less than a decision on the very dignity of the political realm itself" (236-237). Either representatives come to understand their tasks as administrative (where they merely do the people's bidding) or they become the rulers of the people by assuming powers otherwise reserved to the people themselves. In the first instance the public realm disappears, in the second the public realm constricts to such a point that the very purpose of the revolutions—to open up the political spaces to the masses—becomes impossible, and worse, irrelevant.

Moreover, in this system "the only thing which can be represented and delegated is interest, or the welfare of the constituents, but neither their actions nor their opinions" (268). When the actions of citizens cannot be expressed (by being represented) a public realm cannot be created. See 266-275; and Sitton 1994.

4.   For objections to Arendt's conception of council democracy, see Sitton 1994. His most telling critique, and one that applies to the "European revolutionaries" during the post-war period, is that during revolutionary times people stop working, and so only then can they afford the luxury of political engagement to such a degree.

5.   Numerous well-known critics of Arendt' position, including Jurgen Habermas, Sheldon Wolin, Richard Bernstein, and Hannah Pitkin, argue that in ignoring the political importance of the social or economic question, Arendt misunderstands the function of councils historically.

6.   Some theorists admire Arendt's theories not only for their importance for democratic theory, but also for the sake of the expression of the individual citizen. See Villa 1992a and 1992b, and Honig 1993 and 1995.

7.   Keenan's argument is similar to one made earlier by J. Glenn Gray (1979) who highlights the "abyss" that freedom creates in the public realm.

8.   Arendt herself recognized the importance of these matters in three ways: First, she admired the resistance movements, second she gave early support to federalism as the only solution for Europe's problems, and third, she commented constantly on Europe's need for renewal in her letters from there after the war. See her letters to Karl Jaspers (Kohler and Saner 1992, 66, 440); her second essay on Jaspers in *Men in Dark Times* (1968b, 81-94, especially page 93); and many of her essays written during this period, collected in *Essays in Understanding* (Arendt 1994, 101, 112, 114, 149, 150, 269, 416, 417, 426). Young-Bruehl (1982) suggests that Arendt admired the European Movement, but that she had given up hope for its success by the time the French parliament vetoed the European Defense Community (282-285). Young-Bruehl observes that Arendt admired Henri Frénay, a cabinet minister in DeGaulle's government, who, as a leader of the European movement in France, tried to create "a really authentic politics" (282). Arendt understood the importance of a federated European politics for civic and civil relations between individuals and for the very possibility of political action: "The establishment of one sovereign world state, far from being the prerequisite for world citizenship, would be the end of all citizenship. It would not be the climax of world politics, but quite literally its end" (Arendt 1968b, 82).

9.   See also Herriot 1930 and the essays collected in Rijskbaron et al. 1987, for this history. The idea of Europe is of course more complex, and its consequences more problematic, than many historians of the European idea have presented. Geoffrey Barraclough (1963) has made the argument that in fact European unity is, at most, a mythical ideal promoted by only scholars, academics, and a political elite. "If by Europe is meant no more than a nebulous idea of a common culture or civilization, then, rightly or wrongly, only a small minority of cultured people are likely to feel strongly about it. Ordinary people will not support the idea of a united Europe unless they are convinced that it has concrete advantages to offer" (57). J.M. Blaut (1993) has traced the idea of European unity to imperialism and colonialism, and has argued that the presence of a European "mind" or "civilization" is ideological (see especially 50-152).

10.   This was a common complaint by many "Europeanists" of the 1930s. Note Count Carlo Sforza's (1936) claim that there exists "a lowering of the intellectual and moral atmosphere of Europe." H. Stuart Hughes (1977) argues that World War I revealed the "fragility of civilized values" (402).

11. This spirit of resistance was to perpetuate after the end of the war. James D. Wilkinson (1981) notes that German intellectuals, among others, saw the European unity idea as a way to resist the superpower division of Europe after the war. Wilkinson also notes the many former resistance intellectuals who would take part in the pan-Europe congresses and committees designed to unify Europe in the 1940s and 1950s. For more on the role of the resistance in post-war European movements see Burgess 1989.

12. "Federalismo Integrale," *L'Unità Europea*, Number 8 (January-February 1943), 3.

13. Ibid. See also "Federazione Europea e Monopoli Industriali," *L'Unità Europea*, Number 8 (January-February 1943), 7.

14. Solari reflecting on his participation in the movement forty years earlier, in "Il Dibattito," *Comuni d'Europa*, Volume 29, Number 10 (October 1981), xlvi.

15. Cinzia Rognoni Vercelli (1991) calls this the "turning point" in the organization of a European movement (57). On the historical significance of this Manifesto, see also Altiero Spinelli, "Europeismo," *Enciclopedia del Novecento*, Volume II, Roma: Istituto della Enciclopedia Italiano, 1977, 857; Burgess 1989; and Lipgens 1982.

16. Note Spinelli's point here in a letter to Albert Camus, dated 18 March 1945: "We cannot have a popular European sentiment (and consequently European parties) before having created a European federation. We must try hard to set it up by a policy of clarification and by gathering of supervised forces—this is to say politically decisive [forces]—from different countries of Europe, in order to have the federal democratic institutions that determine the formation of a European civic spirit." Spinelli Fonds, microfiche 160/12/G9-13. A note on references: Some references have no official publisher and are taken from archives. All references noted "DEP" or "Spinelli Fonds" come from collections at the Historical Archives of the European Communities, Villa Il Poggiolo, Florence, Italy. Those marked DEP 13 are from the European Movement Deposit, those marked DEP 12 are from the European Union of Federalist Deposit, and those marked Spinelli Fonds are from the Altiero Spinelli papers (DEP 1). For more information, see Jean Marie Palayret, *Guide to the Historical Archives of the European Communities*, 3rd Edition, Florence: European University Institute, 1991.

17. Mario Albertini, "Rapport de la V Assemblée des Militants du Congrès du People Européen," Valkenburg, July 6-11, 1959 (DEP 13; OMF/40).

18. Publius, "Le Letture dei Militanti," *Europa Federata*, Volume 9, Nos. 13-14, 30 August 1956, 3. See also Altiero Spinelli, "Creare una 'Forza' Federalista," *Tesi Federalisti*, Rome: Stab. Tip. S.E.I., January 1955, 9-10, from a speech presented in front of the 5th Congress of the United European Federalists, January 1953.

19. "Ai Cittadini d'Europa," *Europa Federata*, Volume 9, No. 1, 15 October 1956, 1.

20. Mario Albertini, from the July 9th meeting of the "assembly of militants" of the Congress of the European People at Valkenburg, 41, for citation see note 13.

21. Albertini, from meeting of July 8 (DEP 13; p. OMF/38).

22. Altiero Spinelli, "Creare il soldato-cittadino europeo," *Europa Federata*, Vol. IV, No. 41, 8 March 1951, 2.

23. Altiero Spinelli, "L'Italia e L'Europa," radio address on RAI, 25 July 1954. From the Spinelli fonds, microfiche 162/1/A2.

24. On this history, see Spinelli, "Europeismo," op cit, or Burgess 1989.

25. One example of this last point comes in the form of a sort of leader-worship. By the middle of the decade, Spinelli was writing a regular column in *Europa Federata* called "Spinelli Speaks."

26. Note for instance, Ferruccio Parri, "Presentazione" in Parri et al. 1947, 15.

27. Ignazio Silone, "Missione Europea del Socialismo," in Parri et al. 1947, 51. For a detailed history of how these ideas became organized see Vercelli 1991, Burgess 1989, and Malandrino 1988.

28. Altiero Spinelli, "Pour l'union démocratique des peuples d'Europe," in *Cahier de la Fédération Européenne*, No. 1 (March 1945), 14.

29. The Commonweal, Volume 34, Number 23, 26 September 1941, 540-542. Using the Swiss model of federation, Kohr insisted in this article that "true democracy in Europe can only be achieved in little states. Only there the individual can retain his place and dignity" (542). To "retain one's place" is compatible with an Arendtian space of appearance that permits individuals to present themselves, and not to be re-presented by others.

30. As were those of others, for instance Eugen Rosenstock-Huessy (1969).

31. Enrica Costa Bona (1988) argues that the very doctrine of federalism itself was deployed by Italian political leaders as "a more effective means of combating the resistance of the opposition and of public opinion—it was not...dictated by motives of international politics" (471).

32. One might also see the creation of an elite public space as the reemergence of elite publicity for European Union expressed in the ("lost") arguments of Herriot, Briand, and even Coudenhove-Kalergi (as a representative of the aristocracy).

33. As Seabury (1967) indicates, the "crisis" of civilization was also connected to the Cold War, because the USSR was, as Russia had historically been, perceived as a threat to European civilization. However, since the late 1940s and 1950s the chief threat to European civilization according to many "good Europeans" has been that of American culture in general, and Hollywood more specifically (19-36).

34. Even the Pope commented in 1957 that the European community created " a new life in all fields, an enrichment not only economic and cultural, but also spiritual and religious." Speech printed as "Esortazione del Papa all'Unita Europea," in *Relazioni Internazionale* (Milano), 9 November 1957, 1348. The Pope also spoke of the European "patrimony" that refers to a set of intellectual and moral values.

35. All this reflects what Stanley Hoffman (1964) has termed the "procedural illusion" under which these good Europeans fell: "Where social groups remain divided by memories, suspicions and insecurity, where citizens do not recognize themselves in their public authorities, where interest clashes are made more rather than less ferocious by a dearth of ideological beliefs that lends interests a vicarious fierceness, the situation is not auspicious for procedural solutions" (1264).

36. Even one as skeptical of the notion of a European political space as Robert Marjolin (1989) admits that "European union is vital for reasons of international policy, in order to enable Europe to go on playing a world role *and to preserve her freedom*" (267, emphasis added).

37. In what follows, I have relied on Winand (1994).

38. Jean Monnet perceived the committee as such. See Monnet (1978), 414-416. For more on the Action Committee, see François Duchêne, *Jean Monnet: The First Statesman of Interdependence*, New York: W. W. Norton, 1994, 285-288. Stanley Hoffman (1964) referred to the "Monnet method" as the best example of individuals falling into what I noted above as the procedural illusion—"for it does not provide an

answer to the question, Where do we want to go? In fact, it dismisses the question" (1274).

39. See, for instance, Burgess 1989. Some also argue that the popular movements gave birth to a stillborn infant—federalism—and note its failure as early as 1946. Milward 1992 notes the failures of the federalist movements, as do Willis 1971 and Walton 1952 (371, 380, 389).

40. Altiero Spinelli, draft of an essay, "Rapport sur la Assemblée Européenne pour le Pacte," 15 October 1950, 1, Spinelli Fonds 161/19/D8.

41. Wystan H. Auden, "Europe and the Revolutions," *Préparation à la Conférence Européenne de la Culture*, Lausanne, December 8-12, 1949, DEP 13, 538. The image of the baby signified an uncivilized, uncultivated, and unformed being.

42. "Federazione Europea e Monopoli Industriali," op cit; Arnaldo Plateroti, "I lavoratori hanno diritto alla 'cittadinanza europea'," La Giustizia, 24 November 1961. See also the Mouvement Européen, "Conférence Sociale: Résolutions," Rome, 4-8 July 1950, 3-5, 10, DEP 13, 867. At this conference the delegates called on "Europe" to provide rights of social and economic democracy, union rights, property rights, consumer rights, right of habitation and suggested economic and social responsibilities Europeans would have toward the community. The delegates took the central problem of social Europe to be full employment, and presented a Keynesian solution to the problem (14).

43. "Charter of Human Rights: Proposal by European Assembly," The Times (of London), 9 September 1949.

44. "Projet de déclaration fédéraliste," *Cahier de la Fédération Européenne*, Geneva, July 1944, 29, Spinelli Fonds 160/13/E-4.

45. A European supranational state "translates into new individual rights for citizens of all the component states." Piero Calamandrei, "Stato Federale e Confederazione di Stati," in Parri 1947, 29. Calamandrei argued that the effect of such a state would be to "increase the individual rights of citizens where citizens enjoy a double citizenship" (30).

46. For one example of the connection between citizenship rights and European civilization, see the report of an alliance of federalist groups, "La dichiarazione politica del Comitato d'Iniziativa per Il Congresso del popolo europeo," at Stresa, July 14, 1956.

47. Ernesto Rossi, in Parri et al. 1947, 8.

48. The authors of the report dated 15 October 1949, T. Geiger and H. van Buren Cleveland, are quoted in Beloff 1963, 42.

49. I mentioned these reasons in the first section of the chapter.

50. The phenomenology of conferencing around a table might best be explained by Bachelard (1964): "images of full roundness help us to collect ourselves, permit us to confer an initial constitution on ourselves, and to confirm our being intimately, inside" (234). Bachelard's observation may also help us understand the popularity of the "Roundtable" as a form of conferencing in European community affairs and international affairs more generally.

51. "To live together in the world means essentially that a world of things is between those who have it in common, as a table is located between those who sit around it; the world, like every in-between, relates and separates men at the same time" (Arendt 1958b, 48; see also 120). Jennifer Ring (1991) notes that the "tables that provide even our private lives with stability have a counterpart in public: The stable existence of public places is what permits political action to take place, and political action is the basis for human freedom" (438).

52. As will become evident, conferences that focused on political or cultural unification had as their main object the same actor—the European citizen. Political conferences tended to focus on the citizen's rights and responsibilities, while cultural conferences tended to focus on the citizen's "virtues" and character, to borrow Aristotelian terms. In either case, both provide relevant "data" to assess Arendt's argument. Please note the comments of E.P. Wellenstein, a former member of the Committee for a Citizen's Europe on the European Communities, at a conference in 1987: "already in the late forties, when the first steps on the road toward European cooperation were taken, the cultural component was an essential element of the movement" (in Rijksbaron et al. 1987, 26).

53. "Déclaration du Comité français pour la Fédération européenne," *Cahier de la Fédération Européenne*, June 1944, 26, Spinelli Fonds 160/13/E-1.

54. Charter of the "Comité international pour la fédération européenne," April 1945, Spinelli Fonds 160/16/B-14.

55. For the history that follows, I rely on Vercelli 1991 and Malandrino 1988.

56. This trend would be reinforced at the Paris conference of the Extraordinary Assembly of the UEF in October 1949. Vercelli (1991) notes that here the influence of integral federalism declined while that of Spinelli grew (68).

57. Transcript of speeches at the Congress of Europe, in consideration of *Resolutions from the Cultural Committee*, 9 May 1948, 5. DEP 13, No. 446.

58. Draft Resolution, Cultural Section, The Hague Conference of the Council of Europe, May 1948. Out of this a European Study Bureau for Youth and Childhood was formed, and which called for, among other things, a European "civism" to be created among the young. See its memorandum "Historique Objectifs Activités Avenir...," Palais d'Egmont, Brussels, DEP 13, 1261.

59. In what follows, I cite from the "Rapport par le Président du Sous-Comité pour la Campagne Populaire," a subcommittee of the Mouvement Européen (MFE), that was charged by the Hague conferees to develop strategy and which was probably written by Henri Brugmans. DEP 13, 1013.

60. A short time later, on January 29, 1949, the Council of Europe was established at Westminster, which also took itself as a model for Europe. The vision of the conference-as-Europe (or as a future Europe) was reinforced by Spinelli, when he expressed disappointment in the Council: "it is still not European unity" (quoted in Willis 1971, 28).

61. Joint International Committee of the Movements for European Unity, "Cultural Committee Report," 22 June 1949, 2, 5, DEP 13; 658, Doc. IC/P/22.

62. For more on the European Cultural Center, see also "United Europe Movement Rules," 1949, DEP 13, 738; and a draft report "Projet pour un Centre Européen de la Culture," 30 August 1948. The first page of the report expresses the urgency of the cultural center's mission: "if the European union is not founded on a common sentiment, a common conscience, a common opinion, that only the Center can awaken and express, it will fail."

63. The issue of terminological definitions had already been raised and defended by Denis de Rougemont in a paper submitted to the Cultural Sub-Committee of the International Coordinating Committee of Movements for European Unity, on 19 March 1948, 2-3. Doc. IC/P/20. "These definitions should allow the shaping of what the great majority of Europeans believe to be a matter of course, the census of platitudes necessary to their way of life. It is not a question of creating in a few weeks an original doctrine, but of expressing an existing agreement, and of expressing it so as to reach positive

conclusions [.]" De Rougemont insisted that it was important to "register general agreement on a few definitions which can be used for reference by the founders of new institutions, and to which any European citizen can appeal." The key words to define included democracy, liberty, nations, nationalism, national sovereignty, union, federation, and totalitarianism.

64. Speeches from the Lausanne Conference, 8 December 1949, 5, DEP 13, 538.

65. Kenneth Lindsay, "Draft Report for Cultural Committee," Joint International Committee of Movements for European Unity, 1, DEP 13, 658; Doc. IC/P/23. This had also been evident at the Council of Europe—Consultative Assembly meeting, 1st Ordinary Session, 10 August-8 December, 1949, in Strasbourg. Recommendation #28 read that a European plan for cultural cooperation should provide "the methods to be adopted for stimulating popular interest in the cause of European unity by adult education, university extension lectures, etc." (34).

66. "Educational Committee Resolution," European Cultural Conference, Lausanne, 11 December 1949, 1.

67. Prof. Falco, "Pour une histoire de l'Europe," 9 December 1949.

68. "Educational Committee resolution," 1. The "Report on the European Cultural Center" prepared for the Lausanne conference, noted that officers must be formed "to develop their sense of European citizenship...thus forming an elite that is conscious of its responsibilities" (4). DEP 13, 535, Doc. BE/RS/2/A.

69. Note the statement from the College of Europe's "Presentation Brochure," Bruges, 1950: "It is incumbent upon the new generation to put responsible men, who instinctively act and think in function of European unity, in command of associations, institutions, and organs of public opinion. It is undoubtedly good and laudable that statesmen, diplomats and administrators, formed at national schools, make substantial efforts to elevate themselves above traditional contingencies. But in order to produce a novel and lasting work, Europe is entitled to require that its future leaders have received a European formation, right from the start." These educators were quite clear—a European education would form the future leader and would create the public opinion upon which Europe was to be constructed.

70. In the words of the final report of the conference, "civilization is alive when it makes plans. It has its unity, which it proves an defends by setting up its own institutional system and thus shapes its future." Mouvement Européen, *Rapport General*, Lausanne, 13, DEP 13, 531.

71. All this was to be reinforced by rights of social citizenship for all Europeans, as the Conference on Social Europe discussed in Rome in 1950. See its "Résolutions," op cit, as well as the International Report, presented by Gilbert Jaeger, "The Social Aims of Building Europe"; DEP 13, 508. The delegates to the social conference agreed "with the resolutions and the final declaration of the Lausanne European Cultural Conference" concerning education.

72. "Mémoire sur les Activités du Centre Européen de la Culture," 12 February 1951, Geneva, DEP 13, 898 and 901; "Proposition pour Vingt-cinq Causeries sur l'Unité de l'Europe," 11/51; "Draft Statute for European Cultural Center," 1952, DEP 13, 814; Statutes and notes on the functions of the "Secrétariat européen des foyers de culture," 9/52, DEP 13, 864.

73. M. Wigny, "Note on the European Civil Service," Ad Hoc Assembly, Constitutional Committee, Subcommittee on Political Institutions, Paris, 29 November 1952, 3, DEP 13.

74. So much so that, for instance, only "a very small group of decision-makers determined Italy's role in European integration" (Willis 1971, 178). Following the research of the sociologist Jean Meynaud, Willis estimates that only 4900 people, 3000 of them economic leaders, participated in Italy's "functional" integration into Europe.

75. Indeed, this is how many journalists at the time characterized this fight. See, for instance, Jean Picard-Brunswick, "L'Assemblée parlementaire européenne, est une enviable tribune libre," *Combat*, 14 March 1961; J.-F. Dupeyron, "Conscience Européenne," *Sud-Ouest-Bordeaux*, 12 March 1961; Giovanni Acquaviva, "Il Parlamento Europeo," *Corriere del Giorno* (Taranto), 15 April 1961; Jan Hasbrouck, 'Europe Council Seeks New Lease on Life," *New York Herald Tribune*, 7 March 1961; "Le condizioni di lavoro dei minatori in Europa," *Il Popolo* (Rome), 28 June 1961. For arguments surrounding direct elections to the EP, see Assemblea Parlamentare Europeo, Commissione per gli affari politici ed i problemi istituzionali, gruppo di lavoro per le elezioni europee, *Resconto Sommario*, 16 November 1959, especially the remarks of Piero Malvestiti, the President of the High Authority, and L.J.J. Wining answering "four questions" on direct elections.

76. Bonnie Honig (1995) makes a similar claim in suggesting that free spaces are really gaps where political conflicts and differences are permitted. She wants to see action as an event, not a space—"an agonistic disruption of the ordinary sequence of things that makes way for novelty and distinction, a site of resistance of the irresistible, a challenge to the normalizing rules that seek to constitute, govern, and control various behaviors" (146).

77. Conferences and committees, and by extension, councils, are forms of conversation that demand organization. They are, by nature, not spontaneous. And, as I have been arguing with help from Keenan's work, the act of organization precludes the maintenance of freedom within those organizations. This fact is a challenge to Arendt's theory of revolution that has as yet to be explored more fully, for the very act of sustaining councils requires the sort of methodical politics that subverts freedom in Arendt's sense. On the science, or method, of committee and conference management, see Tropman et al. 1979, and Nadler and Nadler 1987. The very existence of books such as these highlights the dilemma faced by non-violent revolutionaries: how do people come together and maintain spaces of spontaneity and freedom when these spaces have to be planned, organized, and administrated?

Chapter 7

The Acting Class

Of all the spaces where citizens may potentially appear, none is more immediate to most readers of this book than the university classroom. In it younger and older adults communicate, debate, deliberate, display themselves, express ideas, and above all, learn together. Though some readers may find this claim surprising, those who teach probably find it a matter of course. The classroom is a common public space where ideas are shared, and the social science classroom is one where ideas about public life are not only transmitted but upon which all members of that public collectively reflect.[1] The social science classroom is that space where *students, as citizens,* can potentially appear. It is often the first time in their lives that late adolescents can take on the persona of the student as an adult and can make their political voices heard, as citizens, without being represented by others (e.g., parents, teachers, advisors, counselors, or politicians). Older, "non-traditional" university students can contribute their ideas and opinions as they help teachers educate the younger members of the class.

Yet the academic community does not often recognize the public nature of the classroom. Many professors demand autonomy over what they can teach, as if they could maintain control over the ideas they present to a captive audience. Faculties defend their classes from both university administrations and influences outside the university, as if to suggest that teaching their subjects can be an experience purified from external, superfluous influence. Professional associations maintain standards, authorize topics through approved graduate programs, and regulate conduct appropriate to university life. It is not surprising, then, that many in academia see their work as open, not to the public, but only to a specialized few who have been trained to analyze ideas and facts according to approved methods.

It is also not surprising that Arendt herself did not believe that college classrooms were spaces of appearance, given the "social" nature of the educational system. Indeed, Arendt emphasized the danger of mixing politics with education among adults.

> Education can play no part in politics, because in politics we always have to deal with those who are already educated. Whoever wants to educate adults really wants to act as their guardian and prevent them from political activity. Since one cannot educate adults, the word "education" has an evil sound in politics; there is a pretense of education, when the real purpose is coercion without the use of force (Arendt 1961, 177).

She is correct if we use the term, "education," in the manner that she uses it, in the European sense of training someone to conduct themselves in a civilized, mature manner. Certainly, in democratic societies, adults cannot dictate to other adults how to behave, much less how to think. But Arendt recognized the public importance of education. In "The Crisis in Education" (Arendt 1961, 173-196) she argued that education rests on the natality of human beings, the fact that new beings enter the world at each moment, and that new beings also enter the world of schooling at each moment. This not only provides new challenges to teachers, but also creates unprecedented possibilities for learning about (and, I would argue, teaching) the world.

Education, she concludes, is about responsibility.

> Education is the point at which we decide whether we love the world enough to assume responsibility for it and by the same token save it from ruin which, except for renewal, except for the coming of the new and the young, would be inevitable (196).

Responsibility for the world demands that we love and respect the young enough "not to leave them to their own devices." This is possible, I believe her to mean, by teaching those principles that demonstrate love for the world— judgment, impartiality, civility, taste, prudent opinion, representative thinking, and intellectual friendship with oneself and with others. I will argue that it is the special responsibility of the political and social sciences at the university level to teach these sorts of principles essential for democratic action.

If we use the term "education" differently than Arendt does, as the means by which individuals learn, not *how* to think about the public world, but *to* think about the public world, then political education becomes not an oxymoron, but redundant. I will use the term education in just such a manner here to argue that among the most political of all potential spaces of appearance in a democracy is the university classroom. Specifically, I contend that in democracies political and social science classrooms ought to be, by virtue of their topics, spaces of appearance.[2] That they do not function as spaces of appearance is obvious, but lamentable, for it is in these classrooms that many, if not most, young adults can (often for the first time) appear before others as citizens. Where faculties of the political and social sciences do not maintain their classrooms as spaces of appearance, they obscure, and even obstruct, democratic action.

This said, I also recognize that maintaining a classroom as a space of appearance is a tremendously difficult, if not impossible, task. I have already characterized the space of appearance as a momentary place where public freedom reigns, where individuals dramatize themselves and communicate their ideas to others, and where they collect and distance themselves in order to establish a truly civil relationship with those who would otherwise be strangers. I have also shown in analyzing the founding of the European Community that spaces of appearance are difficult to maintain, because in the act of authorizing, or founding, a space, freedom may be sacrificed. This freedom may be sacrificed as a result of the form of discourse used to unite participants together in a common project. So to claim that social and political science classrooms at universities can become permanent spaces of appearance in the Arendtian sense of the term is both too broad and potentially self-contradictory.

Nevertheless, I appeal to discerning instructors of political science, sociology, anthropology, history, economics, education, and psychology, to recognize that their topics are appropriate to citizens who deliberate and act. Instructors can instantiate moments of freedom in their pedagogy, and these moments become important for the democratic lessons their students can learn. Even if these moments are transitory, they set examples for our students as we try to help them understand the meaning, if not the truth, of democracy.[3] Indeed, the momentary nature of these spaces expresses the momentary nature of democracy—as a political practice requiring participation, vigilance, and vigor. Where our classrooms lack this, we cannot expect our students to understand the experience of political action. Where our students do not understand this, we cannot expect them, later as adults, to support the democratic, educational, and research activities found at universities. Consequently, it is in the political interest of departments of social science to treat their classrooms as spaces of appearance.

In characterizing classrooms as potential spaces of appearance, I am recommending that political and social science instructors employ examples *periodically* from the setting in which they teach to help students learn politics. Departments need not offer courses on the politics of the university or of the system of higher education (though that may have its place in any university curriculum). Professors can illustrate larger political points and present examples of situations where citizens make judgements by referring to experiences common to the student in the class. Though professors ought to use events in "the world" to help their students comprehend politics, they can also challenge them to be political in the classroom. This is the theater of politics; this is how classrooms can be, *however momentarily*, spaces of appearance.

Before making this case, I would like to state some premises upon which my arguments in this chapter are based. First, students are individuals capable of making informed judgments. University and college teachers are privileged to have students who are generally old enough to have learned something from their pasts, and young enough to want to create more experiences from which they can learn. Students are constantly making judgments, both good and bad, after considering particulars and measuring their understanding from exemplars. Choosing to pursue one course of study over another, choosing to associate with certain people and not with others, choosing to study on a weekend—all of these choices belong to ethics-creating animals. All of these choices are in the most important sense political—they all permit the student to create communities—of friendship, inquiry, and civic association.

Second, students are individuals capable of civility. Certainly this is true in the traditional sense of the term—students can treat each other (and their professors) with respect, kindness, professionalism, collegiality, and warmth. Part of the contemporary American university experience is a kind of re-civilizing youth—introducing them to the adult world by permitting them to make decisions about how, and with whom, they will live. But it is also true in the sense that I have been emphasizing throughout the text—universities help put a sort of distance between individuals. This can have deleterious effects. For instance, first-year students are often intimidated by the bureaucracy which they encounter, a kind of bureaucracy that is unprecedented in their lives (but one that they will surely encounter as they age). This can contribute to psychological crises and lead to "attrition."

But it can also help students enter into mature relations with strangers. University life teaches a kind of "bearing together" characterized not only by common projects (e.g., the life of the mind, communities of inquiry), but also by the capacity to tolerate others. Learning to tolerate others means learning to accept the diversity one finds in a university community, and it means learning that others are distinct individuals worthy of respect, and occasionally, admiration. The "multicultural" experiences found in most, if not all, American universities serve the civic function of establishing both collective and individual identities. Respecting these identities requires that individuals accept others for who, and sometimes what, they are, and this demands a distancing between individuals. In bearing together, the university student recognizes a formal equality between him or herself and those around him or her, and this recognition assumes that the student distinguishes himself from those others. So, at least in theory, civility rests on plurality.

Third, students are capable of deliberation. This assumption would seem obvious to all except professors who spend their allotted fifty minutes per day lecturing at their classes and requiring students to respond to the lectures in kind during the examination period. Deliberation is a kind of conscience—a kind of thinking together—and it is also deliberate, meaning both "on purpose" and "prudent." Students not only can deliberate, but they are deliberate, and they speak their minds deliberately. Even if most students were not to possess these characteristics, there are certainly enough in class who do to assume that students have such capabilities.

Fourth, and resulting from the first three assumptions, students are capable of thinking politically. By "thinking" I make a distinction similar to the one Arendt makes (following Kant) between reason and intellect. Of course, students are capable of understanding facts, ideas, arguments, and concepts. (Otherwise the contemporary American system of higher education would be radically different from what it theoretically is.) But students are also capable of actively engaging their minds to think *through* problems and arguments, to formulate problems and arguments of their own, and to communicate those formulations to others in ways that make sense to the community. In this way, their thinking is tied to the *sensus communis* Arendt describes in her Kant lectures.

Fifth, and finally, I assume that the purpose of teaching political science to university students is to contribute to the education of a world-citizen, in the sense Arendt described in her lecture on Jaspers in *Men in Dark Times*. By this I mean that, *for most students*, political science is not professional training, but rather part of a broader education designed to create the sort of literate public that can think about, and judge, public ideas. It is (part of) a training in public deliberation, one helpful not only to the intellectual development of the individual student, but ultimately necessary for any sort of democracy. Since only very few of our students actually receive the doctorate and find jobs as professional political and social scientists, our reason for being must be this broader, even more public, purpose.

The Site of Learning and Action

Social science classrooms at universities are fixed and plural spaces. They are fixed because there are only so many variations on the theme of chairs, lectern and blackboard, or seminar table,[4] but they are plural because so many different kinds of learning go on within them. More to the point, students experience the plurality of classrooms in a way that teachers do not and cannot. For students each classroom space brings with it different performances, expectations, possibilities, and types of discomfort. Teachers, on the other hand, because they (attempt to) control their own spaces, regulate the kind of space in which they and others appear to a greater degree than students are normally permitted.

In all sorts of classrooms, students learn many lessons. Teachers hope that students learn the subject matter of the course, and professors hope that they take more than a passing interest in that subject matter. But students also learn to socialize with others, proper (and occasionally improper) conduct, and the ways to "get by" in courses. In short, learning is not reserved simply to the subject matter at hand. This constraint permits special opportunities for political and social science instructors to teach ideas about social thought and action, because they teach ideas which appear in their classroom space daily. Social science teachers are thus in an extraordinary position to be self-conscious about the capacities for individuals to appear.

To put it in other terms, the social science classroom is, potentially, the nexus between the *vita activa* and the *vita contemplativa*. It is a place where the life of the mind meets action. To Arendt this is impossible, because the contemplative life demands that the thinker withdraw from the world of appearances and engage in the soundless dialogue of the two-in-one. I am not suggesting that students can withdraw in order to philosophize in the Socratic sense. But the classroom is the place where they can experience the life of the mind as an activity. Often this occurs when the professor, ignoring the scene around him or her, extemporaneously reflects out loud on some topic or another because he or she has been thinking a great deal about that particular topic. While students may not learn anything more about that subject, because the professor is merely talking to him or herself and not teaching, they are experiencing the life of the mind in action.

But this can also occur by design, and by having the student him or herself experience the *vita contemplativa*. In asking pointed questions to them, teachers can require students (who are so self-conscious of the world immediately around them during these moments) to leave the classroom intellectually, in order to understand immanently the requirements of thought. The student is then required to think—to go to the "nowhere" Arendt (1978) discusses in *The Life of the Mind* (197-202)—and this means leaving the world of appearances for even the briefest moment, to call up the memory of an answer or argument.[5] Other teachers can generate conversations that, beyond teaching the subject matter, help students understand the art of conversation, permitting them to employ that skill with themselves when they are by themselves. The act of teaching the social sciences in a university classroom, then, potentially fosters a philosophical temperament in students.[6]

The classroom setting can also be the site of action. I have described Arendt's understanding of action in chapter 2, but recall that it is exhausted in its very performance. She contends in *The Human Condition* that, whereas labor or work leave behind artifacts (i.e., consumable products, works of art, etc.), action is done for its own sake. It disappears during the activity itself, and this is why she makes the analogy to theater. Theater is that form of art which exists only by virtue of its performance, and not by the work it creates; thus it is self-contained. So is politics, for the activity itself is its own reason. Consequently, political action leaves nothing behind. (For Arendt, those activities which build bureaucracies, agencies, and departments are not political, but work toward the administration of society.)

For these reasons, Arendt herself would dismiss the notion of the classroom as a site of political action. Indeed at most times in the class students will acquire information, and be challenged to remember a variety of political facts. If the teacher is skillful enough, the students may come away from the classroom feeling like he or she has made an indelible mark on their lives. Undoubtedly, this is important in the education of young adults. Yet these same young adults can *also* learn the momentary nature of politics when placed in situations where they must act or make choices in the classroom. Students can begin to identify themselves politically through political action in the classroom—disclosing who, and not what, they are. This is an additional lesson to be learned by adults, and for this reason the university classroom is a special place. Unlike a high school civics class, the political science class is a site for students to learn more than simply facts about politics. They learn *to* judge (and not necessarily how to judge) the political world as well. The responsibility is one for adults; providing political moments in the classroom is no more than acknowledging our students as such.[7]

Villa (1996) describes self-contained political action as a combination of various factors: (1) speech—"a certain kind of talk, a variety of conversations or arguments about public matters" (31), (2) deliberation, whose goal is "formed in the course of the 'performance' itself" (32), (3) plurality, (4) equality, (5) commonality, creating the "in-between" that I have called civility, and (6) ability, including judgment integrity, impartiality, and a commitment to the public space. These six factors describe the political science classroom at universities.

The classroom is one of the few sites on campus where public matters can be discussed literally as a matter of course. Other places students are required to be are not public in this sense—think of the registrar's office, the line at the bursar's or financial aid office, the chemistry laboratory, or even the library.[8] None of these spaces are considered "appropriate" for public deliberation, and many of those that are—the bar, the cafeteria, the dormitory common space— are extracurricular. Certainly the classroom is not the only possible site of deliberation, for student organizations and political action committees meet at various places on (and off) campus. But political and social science teachers lose the opportunity to teach politics when they treat the classroom as just another room where students take courses. They miss the opportunity to create an example of political space by talking to, and not with, students, or by treating them as passive consumers of the abundant array of facts and theories that constitute political or social science.

What do we do when we teach politics? In the first place, we perform.[9] Whatever the teacher's personality is outside the classroom, at least some of it is masked in the act of teaching itself. Those teachers who capture the attention of students more easily are particularly histrionic. To be a performer is of course not the sole criterion for good teaching, but performance draws students in to the life of the mind at that particular moment. This is not lost on students, who learn that effective teaching demands theater, and those students who strive to teach others can remember this as they attempt to present what they have learned in the classroom to others. Teaching, then, is a form of appearing before others.[10] When the performance is over, nothing remains. What the students have recorded in their notebooks or have remembered merely represents something that no longer exists.

As teachers we also participate in a space where many possibilities for conversation and action are created. I do not refer to teachers who become side-tracked on some topic or another, but to teachers who recognize the true challenge to their art when a students asks a difficult or unexpected question. Lecture notes become useless,[11] and the teacher him or herself must recognize the novelty of such perspective and interpretation and adapt him or herself to it accordingly. It is not easy, but it is also one of the few experiences that makes teaching unpredictable. This is probably more common at universities than in primary or secondary schools, because of the much broader array of experiences the wider variety of students at universities have upon which to draw. Often the only times lectures become unpredictable, to both teachers and students, are when the students probe more deeply through questioning.

As researchers we present facts and theories to our students, as teachers we offer interpretations. In lecturing on minority re-districting in his Introduction to American Government class, my colleague Alexander Reichl does not merely recount the history of, and definitions surrounding, gerrymandering in the United States, he teaches the different forms of argument relevant to its practice. In so doing, his students learn not only the content of American government, but the form of its discourse. In presenting differing, and often opposing, interpretations of minority redistricting Reichl describes not merely the truth of the practice, but the meaning or significance of the act. This in itself proffers the political to the class—for political action is ultimately about creating meaning, and not establishing truth.[12] He then asks his students to make judgments about the practice of minority re-districting and encourages them to discuss the issue in class with others.

But is not the purpose of social science to present truths? Is it not to instruct the young as to right or wrong answers? Undoubtedly this is one goal, but it is the goal of the researcher, not the teacher. The professor learns a great deal about his or her subject matter in the course of research, but the most important pedagogical lesson that a professor can learn from his or her research is how to ask questions. As researchers we teach ourselves the art of asking questions. We learn which questions are important, significant, and relevant, and in asking questions to our students we try to set an example of the sorts of questions one would want to ask if one wants to learn more about a particular subject matter. The facts we present to our students can be found in books, films, and archival material, but the questions we ask are not so easily found. Part of the training of the university student is in exposing him or her to relevant or significant questions so that he or she may interrogate others, or the texts that they read so that they can create political meaning for themselves. Certainly for those students who aspire to be political or social researchers we want to set examples of truth-finding and truth-telling, but this is a minority of students. For most, the teacher of politics can ask the sorts of questions useful to them as they begin to judge the world from the perspectives of adults.

Our ability to question ourselves and our students is vital for this sort of pedagogy. First, when we ask ourselves questions in lectures we exemplify judging and to some degree thinking. Let us recall the example of the Canadian parliament from chapter 1. If I am a political science professor I can present the facts, gleaned from my own research and reading, of a committee or practice in

Parliament, say that of questioning the prime minister at appointed moments during the week. As a teacher, however, I am interested in asking *myself*, in front of my students, what the point of this parliamentary exercise is. I am also interested in asking them, in front of each other, what the point of the prime minister's question period is. In these simple acts, I accomplish a number of pedagogical goals. First, and however momentarily, I exemplify the Socratic two-in-one to my students because they see me talk to myself, create a dialogue in me. They thereby see the activity of not only the researcher displayed (acted out), but also the thinker, and they can see that in doing so I am showing a concern for the world (because I care enough to want to know the answer to such a seemingly obscure question). I also demonstrate this by connecting lectures with those that have preceded it (or occasionally those that are still to come). In this way, I exemplify the subject as an ongoing conversation, dialogues which they can imitate by themselves or with others.

Second, by questioning them, I give my students the lived, public experience of that dialogue. I make the Socratic dialogue immediately present to them in a way that books, or the simple presentation of facts cannot, and in so doing I hope that they cultivate for themselves a taste for thinking. In answering those questions, or in raising their own, the students learn to present themselves in front of others. For even the most reticent student, who never participates in classroom discussions, the questioning sets an example of how thinking, and thus judging, proceeds. It also exemplifies how action as performing display and communication takes place.

Beyond interrogating themselves or the students, teachers can interrogate texts in classes. This method is used commonly in literature, and much has already been written about its usefulness in the social sciences.[13] Yet there is an Arendtian purpose to the interrogation of texts. In questioning texts in front of the students the teacher presents the author as an actor, performs a dialogue with that author (or those authors), and consequently sets another example for students to observe, and maybe follow. In reading out loud the text under question, the teacher performs a reading of the text and exemplifies the art of reading. Students learn how to treat the text as another part of the performance, and this can make ideas appear alive. In critiquing the text the students are then witness to a conversation between two thinkers. It trains the student in the two-in-one, by presenting a dialogue partner that can be present without there being another living being present. Where students develop an intellectual friendship with the (author of the) book they are reading,[14] they involve themselves more deeply in the material.[15]

Beyond an intellectual friendship with books, the teacher can also help students cultivate civic friendships with one another. Certainly all teachers experience courses in which students are friends, or friendly, with one another. But in many courses these friendships have been brought to the classes or have developed despite the performance of the teacher (e.g., as students commiserate over their mutual bad luck for enrolling in that particular course). What is rarer is to help students establish friendships as a result of their common questioning of the subject material. When such friendships develop they create the space of appearance more easily, because students then are more prepared to perform, in part because they are not performing among total strangers. Active discussion can break down prejudices that some students may have that their classmates have nothing interesting or important to say, because students can witness academic performances by those they had previously perceived as incapable of contributing adequately to their learning.[16] Thus students not only deliberate but in listening to others they cultivate the skills of the reporter who learns through witnessing events and the critic who judges the event by enlarging his or her mentality. This event widens the space of appearance because students become more willing to deliberate over public matters once the class period has ended, as they retire to their dormitories, the bar, or (unfortunately for other professors) their subsequent classes.

There are also instances where professors make theatrical the political science classroom. At LeMoyne College, Professor John Freie casts students as Presidents in a course on the U.S. Presidency and in class they are required to be in character for most of the term. A number of public law classes use role playing to simulate courtroom situations and give students a greater sense of how certain Supreme Court justices might rule in a given case. Modern political theory classes can be conducted by students taking on the voice of various political theorists in mock debates over fundamental philosophical positions. As I have tried to indicate, transforming the classroom into a space of appearance need not entail drama or role playing, but these exercises clearly offer students the opportunity to assume the perspective of others. This, Arendt has argued, is essential for cultivating the enlarged mentality, and empirical evidence points to its success in doing so.[17]

Social science classrooms are spaces of plurality and equality. Many students bring a variety of perspectives to bear on topics, and teachers perform great services by respecting equality of speech. Certainly not all students are equally talented at all subjects, but distinctions are often found on exams, not in classroom discussions. Even the most perceptive student may not be aware during class discussions of how well they are doing in comparison with others.[18] Furthermore, though students may be unequal in talents, this is no reason not to treat them equally in the classroom. In classrooms where individual students are accorded equal respect in conversation, they may feel more comfortable participating and cultivating friendships with fellow students.

In theory, university classrooms could be potential spaces of isonomy, that no-rule found in the democratic polis of ancient Greece. Certainly professors need not monitor student behavior in the same fashion as teachers in high schools or elementary schools. But professors may hesitate in ceding power to their students in other ways—for instance, in lecturing less and conversing more with students, in permitting them a say in the structure of the course and its material, and in encouraging them to critique faculty practices or university policies. It often demands a good deal of self-control, a Nietzschean effort of the will, on the part of the instructor to stop professing and start teaching.[19]

Because they are plural, potentially equal spaces, social science classrooms allow the creation of that in-between space, that *inter-est*, that constitutes civil relations. What brings people together is the subject matter, namely topics upon which all agree are important enough to consider collectively. Yet this is also what distances the participants, for each individual, though sharing an interest in the matter with others, comes to the space with different ideas and vantage points. This will necessarily give rise to differences and conflicts as the participants try to work together to resolve issues of interest to all.

The students learn to resolve issues not only by learning the facts of the matter, but by being presented with varying interpretations as to its meaning. I suggested above that the teacher plays an important role in presenting differing interpretations of a matter. But the students themselves will also offer their own perspectives. It becomes the task of each student to understand these different interpretations, and this can be done by considering the problem from the various standpoints taken. In her Kant lectures, Arendt referred to this as developing an "enlarged mentality."[20] As a consequence students may cultivate in themselves impartiality and ultimately judgment.

Finally, and by means of contrast, new forms of education, such as cyberclassrooms, distance education, or videolearning, do not create spaces of appearance because no one appears in them. They may be appropriate for teaching professions, business, or even sciences, and information technology has been used successfully in the teaching of political science.[21] But entire courses based on these sorts of technologies are inadequate for teaching the social sciences (and probably the humanities and philosophy as well). In learning exclusively through the Internet or by videoscreen students do not have the opportunity to experience thinking or conversation in the manner I have described above. This makes lecturing political science possible, but renders the understanding of politics much more difficult. It negates the tremendous opportunity professors have for sharing the experience of community conversation that constitutes the political world with students. It cannot be recreated through typing messages on a screen, because in doing so the student-citizen conflates the mask with the persona.

In these forms of learning, students are exposed neither to examples of thinking-as-dialogue nor to face-to-face human communities. Both the theory and practice of politics demand the ability to recognize the former as a form of discourse and the latter as constitutive of the polis, and where students lack the lived experience of either their political education is necessarily deficient. Furthermore, distance learning prevents students from recognizing the public realm as a performing one. Both cyber and video classrooms do not expose students to live performances, and the edited presentations of either simulate the representation of a classroom. This poses the sort of problem of representation I mentioned toward the end of chapter 1. Students cannot take the position of the reporter or the theater critic in this instance and do not have adequate opportunities to cultivate their powers of observation. Building on the argument presented in chapter 3 and exemplified in chapter 4, this can hinder their ability to recognize facts, understand the position of other performers, cultivate an enlarged mentality, and ultimately render good judgment about the political world.[22]

Most importantly, students cannot appear, as either students or citizens, and so cannot act publicly. Because they are not acting, surrounded by peers who are presenting themselves to their fellow students, they cannot experience the foundation of public action. In Arendt's terms, by typing their responses over the Internet, or in recording notes from a talking head on a video recorder, they create work, not action. They may not be able to recognize performance in other areas of their political lives, and they may not gain enough experience in the practice of public conduct. While distance learning might be suitable for some forms of education, for the reasons I have just mentioned, they obstruct *political* education.

Can we have true politics without face-to-face contact between people? Without persons immediately (that is, without mediation) present, politics cannot exist, because the very origin of the term presumed this condition. At least, that is how the ancient Greeks assumed political life to be. It is in our appearance before others, and the fact that we can sense people to be in our presence, that we can constitute ourselves into genuine communities. Where our ideas and speech are mediated by people or objects this kind of participatory democracy cannot thrive. Arendt discounts representative democracy as true democracy because the interests of citizens are mediated by their representatives and so they cannot give direct voice to their concerns. Could the same be said of the Internet, for example? Without responding to the physical and verbal cues of the other interlocutors directly can we be said to be creating communities? We certainly create "links" so to speak, but can these be sustained in the way traditional communities have been? If not, then maybe such communities cannot sustain democracy as a tradition. Where democracy cannot be institutionalized—that is, where it cannot be part of a community's tradition—then what is to prevent it from disintegrating? In other words, what is the interest in sustaining democratic community among Internet interlocuters if they are not in each other's physical presence? Can we really care enough about these others to want to maintain this sort of relationship with them? Or does it become just another alienating form of discourse?

In short, traditional classroom instruction can be sufficient to teach politics. Creative teachers might use simulations, role-playing, interactive journals, or even theater to teach their students. But even the simple, conservative lecturer can open up political moments in the classroom with a minimum of effort. He or she need only treat students as the adult actors and spectators that they are, and begin to challenge them to make judgments in, and about, the classroom. What is important is not that students must be taught using one method or another, but that they recognize the political nature of their experience, so that they can self-consciously act as citizens in the classroom. The classroom itself can help cultivate judgment in students by permitting them to validate an exemplary political experience. In the process it may deepen their interest in the subject and motivate them as citizens and scholars. In this sense, I recommend that my ideas *supplement* contemporary pedagogical practices in the political and social sciences. Yet more can be done to present the university as a theater of politics.

Class Politics

Spaces of appearance are, by definition, political, and this implies certain things for the social and political science classroom. First, those teachers who are concerned with educating their students politically ought to politicize their classrooms. By virtue of their subject matter, political and social scientists are concerned with the public sphere, so in theory their classrooms ought to be public spaces. In practice this is often not the case because professors of political science consider their research methodology (i.e., the objective, scientific approach however defined) relevant to the undergraduate classroom where it is not. Thus it is difficult to persuade professors of political science to become teachers of that subject.

In the past, to politicize classrooms meant to infuse one's lectures with political significance or force, or to activate students in some broader political movement. Marcuse's cry for the Great Refusal was one such example from the sixties, and other political movements from situationalism to feminism to anti-apartheid rallies have regularly been introduced into classrooms from Berkeley to Cambridge and Morningside Heights, via Madison and Ann Arbor. All of these politicizing moments have their place at the university, but I do not refer to this sort of politics when I describe the classroom as a potential space of appearance.

Rather the teacher ought to be conscious that the class itself is nestled in a matrix of political and economic possibilities.[23] Certainly individual students come from different socioeconomic and racial backgrounds, and this has political importance, but the experience of being in a social science class at an American university or college also has implications for the public life of students. To politicize this or that class at the university means to make students aware that they are engaged in some artificial practice. The class results from certain political and economic forces and institutions and is not a given experience of one's late adolescence. To do this, I would argue, requires a kind of staging—making students aware that they are acting in a manner that is by definition unnatural. Conveying to students an awareness of the politics of higher education is not an easy task, nor is it one that the students themselves necessarily want to assume. But it is part of their political education in a democracy, an education that gives them space to appear, and teaches them how and why the conditions of their own world arose.

Almost any topic relevant to the politics or economics of higher education is appropriate to this end. For instance, the economic relationship the students have with the university is relevant to this matter. Their financial aid status, the financial aid practices of the university, their ability to receive loans or grants—all of these issues concern their immediate well-being, but they also reflect the university's need for students. Why does the university have an interest in securing loans or grants for its students? Why do so many of them lose aid money upon entering their third year? Do students at, for instance, Ivy League schools enjoy unfair advantages vis-à-vis those at other universities or colleges? What are the political and economic advantages or disadvantages of attending a certain school? A four-year university? A two-year college? How do colleges and universities garner federal and state assistance if they need them? How are curricular decisions made, and who makes them? Is there a role for students in such decisions? At the university level? At the departmental level? Which resources are available to students to give voice to their interests and opinions? All of these questions are political ones, and the political science classroom is an appropriate venue for entertaining them.

Some will object that these topics, while relevant to the life of students at universities, are not the special provenance of the political or social sciences. But if not these fields of study, then which others are relevant? Which topics are more immediate, more pressing, to students in their roles as democratic citizens? Moreover, the task of teaching political science is, as I have argued above, a special one. Because his or her subject matter is, literally, the public realm, the political science teacher helps students care for the world. The teacher needs to remember that the world is also their world, the unmediated world of the students. In so doing, the teacher is then better able to connect their world with other worlds, the worlds about which the teacher would otherwise normally instruct.

Permitting students to assume responsibility for the world can be done in the context of teaching students new ideas or other ways of the world. It requires, first of all, recognizing the "staging" of the class and of political or social science more generally. The social science teacher ought to discuss with the students the ways in which their educational experience is constructed. This means, for instance, discussing the possibilities inherent in syllabi. On the first day of class, professors often distribute syllabi as if they represented the way in which the subject matter of the course must necessarily proceed. Alternatively, they could distribute syllabi while mentioning the choices that went into deciding upon particular topics or texts, or reflecting upon how the choice of the topics or texts was made. Was it the decision of the professor alone? Was there a committee involved? If the choice was made by others, does the instructor agree with that choice?

Subsequent to the handing out of syllabi, the teacher can present him or herself (dramatically if he or she wishes) to the students. This means not merely giving names or office numbers, as if that teacher was to be treated bureaucratically. Rather, students might be interested in knowing how one becomes a professor of this or that subject. This would not only satisfy their curiosity, but it would establish the professor as an actor who has appeared on other stages. This may also begin to equalize relationships in the class, as students come to recognize the teacher as a being who appears in public. At the very least it would introduce the notion of plurality to those students who realize what sorts of experiences the teacher registered in order to possess a vantage point different from theirs. Almost any information about his or her training the teacher reveals will help convey the message that the course is a political one, one concerned with the public realm.

I am not suggesting that professors remove whatever masks they have on in order to draw closer to the students. I am recommending that they inform their students of the masks professors normally wear.[24] Nor am I advising that professors be casual or friendly (or standoffish), but that they make their students aware of the work that is involved in assembling classes. In being aware of the work involved, students can then recognize the classroom for what it is—the result of artifice. But in so doing, they can also, however slowly over the semester, come to recognize the action inside the classroom as something fundamentally new. For whatever occurs from that first day on will be an experience shared by both teacher and student, and something that neither has ever experienced precisely in that manner before. It is the experience of novelty that conveys the possibility of the political to students. The possibility of creating something out of nothing is analogous to art (in this case performance), and it also conveys the idea to students that creation is possible. Whatever else the professor then lectures to his or her students, they will at least understand the inherent possibility of creation when individuals join together. In a democracy, this may belie messages conveyed during lectures about the failings of individual human agency (e.g., lectures on bureaucracy, authoritarian regimes, international organizations far removed from the average citizen, or clientelist politics). If participatory citizenship is important in the polity, the message ought not to be taken lightly.[25]

One way of teaching students the public nature, and staged character, of their classes is through Individual Learning Contracts (ILC). The ILC is an agreement between student and teacher delineating a program of study based on the student's interests. Contracts are developed by negotiating with students, who are asked to enumerate their goals for the course, the activities in which they will be engaged, and the criteria by which they will be evaluated. Most professors agree informally to a version of the ILC in directing senior theses or independent study projects, but such contracts can be used in standard political and social science courses as well.[26] The ILC has many advantages for classroom teaching—it permits students to recognize and develop their own interests, it encourages student-teacher interaction, it makes the student more responsible for his or her own learning, and it permits each student to learn according to his or her own learning style.

Most importantly, it makes students political within the classroom. By negotiating their class projects students learn the political arts, and they learn that they can be involved in structuring their own learning. They learn to play roles in what they will take from the course and that the course itself is experienced differently by different students (which, as I have argued, is a step toward an enlarged mentality). The ILC also challenges the traditional ways of structuring a course and thus demonstrates to the student that courses are indeed constructed practices. It may teach them that those traditional courses do not legitimize their own interests or articulate them and exemplifies the possibility that authority can be shared between student and teacher. Finally, because the student negotiates the subject matter of the course as well as the evaluation criteria he or she can begin to see that education is something that is malleable. They recognize that education itself is a political practice.[27]

As the students come to realize the staged, political character of their political and social science courses, they will then be able to examine more critically the stages upon which their other classes are performed. Students, faculty, and administration will derive multiple benefits from this knowledge. They will understand the political nature of the modern university or college and will understand better the financial interests that drive it. They will recognize the power relationships inherent in higher education, both within their institutions, and between their institution and others. Administrators may find that this makes it easier to recruit students for economic and political tasks—e.g., raising funds from alumni, lobbying state capitols for capital, defending university educational practices in front of a skeptical public, etc. Faculties may also inaugurate and institute service-learning programs more easily, as students better understand the connection between classroom and "life" (see chapter 8). Professors may find that students grasp sophisticated concepts more readily by being able to act them out in class, and this may catalyze greater interest on the part of at least some students in the intellectual work of that professor. It may thus, ironically, serve as a recruiting tool into the profession. Even where students are unwilling or unable to continue higher training in the social science, it may engender within them a greater respect for the work of academics.[28]

A university or college which permits students to appear as citizens is one that offers these adults a chance to participate in its governance, as a part of the *pedagogical* task of those universities. University bureaucrats may balk at such democratization, but with assistance from faculty, students can organize themselves in effective ways.[29] Student groups can represent majors in departmental meetings over curriculum requirements. These same groups can implement ongoing teacher evaluations so that underclass students can refer to them in choosing classes. They can also be sources for tenure decisions, as well as salary and benefit increases (or, if advisable, reductions) among tenured faculty. Universities might schedule special sessions on faculty evaluations during orientation week for first-year students and invite former students to write annual letters of evaluation. Majors can organize clubs and societies to investigate the purposes of graduate education and university teaching. In each of these ways, students and teachers create new types of classrooms and new subject matters, immediately relevant to their experiences as students and teachers.

Because most students normally spend only four or five years at their university or college, it may be up to faculty members committed to democratic education to maintain continuity. The role of the faculty advisor becomes crucial then—not merely as a mentor to individual students interested in the major, but as one who helps organize students to participate politically in that major. Along these lines, the faculty advisor serves a number of different purposes. First, he or she is among the first to treat the university student as an adult in a one-on-one setting. By this act students live the experience of being treated with respect and dignity as adults. Second, by recruiting students, maintaining records, or teaching parliamentary procedure, advisors help perpetuate the life-span of the student organization. This makes it easier for new students to join and helps all students recognize the importance of institutional tradition. This in turn may further entice students to treat that organization with care and advise their younger classmates to do the same. Student organizations thus become an important means by which students themselves become advisors and mentors.

Finally, faculty advisors become the bridge between students and faculty (and possibly the administration). They widen the spaces in which students may appear by integrating students into departmental decision-making, by introducing students to faculty members, and by defending the rights of students to other members of the faculty or administration. They do not represent students in front of the faculty; they permit students the possibility of presenting themselves. In so doing, they facilitate student action. This is especially useful in departments of political science or sociology where the very subject matter demands a sense of, and concern for, community.

Social science professors can go beyond these roles, widen the space of appearance even further, and concern themselves and their students with broader issues. For example, colleges and teaching universities engage in a fiscal struggle for their very survival in a system of higher education biased toward research, not teaching. Federal and state dollars are directed at predominantly research universities (Gorham 1993, 613-618), so faculties could involve their students in the political and economic debates surrounding the very existence of these smaller institutions. They can encourage students to defend actively the place of smaller colleges and universities in the competition existing among institutions of higher education. In discussing these sorts of issues, students exemplify the nature of their citizenship, for they are topics that reflect their *immediate* public concerns. Consequently, they learn how to recognize what their public concerns are, and this is an essential skill for any citizen or future citizen of a larger polity.

Professors can help students learn about the relative weight of research and teaching at that university or give a mini-course in the administrative politics of the university. They can teach students the politics of federal and state funding of higher research. In turn, students can insist that professors demonstrate that their research contributes not only to the general information base of American society but also to the pedagogical activities of the university. Student organizations could lobby state legislatures to reform higher education funding laws in ways that encourage professors to incorporate the fruits of their research into graduate and undergraduate coursework. This is an alternative for those who complain that university professors do not teach their share of courses. Instead of coercing professors into teaching more courses, they might be provided with more material incentive to incorporate the results of their research into undergraduate teaching. This informs students and teaches them the importance of freedom of inquiry. It also helps students make professors more accountable not only for their teaching abilities but for their research agendas as well.

Teachers might involve student organizations in the fight for state financing of all colleges and universities at the capitol. Administrators might invite more students to plan university budgets and become part of grant-writing committees. They might also encourage students to combat a financial aid system "devoted as much to white middle- and upper-income students who frequently attend higher-cost public or private institutions as it is to low-income students" (Eaton 1991, 121). Students could be given course credit to work on this issue—conduct letter-writing campaigns, protest at the state capitol, or talk at local Rotary club functions. Insofar as universities and colleges rely on public moneys for support, their students can work for a more equitable distribution of funds at the same time that they teach themselves to appear in public.

Students at public universities and colleges might also learn about the structure of higher educational governance by attending meetings of, and lobbying, state governing boards. Hugh Davis Graham (1989, 96-97) argues that state governing and coordinating boards have become captive to the interests they serve, the colleges and universities themselves. By encouraging student participation in the policy process, universities not only encourage experiential education, they also promote an institutional check on themselves as special interests. Here students have closer ties to the general public (i.e., their parents, relatives, and friends who are not academics), and they can serve as public watchdogs over an obscure but political process. Again this fosters their abilities to appear as both students and citizens.

By encouraging students to participate in politics, universities promote a number of public goods: (1) they involve professors in the political education of students, (2) they promote democratic pedagogy as an example for students who will become future teachers, (3) they reflect the collective, participatory, nature of the practice of acquiring and discussing knowledge, (4) they keep an open society by giving students access to information, (5) they give faculty a stake in the university and in the profession of teaching, and (6) they help students recognize the economic concerns that drive higher education in capitalist democracies. All of these practices not only permit students to appear in public as citizens and to enjoy wider spaces for their appearance, they teach judgment by exposing students to a variety of opinions with which they can enlarge their mentality.

Notes

1. In describing university classrooms as potential spaces of appearance, I limit my discussion to campuses in the United States. I do this because the United States is distinct among post-industrial nations in its system of undergraduate education in the arts

and sciences. Many if not most American colleges and universities require some sort of liberal education, where those in Canada and Europe require their students to concentrate in one subject or another. Thus my remarks that social sciences classrooms are distinct because they can function as spaces of appearance are not incorrect in the European or Canadian context, just irrelevant to their purposes. The system of liberal higher education in the United States permits (if not requires) most students to register for sociology, political science, history, or anthropology. Thus my reference to "students" in this chapter is not only to the student majoring in the subject, but to the "average" undergraduate as well.

2.   In this manner, I am following the lead of other critical admirers of Arendt's work, who apply her concept of the space of appearance to movements she might not have considered properly political—e.g., socioeconomic issues such as housing, welfare, or sociopolitical movements such as the women's movement. For examples, see Honig 1995, Isaac 1996, and Benhabib 1996. Benhabib (1996) goes so far as to argue that "it is only under certain very specific historical and institutional conditions that the human space of appearance assumes the form of a *public space*" (127). Under other conditions (for instance, totalitarianism) the public realm "migrates into the private sphere" (128), and household work she (as opposed to Arendt) argues is filled with action. Benhabib sums up the way many contemporary thinkers appropriate Arendt for participatory politics: "Engaging in politics does not mean abandoning economic or social issues; it means fighting for them in the name of principles, interests, values that have a generalizable basis, and that concern us as members of a collectivity. The political for Arendt involves the transformation of the partial and limited perspective of each class, group, or individual into a broader vision of the 'enlarged mentality'" (145). Consequently, the political is not a set of issues or specific institutions, rather it is "a certain quality of the life of speech and action...characterized by the willingness to give reasons in public, to entertain others' point of view and interests, even when they contradict one's own, and by the attempt to transform the dictates of self-interest into a common public goal" (146). If we follow the lead of scholars such as Benhabib, there ought to be no better example of this task than the social science classroom in institutions of higher education.

3.   At least in departments of political science, professors often seek the truth of democracy for the sake of its meaning. That is to say, they concern themselves with research agendas and methodological rigor and in doing so can sacrifice teaching. I am arguing in this chapter that while this may inspire a few students to imitate those professors in their careers, "poor" teaching (in the Arendtian sense I am arguing here) confuses students as to the idea of, and potential behind, democratic action.

4.   I consider some "alternatives" to these sites below—e.g., distance learning, video classrooms, cyberclassrooms, and adult education.

5.   In this regard, *The Life of the Mind* is not only philosophy, but a kind of social scientific inquiry into thinking. Arendt is interested in the "where" of thought—the location of the individual during the thinking process. Thus, the book is as much a kind of epistemological geography as it is a formal treatise in the philosophy of mind.

6.   "Action creates a disclosive relation between plural individuals and their common world, a relation that is constantly threatened by the philosophical/human-all-too-human desire to escape its contingency and groundlessness and find a more stable alternative (politics as *techne*, as *episteme*, or as an instrumentality)" (Villa 1996, 11). A critical site of this struggle is the social science classroom, where students are exposed to the demands of the world and the demands of the mind simultaneously. The teacher, and

his or her presentation, can serve as exemplars to these students in order for them to understand what it means to make these sorts of choices.

7. As I suggest in note 25, the teacher who dramatizes politics or opens up the classroom as a space of freedom should not do it all the time. Even though they are adults, they are still students, and they come to class to learn something. This means they must leave with something (in Arendt's terms, "work"). So learning still involves exams, lectures, and other required activities. I am not suggesting that the classroom is solely a political space, merely that political science professors can use it as a political space occasionally to illustrate the subject matter of the course. This helps students learn politics by experiencing it directly.

8. Though, at least in terms of the last of these spaces, this may be changing. Universities such as my own are beginning to institute "active research rooms" in libraries where students are encouraged to deliberate in groups, and thus in my terms perform in front of each other. But even these rooms are placed away from the central reading rooms, so as not to disturb the typical library user who is required to study in silence.

9. Some anecdotal examples: "Teachers learn they are always on stage and that who they are, how they act, and what they believe, are as important as what they say and teach. . . . Teaching, like leadership, is a performing art." Thomas E. Cronin, "On Celebrating College Teaching," *PS: Political Science and Politics*, September 1991, 482. Cronin cites approvingly the words of historian Page Smith: "enactment, performance, dramatization are the most successful forms of teaching" (487). Stephen Brookfield (1995) observes that university and college teachers suffer from an "impostor syndrome"—a fear that they will be revealed to be charlatans by either students or colleagues. The very concept of the impostor syndrome suggests the dramaturgical nature of teaching and implies that in the classroom professors put up a façade, a false face, or in Arendtian terms, a persona.

10. We can also create a space where being a student is a form of appearing before others. Where we encourage our students to actively take part in their own classroom education, we permit them to try on the persona of the student in public. In Goffman's terms, we welcome them from the audience into the performance itself. For those few outstanding students who we try to encourage to pursue graduate studies, we may find that we permit them entry into back regions, where we teach them the trials of becoming teachers, researchers, and professors. In classical terms, we recreate the Dionysian experience of the theater of appearance, where audience and stage become not two separate realms but extensions of each other. By participating, students come to appreciate the complexity of and preparation involved in teaching, and this allow them to understand the dynamics of the classroom more deeply than as passive consumers of information.

11. As a former student of mine, Richard Parrish, wrote me in November 1998: "In my experience a professor who reads from notes gets fewer questions, and fewer interesting questions, because students—besides being bored—do not think that the professor will be capable of issuing a serious reply, hampered as he or she is by reliance on lecture notes. In addition to that, professors who constantly read from notes appear uninterested in the fact that they are conveying information to actual people who are present in the room." In my terms, the professor who simply reads from his or her notes transforms an essentially public space into a private recitation of collected knowledge. In teaching other disciplines this may be perfectly adequate to his or her task; in teaching politics it violates the very subject matter, namely the public space. Students cannot be

exposed to the benefits of public deliberation, though they may be exposed to an insidious and ersatz form of political discourse, administrative and technocratic jargon. This sort of classroom experience cannot prepare them practically for democratic life, though it may acclimate them to a bureaucratic imperative.

12. As I describe in chapter 3, presenting truth is the task of the social scientist. But, I would argue, it is the task of the social scientist as social and political researcher to do so. In his or her job as a teacher of politics, presenting truth must coexist with helping students create meaning for themselves. That task requires the professor to offer a stage upon which his or her students may perform, so that they can make meaning for themselves.

13. Note, for instance, the work of Jean Baudrillard, Michael Shapiro, Michael Ryan, or Diane Rubenstein.

14. The friendship is measured by how difficult it becomes to put down a book we are reading, or how sad we are when we have read the final page.

15. An excellent example of this is the quote analysis, a two or three paragraph assignment in which the student chooses a quotation of not more than three or four sentences from the reading and discusses it in a short essay. In the first paragraph the student explains the argument of the quote in his or her own words, and in the second and third paragraphs he or she presents reasoned arguments supporting, extending, or criticizing the thesis of the quotation. This exercise helps focus the student's attention on particular issues and helps him or her discern both the particular argument in the text he or she has chosen and the nature of argument itself. For a more detailed description, see Charles Hersch, "The Quote Analysis: Teaching Political Science Students to Read with Focus," *PS: Political Science and Politics*, September 1995, 523-524. See also the "five-word game" as described by Mel Cohen, "Making Class Participation a Reality," *PS: Political Science and Politics*, December 1991, 699-700. Finally, Allan McBride notes the importance of "reading aloud and subvocalizing" in learning statistics. Allan B. McBride, "Creating a Critical Thinking Learning Environment: Teaching Statistics to Social Science Undergraduates," *PS: Political Science and Politics*, September 1996, 517-521.

16. I owe this very wise observation to my former student, Richard Parrish.

17. See John F. Freie, "A Dramaturgical Approach to Teaching Political Science," *PS: Political Science and Politics*, December 1997, 728-732; Dean C. Hammer, "Giving Flesh to Ideas: Constructing a Cultural Dialogue," *PS: Political Science and Politics*, June 1994, 259-261; Thomas R. Hensley, "Come to the Edge: Role Playing Activities in a Constitutional Law Class," *PS: Political Science and Politics*, March 1993, 64-68; Frank Guliuzza III, "In-Class Debating in Public Law Classes as a Complement to the Socratic Method," *PS: Political Science and Politics*, December 1991, 703-705; Mel Cohen, "Making Class Participation a Reality," *PS: Political Science and Politics*, December 1991, 700-701; and Elizabeth T. Smith and Mark A. Boyer, "Designing In-Class Simulations," *PS: Political Science and Politics*, December 1996, 690-694. Stephen Brookfield (1995) has demonstrated that role-playing helps generate classroom conversation in a variety of university classes (152-153).

18. Without asking the other students, of course. But that requires the kind of informality between students that benefits the class as a space of appearance anyway.

19. It requires teachers to become like Schopenhauer's elephant, who recognizes the futility of the struggle against its trainers and permits itself to be led. Arthur Schopenhauer, *The World as Will and Representation, Volume I*, E.F.J. Payne, tr., New York: Dover, 1969, 306: "We are like entrapped elephants, which rage and struggle

fearfully, for many days, until they see that it is fruitless, and then suddenly offer their necks calmly to the yoke, tamed forever." As I indicate in note 7 above, though, the classroom should not be organized as isonomy all the time. Teaching involves more than giving students the opportunity to perform all the time; it involves not only action, but work. The political science instructor exemplifies isonomy, democracy, or egalitarianism by providing *moments* where students experience the power of no-rule.

20. I have examined this concept more closely in chapter 3.

21. For example, computer simulations are often used with great success in political science, and e-mail or interactive learning journals can encourage students to participate and help them comprehend difficult philosophical and theoretical concepts. See Barbara Welling Hall, "Using E-Mail to Enhance Class Participation," *PS: Political Science and Politics*, December 1993, 757-758; Dean Hammer, "The Interactive Journal: Creating a Learning Space," *PS: Political Science and Politics*, March 1997, 70-73; and the examples discussed by various authors in *PS: Political Science and Politics*, September 1998, 568-590. As a supplement to classroom experience, information technology can certainly enhance the understanding of students, but it is no substitute for this experience.

22. Etymologically, "performance" derives from the Latin *per-fournir*, to thoroughly complete in the sense of furnishing. This demands a material presence, so to perform politics means to furnish the people who actually engage in the activity. Where the classroom remains unfurnished with the constituent material of politics—people— then can individuals learn politics?

23. I would further suggest that if professors want to politicize their classrooms along the lines I described in the preceding paragraph, they may be more successful at doing so if they also recognize the political economy of higher education in their classrooms. I return to this idea below.

24. Brookfield (1995) recommends this strategy as a way of combating the above-mentioned "impostor syndrome."

25. The radical democratization of a political science class was courageously attempted by Professor Mark Mattern at Chapman University. In a class on democratic theory he sought to teach his students by sharing power with them. Slowly, over the course of the term, he ceded his own power over curriculum, instruction, and grading to the students. By establishing, and then dissolving, intermediate institutions for a few weeks modeled on the U.S. government he permitted the checking and balancing of powers between he and his students before they assumed full responsibility. In the end, he deemed the attempt a failure because the classroom became chaotic and ungovernable, and, given their newly acquired powers, too many students chose to stop working in the course and reward themselves with high grades. He found that "students gained a greater appreciation for the philosophy of democratic education and for the mechanics of teaching that most instructors take for granted but of which most students tend to be unaware," though he was "less certain of how much of the substance of democratic theory students learned in this course." Mark Mattern, "Teaching Democratic Theory Democratically," *PS: Political Science and Politics*, September 1997, 510-515.

It should not be surprising that the attempt ended in that fashion because the students simply acted in their own short-term interests. But I would not necessarily judge the attempt as a failure because the students learned the mechanics of democratic education, thus given the space in which they were permitted to appear, the students learned the appropriate lesson of the exercise. They might also have learned that democracy requires vigilance on the part of citizens, or they might have learned that democracy is not necessarily the most efficient way of organizing their political lives. But they were permitted the chance to exercise that judgment because they were put in alternate positions in the classroom and so could view it as a social construct that is created, and not natural. The exercise also indicates that giving over an entire classroom to the actual practice of democratic politics may not be the best way of conveying intellectually the power of democracy to students. Because these students are still *learning* civic judgment maintaining some authority is beneficial to not only keep order, but to exemplify an alternative to democracy in the classroom. In doing so, students can learn to recognize exemplary validity and can come to their own conclusions about which form of government or political power suits them as citizens. Furthermore, while students may have learned to act democratically, they did not learn how to judge democracy. Professor Mattern's class fell victim to the difficulty that Arendt's theory would predict: democracy requires not only political actors but also citizens who are willing to distance themselves critically from the action and judge. This means providing opportunities for students to not participate all the time, and this can only be done in more conventional classrooms where the professor can enforce non-participation and enforce assignments designed to enhance judgment.

26. See John F. Freie, "The Individual Learning Contract," *PS: Political Science and Politics*, June 1992, 230-234.

27. The most systematic use of the ILC has been at Evergreen State College in Washington, and its success in accomplishing these goals has been well documented. See, for instance, George D. Kuh, John H. Schuh, Elizabeth J. Whitt and Associates, *Involving Colleges: Successful Approaches to Fostering Student Learning and Development Outside the Classroom* (San Francisco: Jossey Bass, 1991).

28. If for no other reason than they will begin to see that the work of academics is political—that is, concerned with not simply the public realm in abstract terms, but *their* public realm, the world as they experience it immediately as students. Administrators may want this sort of understanding inculcated in students so that those administrators can turn to them as alumni for donations without having to spend so much time and energy justifying either the purposes of the university or the failings of the football team.

29. Much of what I discuss over the next few pages can be found in more developed form in Gorham 1993.

Chapter 8

Participation and Judgment in the University Community

"Since men appear in the world of appearances, they need spectators, and those who come as spectators to the festival of life are filled with admiring thoughts which are then uttered in words. Without spectators the world would be imperfect; the participant, absorbed as he is in particular things and pressed by urgent business, cannot see how all the particular things in the world and every particular deed in the realm of human affairs fit together and produce a harmony, which is not given to sense perception, and this invisible in the visible would remain forever unknown if there were no spectator to look out for it, admire it, straighten out the stories and put them into words."

Hannah Arendt (1978, 132-133)

In the last two chapters I have suggested examples of how certain university practices can be adapted to suit the twin public goals of political action and political judgment. I have argued that political research ought to be conducted for the sake of teaching our students about the university and the world, and that our classroom settings can be models of political action for those students. In this chapter I want to discuss the third pillar of university life, community service. Community service has been part of the job description of the American professoriate for quite some time now, and it is becoming a more common part of the required curriculum for students at many of our nation's universities. I want to examine more closely how universities can rearticulate service in order to render its members active and judicious. Proponents of service invariably emphasize the former of these terms, but I want to emphasize the latter, because community service has a role to play in teaching judgment. I imagine alternative forms of community service that I believe incorporate this sometimes overlooked public purpose of higher learning.

In the first section I sketch the most significant secular arguments for community service, analyze their most important components, and discuss ways in which political judgment might supplement all of them. I examine arguments based on tradition, institution-building, democracy and participation, and citizenship. None of these are mutually exclusive of the others, but by distinguishing them analytically, I can make my own points more precisely. Each argument articulates important, and often necessary, reasons for continuing the practice, but, I argue, none of them provide sufficient reasons for justifying community service.

In the section that follows these sketches I suggest ways in which community service practices, for both professors and students, and incorporate the learning of political judgment. I give practical examples, but ones that would require substantive changes in the ways in which service program designers both think about and implement projects. They also imply significant changes in the manner in which universities are governed, and ultimately, structured. However, to actually implement these suggestions would take relatively little time, money, or effort on the part of administrations. But they would not make sense both to the university community or the public at large without an appeal to both learning and political judgment.

In the final section of the chapter, I reintroduce the university as a theater of politics. I argue that if the university is to be conceptualized theatrically, as I have used the term "theater" in this book, then community service becomes in some ways the most important component of university public life. Just as classrooms can be re-structured into momentary spaces of appearances, so I would argue, can service practices. But this means turning university governance into both a political and an educational experience. It also means encouraging members of universities to perform and critically appraising their performances. Whether or not universities are prepared to do this in the years to come is another matter.

Arguments for Community Service

Arguments for community service take a variety of forms, but all conclude that community service is indispensably good for the self-government of any campus and for the cultivation of university citizens. In what follows I would like to review the most significant arguments for community service, based on tradition, institution-building, democracy and participation, citizenship, and religious commitment. I contend that while each argument raises important and often persuasive cases for community service, they are not sufficient to be wholly persuasive. For none of them account for political judgment and each lacks a conception of the political space in which servers can appear. I offer an

Arendtian interpretation here to supplement these sorts of arguments that would otherwise remain incomplete.

Tradition

Community service extends the life of an institution and its relationship to the public sphere, and this is both a good in and of itself and a source of moral support for both the community and the individual. Citing service practices in the Revolutionary War or in the small town democracy observed by Tocqueville in the early eighteenth century, proponents maintain that community service is a long-standing tradition in the United States; one that has sustained not only particular institutions, but the very fabric of the nation. In the context of contemporary higher education the argument goes something like this: our students need to be aware of the culture in which they have been nurtured and which they share with both their fellow students and people outside the university. They ought to recognize the value of sharing a society that permits them to be educated in the manner that they have, and they should be grateful for being able to live in such a society. Such gratitude (Buckley 1990) can be expressed by serving the people who have extended the life of the society in which these students learn.

In regard to the professoriate, some argue that service is necessary to build institutional loyalty on the part of individuals who might otherwise be critical of large institutions. Universities and colleges are not simply places where professors are employed, they are also structures of public education and common governance. As pillars of academic freedom, universities protect first amendment rights, not only of the professors themselves, but for society in general, because even those who do not work at universities know that it is a place where freedom of expression, as a cherished American tradition, can be protected. Thus the place of universities in American public life is a defensible one, and the institution has traditionally provided sanctuaries for both individuals and ideas who might otherwise be left unprotected outside the ivory tower. Moreover, universities, since the middle ages, have been self-governing guilds that determine their own rules and purposes. Consequently universities protect another sort of traditional freedom—that of collective self-governance— and professors ought to serve both the university that enjoys this privilege and the community at large that is willing to permit its self-governance.

Arguments from tradition can be popular ones, except we know that tradition itself is no guarantee of good government, or academic freedom. For instance, it was not tradition that permitted African-Americans free entry into universities, nor was it tradition that encouraged women to study medicine, law, or business. Even today, tradition permits the existence of fraternity hazing, a practice that one may enter into willingly, but not necessarily by using good judgment. By holding to tradition, one is not challenged to think about the reasons for engaging in certain practices, and this is problematic, not because reason ought to be the source of understanding for our actions, but because reasons provide us with a tool for exercising judgment. Where we stop-and-think about our traditions we can then assess their advantages and disadvantages, and the collective and individual benefits that might accrue from continuing this or that practice. So tradition itself cannot justify community service, but rather the judgment rendered over that service ought to determine whether the practice should be continued. What is valuable about any tradition is not the tradition itself, but whether that tradition permits individuals to judge well the communities in which they serve.

This is one important consideration to any theory of community service. Does service, on the part of students or professors, foster judgment? Does it permit the members of the community to reflect upon their institutions in a careful and deliberate manner, or does it invite them to participate unreflectively in common practices for the simple sake of the institution itself? Traditions that teach political judgment ought to be worth preserving, and community service should be oriented around this practice. Likewise, nontraditional services that teach judgment are worth considering, because they may initiate traditions that give people pause to think about their traditions, which in turn may help them think more clearly about whether to preserve or give up their traditions.

Institution-Building

Some proponents, especially conservatives, contend that community service strengthens the connection between the individual who serves and the institution under which they serve. This does not defend the practice of community service on the grounds of preserving a tradition, rather it defends community service as a central component of the structure of public institutions. In this regard, community service does not maintain institutions for the sake of tradition, rather they strengthen the bonds of the institution because strong institutions are a good in themselves.

Not only do strong institutions preserve traditions, they also shape the character of individuals, provide order in their lives, give their members both financial and moral security, and mediate connections between their members and the outside world. In the case of universities and colleges, both students and professors are taught good habits, and are given the security of a place in the world, not to mention the financial security to those who earn their living or who are supported with scholarship money there. Individuals receive benefits by being part of universities—not only do they earn their livelihood, or receive an education (so that they may have more options in earning their livelihood in the future), but universities help to establish individuals with a class or status position. Beyond claiming membership in a university in some capacity, an individual can sometimes boast that it is an Ivy-League university, or a medical school with Nobel prize winners, or the state university that has recently won a basketball championship. The institution itself, then, partially provides identities to some individuals.

Individuals ought to serve their communities because in doing so they extend the lifetime of that university, strengthen its institutions, and integrate it more fully with the world. Unlike the argument from tradition, this is a good not for its own sake, but because the university, as an institution, provides vital services to its members and the community at large. So students and professors are responsible to their institutions, to support them by serving either the university community itself or the larger community within which the university or college plays a role, in order to enhance the status and power of that university or college. Doing so will continue to permit individuals to accrue benefits from that university in the future and may even expand the number of individuals who are positively affected.

Though what is good for one institution is not always good for another. Take the case of reform-minded professors who sit on election boards or watchdog committees to ferret out corruption and graft in city politics. Of course the public service they perform may enhance the status of the university in the eyes of many citizens of that city, by weakening machine or clientelist politics. But this very act also destroys the lives of those individuals dependent upon these antiquated systems for their livelihood, such as recent immigrants or tavern owners. I do not mean to argue that taverns or ward politics are more important institutions than universities, only that they too are institutions of American life in a number of places. The fact that they are institutions means that one cannot argue for service on the grounds of institution-building. Because there are extant institutions that one may judge to be harmful to the public good, institution-building itself is no argument for community service. One need not be William Plunkitt, Boss Tweed, Richard Daley, or even Marion Barry, to recognize that machine politics is an institution that benefits more than just a few of its participants.

The question that remains is, how do we judge which institutions are worthy of building and which are not? This brings us back to that criterion of service I proposed above—political judgment. Community service ought to teach us how to think about our institutions, how to understand their functions, how to determine if they are worth preserving, and how to reform them when we judge them to be in need of reform. Furthermore, we should think about how we act in institutions—how we contribute to their strength, how we can contribute to making them more just (however we define the concept). So we need to learn to think about action within institutions. This is something a theatrical notion of politics can help us discover, and it is something that community services ought to incorporate. Service practices can teach its participants not simply how to serve, but how to act, in the Arendtian sense, in institutions. In serving the university or the broader community, the student or professor can learn the importance of performance and communication (see the appendix). In engaging in action the person does not merely provide labor or work for others, but communicates, debates, deliberates, and educates others, and is educated in return. The participant performs while serving the community, and this means he or she does not simply render tasks for others or the public, but that he or she expresses his or her identity in the process. Service could be a means by which individuals make their appearance in the world and invigorate the public world by creating spaces of appearance. Acting within institutions, as citizens, means politicizing them, and this means politicizing the notion of community service.

The university citizen energizes university institutions by recreating them as public spaces, in the sense of the term as I have used it in this book. But as we have seen in chapters 3, 4, and 5 citizenship implies more than simply participating, it requires the aforementioned capacity to judge. This demands an ability to withdraw from participation, from the institution itself in order to come to a reasoned understanding of the worth of that institution and its practices. As I will argue below, community service must incorporate into its practices means by which individuals can withdraw from service in order to judge the fairness and effectiveness of the institutions within which they act. Necessary to the strength of the university as a democratic institution, it articulates university institutions as centers of both participation and public reason.

Democracy and Participation

A third line of argument defends community service on public, communal grounds. The contemporary impetus for community service came from philosophical movements that emerged in response to the individualist excesses of Reaganism. Books, such as Benjamin Barber's *Strong Democracy* (1984), Robert Bellah et al.'s, *Habits of the Heart* (1985), and Philip Selznick's *The Moral Commonwealth* (1992), called for reinvigorating communities and communal relationships through greater participation in public institutions. Called communitarianism or civic republicanism, these movements were supported by philosophers of varying stripes who argued that America was in dire need of a new public philosophy of service. The arguments were assumed quickly by the Clinton Administration in their campaign rhetoric and policy pronouncements, and the administration has proposed rather frequently bills encouraging community service in various forms.

Though there are subtleties that differentiate the various arguments from one another, the participatory argument for community service possesses certain fundamental characteristics. Proponents argue that Americans do not participate enough in public life—either because they choose to privatize their lives, or because public institutions prevent them from doing so, or because the political culture of participation has atrophied, or because of any combination of these factors. This is both a moral and political crisis—moral because citizens become ever more atomized and distant from each other, political because legitimate government becomes difficult, if not impossible, to sustain when individuals are alienated from each other and from the government itself.

Active participation in the social and political life of the country results in various benefits to the individual citizen and the country itself. The citizen learns to feel part of a larger community and learns about that community. This in turn empowers that citizen in that he or she begins to understand better how his or her society works and begins to feel more confident that he or she can contribute to the maintenance or reform of that society. As an exercise in self-government, it is also an educational program for the citizen, who comes to appreciate the importance of collective liberty for its own sake, and as part of a greater American tradition. In uniting with others in a common project, such as community service, the citizen weaves a tighter web between him or herself and others, and as all citizens do so, each is provided with a greater sense of collective security. People learn to help, and count on, their neighbors, and with this comes a feeling of both empowerment and relief—the belief that the citizen can make the lives of other citizens better, and the security in knowing that other citizens will be there to help should the citizen need them. But, the communitarians and civic republicans are quick to note, this is not an entitlement ideology, people can only earn this sense of security where they do their part and share in the welfare of others by demonstrating a responsibility toward the public.

For its part, the government, by encouraging service, legitimates itself. By involving more participants into the fabric of American life, the government integrates its citizens into both its activities and into the activities of the society which it is designated to protect and defend. Because citizens feel that they have some sort of say in how both government and society operate they will support that government more openly and forcefully than if, sensing their own powerlessness, they perceived government to be an institution apart from their everyday lives and concerns. By engaging with others in collective projects the common life of the polity is enriched, and the government both democratized and strengthened.

Clearly the benefits of participating are one important justification of community service. Yet participation and democratization by themselves cannot be sufficient arguments for this practice. Being an active, involved member of a community, while potentially honorable and praiseworthy, is also potentially dangerous, depending on the political context. Participating in, say, the Nazi regime hardly speaks to any of the characteristics and benefits of participation that I have mentioned. But we do not even have to take an example as extreme as this one.

Let us take the example of a professor who is encouraged to participate in the university community by serving on committees, attending college assemblies, or advising agencies of government or non-profit institutions. Certainly it is possible, and even probable, that tremendous benefits will accrue to both the professor and the university by his or her participation in these activities. The professor would learn the art of collective self-government and thus feel him or herself to be integrated more deeply into the life of the university, the university would enjoy the added legitimacy of each professor who enriched his or her professional life in this manner.

But there exists the possibility of loss as well. First, that professor might involve him or herself in his or her committee work to such a degree that his or her other responsibilities (e.g., teaching and research, not to mention family life) may suffer as a result. Second, that professor may involve himself to the degree that he begins to use his or her positions on that committee to exercise power unfairly over other professors or members of the administration. Third, involving him or herself in the minute details of committee work may blind him or her to the true effectiveness of that committee. It may obstruct his or her thinking through whether or not such a committee is even necessary to the efficient operation of the university. Fourth, as the professor involves him or herself more thoroughly in the life of the university, he or she may indeed come to feel closer to his or her colleagues, but he or she may also come to recognize his or her colleagues as inadequate to the tasks at hand, thus paradoxically alienating him or her from the life of the university. Fifth, he or she may find him or herself as an opponent or ally of the administration to such a degree that, if the former, he or she obstructs what might otherwise be good policy. If the latter, he or she discounts too quickly the ideas of other faculty who oppose the administration on one issue or another. In either case, the professor may not be open to *learn* from others, in the first instance from administrators, in the second instance from other faculty members.

I have not exhausted the list of potential problems here, and I do not claim that these problems trouble most institutions of higher learning. I would not even suggest that they are likely to occur. I am only proposing that because these results are possible, participation by itself cannot be a defense of community service. The act of participating involves the person in a collective activity, but does not ensure that the person thinks clearly about the ways in which he or she acts. Nor, as I suggest in point four above, can it ensure that people actually feel more integrated into their community. Participation requires judgment as well. To serve one's community effectively, one must not only participate, but one must do so with the sort of judgment that helps him or her distinguish between right and wrong, truth and falsity. This is the sort of judgment that Aristotle argues derives from the wisdom of our every day experiences (*phronesis*). But as I have tried to indicate, everyday experience is no guarantee of wisdom.

Participants do not always have the opportunity to reflect upon the activities in which they are engaged. In my example here, professors do not remove themselves from the activity in order to achieve the sort of distance sufficient to render judgment about it. In a few cases this is because that professor is so involved in community activities that there is not time to do so. But in most cases it is because there is no institutionalized means of rendering judgment. Of course there exist study committees, or academic review committees, which in theory are supposed to do this. But they themselves are committees, and professors often treat them as another committee obligation. Additionally, as I have indicated in chapter 6, the committee structure itself, while sometimes permitting individuals to appear as distinct and expressive beings, does not sanction the kind of collective judgment that checks the bureaucratic imperative I mentioned in the Introduction.

Following Kant and Arendt, I would argue that judgment has something to do with taste, and the ability of the person to both think about his or her common experiences and articulate opinions about those experiences to others. Rather than encouraging individuals to participate in community service, and thus to multiply their everyday experiences in the hopes that their judgment is improved, I would argue that *judicious* community service is one that provides opportunities for people to stop participating in order that they may become spectators to the action in which they may have previously engaged. But, and this is crucial, this cannot be institutionalized in the manner in which it is usually done so—by assigning professors to committees which look at the usefulness of committees. Rather, as I will elaborate below, professors need to be able to think systematically about university governance taken as a whole. Why not, for instance, require professors to audit a course on both university governance and the government of their particular university? Asking professors to think, in a *learning* setting and not a bureaucratic one, might facilitate their ability to reflect upon the topic. Such reflection would be deeper and more comprehensive than sitting on study committees, because, among other things, they would be required to read about issues relevant to their everyday, and thus (following Arendt) *political*, lives. They could deliberate more intelligently on these matters, and they could, to employ our term here, create at least one type of space of appearance at the university—a space for expression, communication, deliberation, and, above all, learning.

Citizenship

A fourth argument, that shares characteristics of the previous three types of arguments, is the argument for community service from citizenship. Making this sort of argument, though, is not as easy as it may appear, because citizenship can mean all things to all people. Conversely, it can mean nothing to anyone. Some theorists emphasize the rights of a citizen—political, civil, and socioeconomic—and argue that community service plays an important role in earning such rights. They perceive it as a sort of obligation necessary to enjoy the freedoms and social benefits of living in a state such as the United States.

Others focus on the importance of civic virtue—those mores, values, and principles that citizens ought to hold in order to be accorded political respect in a democracy. Some of these virtues may include holding public office, tolerating other citizens, understanding and respecting the laws and obligations in our society, and maintaining a commitment to the political community above and beyond a commitment to the self. Community service, it is argued, can foster any or all of these virtues, and more.

Still others tie the citizenship argument into one of the others I have already mentioned. Some argue, for instance, that good citizens are those who respect and cherish traditions. They act publicly because they recognize that those traditions are in some sense greater and more durable than their own individual interests. Institutionalists note that citizenship itself is an institution, composed of historic civil, political, and socioeconomic rights and responsibilities (Gorham 1995). Participatory democrats often suggest that participation is the focal point around which citizenship is developed, and democracy is distinctive because it is the sole form of government that respects equally the rights and obligations of all citizens. More radical democrats argue that democratic government should not simply respect rights and obligations equally, but guarantee that each citizen equalize their rights and obligations and that those who receive more from the public coffers contribute more to those same coffers. Thus, for instance, students who receive financial aid money ought to serve their country in a voluntary capacity for one or two years.

Regardless of the source of the civic argument, proponents of community service claim that such service will make better citizens and this will benefit the country as a whole. Community service teaches self-sacrifice because servers must put the needs of others before themselves. It teaches equality, because all who participate do so roughly on the same footing. It strengthens communities because it exposes citizens to the lives of others in need, or to other citizens with whom they can discourse. Moreover, it teaches the individual citizen how he or she can change people's lives (presumably for the better), and, in the process, how social institutions work. Finally, by working together with others in the service of a greater good, citizens learn the virtue of collective liberty—a value essential to democracies and a source of the American tradition.

But, as with the other arguments, the one from citizenship lacks an account of political judgment. Or more accurately, for a theory of citizenship to account for the benefits of community service, it must first include an account of political judgment. As I have argued above, simply serving one's community is no guarantee of political learning; likewise, it is no guarantee that one will acquire either civic virtue or a greater understanding of one's rights and obligations. Indeed the very definition of the term service, even when modified by the adjective community, is not civic. To serve implies subservience, and even where one serves the public, one is placing oneself under the power of something else, and not in a position equal to that which one serves. So there is already a tenuous connection between service and democracy.

This connection has been periodically contradicted by the history of western political theory as well. The ancient Greeks did not include service in the responsibilities of the citizen, and they relied on slaves, women, foreigners, and occasionally members of the lower classes to provide services. To serve the Greek community meant *not* to be a part of that community and not to be capable of sharing in the public life around which that community theoretically thrived. The service ethic in the west was first justified by the pan-Hellenic philosophical schools that emerged after the death of Aristotle and the decline of the Athenian Empire. The most famous of these, Stoicism, influenced the Roman leadership who subscribed to it as a philosophy of leadership. It was Christ and his followers who democratized the concept, making service possible for all believers. But under Christ one served God, not the earthly community. Of course, words can change and new definitions can be asserted, but I present these facts to maintain that there is no necessary or historical connection between citizenship, democracy, and service.

The necessary connection between the three concepts derives from two affiliated concepts—a place for individuals to appear as citizens, and their capacity to exercise political judgment. Where individuals can make their voices heard, where they can be guaranteed a space to appear as public actors without fear of persecution, and where they can act prudently and judiciously, then individuals can be considered to act as citizens. With a space to appear, they can express who they are and can contribute to the public life of the community. By using their good judgment, they preserve that space as an open, deliberative, and democratic one.

Community service, then, ought to be an act performed in such public spaces and with the judgment necessary to secure these sorts of spaces in the future. Community service in universities is a special case of this. In institutions of higher learning, community servers ought to act in ways that preserve the educational character of the institutions. Thus such service ought to exist in spaces that not only permit people to act judiciously or encourage them to do so, but should teach them judgment at the same time. Of course, it is not likely, or even possible, to teach judgment, and both Kant and Arendt would argue that taste, the faculty upon which judgment is cultivated, is ultimately a private sense. I am not arguing that community servers can be taught judgment by other community servers or by teachers of community service or even by professional servers (e.g., those in the helping professions).

I am suggesting that community service activities should be practiced in a context that permits individuals to cultivate their own sense of taste and the capacity to articulate this sense to others. To serve in a truly civic capacity, as, that is, a citizen, is to do so while becoming wiser and while possessing a deeper understanding of public life. But the citizen does not achieve this simply by acting; I have argued above that acting in public is no guarantee of either taste or wisdom. Contributing to this, as I argue in chapters 3 and 4, is the ability to withdraw from action in order to reflect critically upon that action. Politically speaking, this means that community service ought to include a component where individuals have the right not to serve, in order to spend time thinking about the community. In this sense, I am redefining community service, for within this rubric I am including individuals who do not act publicly, or who do not act publicly for a specified amount of time, if that period of detachment gives them the opportunity to reflect (most productively with others, it seems to me) on the nature of the public, and by extension, community service itself.

At universities, this means rethinking the nature of the university citizen. It means thinking about whether and/or to what degree both students and faculty should be required to serve the university community (or the community at large as representatives of that university). It also means considering the possibility that non-participating students and citizens can cultivate civic virtue. It means considering the possibility that professors who rarely participate in service activities can theoretically be as civic-minded and as publicly useful as (if not more than) those who engage in public activities constantly. For those professors who withdraw may display a sort of political judgment that is not displayed by the very active participant. Again, I am not saying that this is always, or even often, the case. I am simply asserting that it is a possibility, and that if the university is to reward its professors and students justly for being good community citizens, then it needs to at least *consider* this possibility in establishing just systems of distribution for these rewards. I make a few suggestions below on how institutions of higher learning can begin to consider this possibility in practice.[1]

Service Practice: Learning Political Judgment

I have been arguing that community service is a practice that can be justified on various grounds, all of which rely ultimately on the ability of individuals to judge the world in which they live. I would like to enumerate here ways in which I believe these practices, on the parts of both professors and students, can be made to help their participants practice political judgment. In keeping with another theme of the book, the theatrical nature of politics, I will also recommend community stages upon which servers may perform, and community theaters within which they may learn the arts of observation and criticism. I have argued that participation without a kind of critical, reflective judgment is insufficient to create good university citizens, and we can re-design institutional practices so that individuals can learn to articulate their tastes to others. In the process, they may better appreciate civic virtue and the power of learning.

Are You Being Served?

Whether it is called community service, public service, or, simply, service, universities require members of their faculty, staff, and administration to devote time and energy to the function of the public world. The public world can be the department, the college, the university itself, or the larger community within which the university plays an important role, but in any case the good university citizen is one who maintains and invigorates the relevant sphere. Within the campus itself, tasks can include serving on committees, attending public assemblies, giving public lectures, and fundraising. Committees themselves may concern everything from admissions to allocating classroom space and parking permits. A few lucky individuals are permitted to sit on "task forces" and the most fortunate ones enjoy being members of "special task forces." For faculty members, committee service, measured by quantity and quality, is an important criterion for tenure, promotion, and increases in salary.

Sitting on a university committee is, at least in theory, a lesson in democracy, because in doing so faculty members participate in the governance of the university. But, as I have argued above, it is not necessarily a lesson in political judgment. The stated purposes of committees are not to inculcate judgment, reason, wisdom, or learning in general; the idea is to get things done. Committee members are charged with administering some task and are judged by others on how well they have done so. Indeed many committee members become frustrated when objectives are not met, even (and sometimes especially) when the situation is caused by one or more obstinate members filibustering a proposal. Committee members who talk too much often frustrate their fellow members who do not want to discuss items *ad nauseum*, but want to conclude with the day's business. Yet isn't democracy about deliberation, discussion, and participation?[2]

I would argue that (at least in this instance) the offending member is often not talking too much, but listening too little. In this state of affairs he or she treats the other members of the committee as means to his or her own end, rather than as ends in themselves. In the context of higher education, this Kantian observation reflects a situation where individuals are more than willing to teach others about their position, but less than willing to learn from those same others. In the midst of thousands of examples that surround them, they have forgotten how to be students. I have been arguing throughout the book that learning how to be a student is one important element of learning political judgment, at least in the context of higher education.

How can committee service be reinvigorated to help cultivate political judgment within the university community? Clearly committees that accomplish tasks ought to continue, but all faculty members should serve at least one term, every ten years or so, on a committee that discusses the philosophy of serving on committees. This would be the only committee on campus that would conduct its affairs as if in a classroom setting, with the chair as a sort of facilitator. The chair would provide assigned reading materials and would encourage participation and discussion in weekly meetings. Of course, the subject matter would range beyond the role of committees, hopefully into the governance of the university itself; but any discussion would institutionalize discourse on the practice of university politics.

The benefits could be significant. Individuals would learn more about their own university, and about university governance in general. They would also learn about the philosophy of governing universities, which may help put their experiences into context. It may make the jobs of administrators easier because they would be working with others who are learning what their responsibilities are. Of course, it may also make their jobs more difficult, for the very same reason. But most importantly, it brings together faculty members, not to get things done, but in a spirit of learning collectively about the public world that they share in common.[3] They would have the opportunity to bring their common experiences to the table and reflect upon those experiences in light of readings that they have discussed together. By articulating their personal experience, and by offering to others particular problems, solutions, and examples, the members of this committee can begin to teach and learn from others a sort of political judgment.

Moreover, it would be a space where professors would appear in academic roles. They would take the personae of *both* the teacher and the student, and in doing so perform both these roles for benefit of the other members of the committee. This helps those other members appreciate both of these sorts of roles (many of whom ought to learn to appreciate the latter). Such appreciation could benefit them when they return to the classroom and summon their own students to appear before them and the rest of the class. In being students (again) in this sort of committee, they imagine how students perceive the class and the instructor, and thus enlarge their mentality, to use Arendt's term. Also, because the committee is one that discusses the governance of the university, it is also a theater of spectators. In it professors can observe collectively the functioning of both their university and universities in general and in doing so can develop the sort of judgment I describe in chapter 3.[4]

This could also render the experience of being at a university more meaningful or significant to the individual professor. At the very least, by encouraging professors not simply to act, but to take the position of a spectator, they would be able to make their experience at their university mean something to them, and possibly to others. In withdrawing from the university theater, they would be in a better position to view the whole of the drama as it unfolds daily before them. They would better be able to determine the purposes of the university, but also the means by which it accomplishes these purposes. They would do so collectively, and thus both recreate the conditions for public action and learn the requirements for public reason. It would also teach them that in distancing themselves from the activity of the university they can come to better appreciate the virtues of that activity (if there are any). Finally, they could bring these perspectives back to their own classrooms should they choose to turn these into spaces of appearance (see chapter 7).

I would take this idea of learning from other faculty members one step further and recommend that universities institutionalize a program, as part of the faculty service requirement, to encourage professors to take classes from other professors in departments other than their home department.[5] Periodically professors would audit classes in other subjects, not simply to learn those subjects, but to re-learn the practice of learning. This in turn would help them appreciate anew the experience of their students, which may help them transform their own classes. Obviously this could take a variety of forms—it might be required, or assigned in lieu of sitting on other committees; faculty members ought not to be permitted to audit the same class twice, nor should they audit a class in a field that they know well. In order for professors to learn how to learn again, they ought to place themselves in the position of their students and approach subjects from a place of relative ignorance.[6] The practice might also serve as a kind of peer-teaching program as faculty members come to know each other better, and share teaching styles more regularly. Instead of service, then, professors would be exposed to service-*learning*.

Another version of this form of service-learning could be practiced through what Charles Anderson (1993) has called "education forums"—panels composed of faculty and alumni to judge the performance of the institutions and the disciplines that constitute them (146-160). According to Anderson the fora would receive a report from the faculty justifying the present curriculum and then begin to examine each department in depth before turning to the university at large. He argues that both faculty and alumni have the depth of experience and the interest to judge the future of the university and recommends that departments in the leading graduate schools initiate these fora. This guild-like arrangement would serve as a form of governance of the various academic professions.

I would modify his suggestion in two ways. First, insofar as an undergraduate education involves something more than professional training it is also important to create these fora at colleges and teaching universities. This offers alumni the opportunity to grade not only the professors but both the departmental and university curriculum with regards to how well the university has taught reflective judgment and has generated interest in the various disciplines. Second, these educational forums might be structured to give relatively more influence to the alumni, because they are in a position to judge the institution more perspicaciously than the professors who teach there. The alumni do not participate in the academic programs of the institution (anymore) and so possess the requisite detachment to be critical spectators. But as alumni they already possess interests in the institution—both material and moral—so that they can still be considered citizens of that particular university or college. In short, alumni are situated well to be critics of the ongoing dramatic performance of the academy. Alumni can possess more influence relative to the professoriate in educational forums where alumni are facilitators or instructors who teach professors about their own institutions. In the process, professors may learn to listen better because they have taken the position of students.

At the level of community-wide service, the idea ought to be the same—creating opportunities for professors not simply to act, but also to learn, to observe, and to cultivate good public judgment. In so doing professors can appreciate the lives and struggles of individuals outside the university community and may be able to incorporate that learning in the classroom or with other professors in their university committee work. In this regard an example from the city of New Orleans is instructive.[7]

The St. Thomas Housing Project is a residence of publicly owned low-rise apartment buildings situated in the Lower Garden District of the city of New Orleans. Its residents are extremely low-income African-Americans, and the project is beset by the problems of drugs, gangs, and crime that afflict so many of the housing projects in the United States. As a result, the project is served by a variety of public and private agencies—including the local police, the Drug Enforcement Agency, the state police, and welfare providers from local, state, and federal agencies. All of the members of the "security" and "helping" professions (including advisors from local universities) intend on maintaining peace, order, and some measure of economic security to the residents. Thus many programs are furnished to the residents in order to educate them on matters of health, social welfare, safety, and employment.

But St. Thomas is also a neighborhood of active, intelligent citizens who have set out to solve problems on their own initiative. In doing so, they have established the St. Thomas Residents' Council (STRC), a committee of residents concerned with establishing and maintaining some degree of self-governance (already a difficult task in communities run by public housing authorities). The STRC has thus assumed the task of educating the service providers as to the role and responsibility of the service provider in St. Thomas. In 1989, STRC president Barbara Jackson notified all service providers in the community that the residents were going to be active participants in any decisionmaking that affected their community. The service providers were required to sign an "accountability statement" committing themselves to power-sharing and anti-racist education.

The result was the formation of the St. Thomas/Irish Channel Consortium (STICC), an organization made up of the STRC and approximately twelve social service and community organizations. STICC is effectively an advisory board created by the STRC that can be used to promote the interests of the residents and yet one that remains under the direction of those residents. To ensure this, the STRC holds a majority of seats on STICC and retains veto power over all decisions the Consortium makes. Furthermore it has served to educate service providers and render them accountable for their actions within the community. It hands out "report cards" to service providers, marking their success at serving the residents' needs, and it requires all participating agencies to attend intensive workshops on "undoing racism." They have furthered their demands in the past by threatening to challenge the flow of funding to service providers if the providers do not accede to the power-sharing and educational arrangement.

They have also requested that any academics who wish to use their neighborhood as a topic of research consult with members of STICC. The logic behind this is clear—in publishing works on the STRC or STICC, academics may in effect exploit the plight of its members to better the lives of academics without returning any service to the residents. They are suggesting, then, that servers—both in the helping professions and in academia—may be serving themselves rather than the residents. As a result, they want to redefine the parameters of community service.

In order for a professor to participate in the meetings of STICC he or she would need to learn how to listen. Listening would be a prerequisite for good judgment in this situation, because the residents are demanding that such visitors try to understand the plight of a resident from the perspective of a resident. Moreover, the experience is necessarily educational, both because STICC demands it and because most academics have a great deal to learn from residents of housing projects (if for no other reason than they have never shared in this experience).

This is a potential model of judicious community service for academics. Why not assign community tasks to professors, not as advisors, not as members of "blue ribbon" committees, not as so-called experts, but as potential students of the social classroom in which they live? Learning from other members of the larger community is essential in helping professors learn good political judgment, because in participating in experiences which they have not previously shared, they expand the domain of their visiting imagination.[8] But they must be prepared to learn, they cannot expect to teach others from the position of "expert." In this light, democracy truly becomes a laboratory of learning, rather than a means by which expert ideas are popularized. Most importantly, what is learned are not facts or theories, but political judgment—the capacity to reason appropriately in public circumstances, and with others, by letting one's imagination visit the positions of others within the communities in which they act.

Are They Being Served?

Community service for students is a different matter. Most students, called to serve their communities, are not called to sit on committees deliberating over this or that (seemingly obscure) point. Rather they are called to "action"—to help others either on campus, or, more likely, in the surrounding community. In serving others, students learn to reach beyond their immediate surroundings, and experience life in the so-called real world. This, it is argued, is an education in itself. But for reasons I have suggested briefly above, and more extensively elsewhere (see Gorham 1992, 107-128), service and learning do not necessarily go hand-in-hand.

I would like to suggest ways in which service and political learning may be structured for students at universities. More precisely, and in keeping with my theme here, I want to suggest ways in which universities can give their students opportunities to appear in public and exercise political judgment. Both lessons can be learned simultaneously if care is taken to design appropriate service activities and projects.

How can this be done? In the first instance, we ought to treat community service projects as extensions of the classroom experience. I do not mean that participants should reproduce their classroom experiences in service contexts. Rather, I want to extend points I discussed in the previous chapter to service work. Just as classrooms are to be treated as spaces of appearance, community service projects can be imagined *politically* as potential spaces of appearance. That is, we can imagine them as places where students can act as citizens for what may be the first times in their adult lives. Consequently, service projects can be those designed to educate students politically, permit them to express their opinions on an issue or variety of issues, help them participate in order to develop greater civil relations with others (as I have defined civility in previous chapters), and learn the power of observation and criticism by detaching themselves from their immediate surroundings (in this case the campus) in order to render good opinion about those surroundings. In sum, service projects can nurture their capacity to articulate their tastes and subsequently help them exercise judgment about the world.

Already many political science classes successfully incorporate these experiences into their curricula. Rob Koulish at Bentley College engages his students in an immigrant assistance program where they learn immigration policy through practice, and where they are required to negotiate bureaucracies on behalf of their clients. At the University of Virginia students in an urban politics class learn about homelessness and housing policy by serving needy individuals in Yonkers, New York. The University of Maryland's department of political science encourages its graduate students to work in the field as part of their studies through a public service fellowship program. Project Public Life in Minnesota teaches students political concepts such as "interest" and "power" by having them participate in public service projects and by writing public life journals. Finally, universities throughout the United States are beginning to incorporate service learning into their curricula, and these practices are being documented systematically by a veritable army of researchers.[9]

But in extending the classroom experience in this manner, students can also learn both the importance of teaching and how to teach. Service ought to be an opportunity for students to teach others, both to gain greater mastery over their experiences and knowledge of the world and to permit their imagination to go visiting as they assume the position of the teacher. In so doing, they can learn to appreciate the difficulties involved in teaching and the complex interaction between teachers and students. Community service projects are a particularly good place to experience this because they can teach without being under the watchful eyes of their professor. They do not have to worry about their performances and consequently their grades, and so do not need to alter their persona as dramatically to accommodate what they perceive as their harshest critic.

In teaching in a context away from the classrooms in which they themselves are students, they learn to *act*, and not to distance themselves. This exercise is particularly useful for students unaccustomed to acting, who seek refuge at the back of the class, so to speak. By permitting them to articulate what they know to people who do not govern their academic futures, even the most reticent student knows that he or she does not have as much to lose. Thus there is a greater chance that the student will abandon his or her position as spectator, and will perform on a stage unfamiliar to him or her, but relatively unknown to his or her professor as well. This may in turn give that student a greater understanding of how to be an active spectator when he or she returns as a student to the university classroom, because the student will have seen examples in other contexts of how other students behave, and because he or she will have a more intimate appreciation of performance anxiety.

Some forms of community service can (and already do) require student teaching in public school systems. But even other types of service can incorporate a teaching component. In cleaning up environmental damage, students might also research the causes of the environmental damage by playing the role of reporter. The could investigate the history and sources of pollution to the region and interview the private and public officials responsible for the problems. They might present the results of that reportage, not (only) to their class at the university, but also to a public assembly in the town or locality where they have been working and researching. Or in providing meals on wheels to the elderly or infirm, they could interview the service recipients. They would learn more about the lives of individuals unlike theirs, they could learn the history of how one becomes a service recipient, and they could then share their findings with fellow students, service providing agencies, and public interest groups concerned about the rights of the elderly (e.g., the Grey Panthers). Literacy volunteers could use the opportunity to help the people they teach how to tell their own stories in print. This would allow those volunteers, as well as those who read the stories, to enlarge their own mentalities by learning languages of perspicuous contrast.

Community service at universities could examine the practices of universities themselves. As a service to their fellow students, volunteers might investigate Boards of Trustees and encourage greater student attendance at their meeting, which would bring their meetings and decisions to a broader public. Volunteer reporters might also research the offices and decision-making practices of the administration—e.g., presidents, vice-presidents, and deans. They could ask to sit in on department meetings in order to better comprehend how faculties make decisions on curriculum, courses, salaries, tenure, hiring and firing, electing chairs, and anything else relevant to their lives as students. They might also investigate how decisions are made on financial aid awards, and publicize their findings to the student body. Finally, they might serve on review committees in order to observe how professors teach, in order to publicize their findings to the student body. This may help their fellow students make more informed decisions about which courses to take or which majors might have the most appeal.

Such research could have great impact on how students understand the structure of power at their university. They might come to understand in more detail why certain university departments and offices increase their institutional power at the expense of others. They might begin to comprehend the political significance of research, and its importance relative to teaching, by investigating the reasons why professors and administrators alike emphasize one or the other in making salary, hiring, and tenure decisions. In short, student community service could be politicized by permitting students to observe action in the university as a critic might observe live theater. They could then write their review of the performance in order to illuminate political truth and share it with the other members of the academic community. Community service, then, can be another way that students learn to treat their immediate lives in a political fashion and to connect their daily experiences with broader understanding of their own community.[10]

Indeed, the first people to be investigated might be those professors and administrators set upon requiring or compelling community service for students.

Do they have good, public reasons to do so? Are there also private reasons of personal aggrandizement that come into play? What are the psychological factors that motivate some to encourage others to participate in public projects? Is there anything in the personal histories of professors or administrators that has contributed to their desire to establish and propagate such programs? Finally, in whose interest do such programs serve? Is it only for the good of the student? Community service at universities could be quite an education.

I have been arguing that judicious community service is one that permits individuals the time and means to reflect upon their acts. Therefore such a program would require that those students who have over-extended themselves be encouraged not to participate in the serving activity as it is normally conceived. Rather incentives would be built in the system to help those students "stop-and-think" about what they have done or are doing.

As teachers we have all met students so enamored with public service—either from religious, political, personal, or moral beliefs—that they continually act for the public good. They involve themselves in church fund-raisers, student government, hunger awareness projects, literacy campaigns, and save-the-whales schemes—sometimes simultaneously. Obviously such students are rare (though prominent on campus), and social science educators often do their best to encourage these activities. Certainly these students serve their communities more than peers concerned primarily with finding the cheapest beer for a Friday night keg party.

But I would argue that they do not necessarily serve their communities more than the student who is not involved in service activities to this extent, but who spends his or her time reflecting on the justice of the world. Because political judgment originates in the capacity for the person to be a spectator, those students who do not spend sufficient time as a reflective political spectator cannot cultivate an appreciation of the entirety of the political world in which they work. I have suggested in chapter 4 that this was one reason why Eichmann had such difficulty making moral decisions, and Arendt has argued that it is one component of the *banality* of evil. I do not mean to imply that there is a potential Eichmann in all over-active community servers, only that where political action prevents individuals from taking the time to stop and reflect upon the public world, there is a danger that they will not develop political judgment as quickly as if they had more opportunities to stop and reflect. Thus the problem of thoughtlessness is not only a problem for those students who spend their time distracted from studying and thinking; it is also one afflicting those who are too active politically to reflect deeply on what they are doing.

Of course, one ought not prevent students from participating in whatever causes they see fit, but maybe those causes could have a judging component inscribed in them. Let us take student government for instance. It is quite easy for certain students to become involved in student government very early and very deeply in their college careers. Indeed, political science professors meet more than a few of these students who see the exercise as a training ground for a future career in politics. Why not require those students participating in student government to attend regular discussion sections on the relationship between morality and politics, on the civic responsibilities of politicians in contemporary America, or even on the psychological needs of the politician?

Making these requirements for only those students involved in government may seem unfair, but these students voluntarily accept the power and responsibility of public office. Because these students have public responsibilities, they also have the responsibility to deliberate prudentially over the reasons they want to be in government, and what their responsibilities are as governors. For those participants unwilling to do so we may ask what their motivations are in wanting to represent the student body. Are they concerned enough about the public sphere to spend enough time to think about their own relationship to it as the political representative of others?

At the other end of the spectrum, so to speak, why not offer discussion groups for those students who do not participate in service activities? In them students can think about why they avoid community service, whether it be for personal, psychological, political, or moral reasons, in order that they learn to judge whether or not their reasons are good ones. This would not require them to participate in community programs, it would make them defend their positions thoughtfully, and it would do so while keeping in mind the learning character of higher education. This might be a more just alternative than requiring students to participate in community service, as an increasing number of high schools, colleges, and universities are now doing. It would be a means of rationally persuading students to consider community service, if they cannot give good reasons why they ought not to participate, and thus appeal to their faculty of judgment. For those democrats who believe in the citizen's ability to choose, this alternative is certainly fairer than requiring participation, or even strongly recommending it by the carrot or the stick. As an alternative to community service, it emphasizes a public concern while it respects the higher learning upon which universities and colleges are founded. Finally, it preserves the principle of choice underlying democratic institutions, and thus may make those students appreciate more deeply such virtues inherent in them.

Performing Liberal Arts

Politics in universities is theatrical: to paraphrase a well-known claim, the action is so dramatic because the stakes are so low. Though most professors do not control biological weapons or manipulate junk bonds, we do attempt to influence the minds of millions of individuals daily. While university politics may not revolve around life-or-death issues for many people in the world, it does have something to do with the intellectual and moral well-being of American society. If we decide to act on this stage, we can try to do it without hypocrisy. We can also try to learn how to judge those who act in a reasonable manner.

Politicizing the university means generating spaces of appearance in them, and I have argued that the classroom is potentially one of the most effective means of permitting individuals to appear. But this means transforming research and service practices to support the creation of these spaces. Research topics and methods can, and ought, to be subsumed under the sign of learning, if they are to be justified on public grounds. In other words, if research findings are to be defended as benefiting the community in some sense, and not just as articulating knowledge for its own sake, then that justification must consist of a public learning component compatible with classroom experience. Otherwise its justification remains private—for instance, advancing the career of academics who seek to appeal to a narrow band of specialized researchers because that is the most efficient means for them to succeed in achieving fame or fortune. An effective way to share one's learning with the public is in the form of a critical report—an observation on a part of our world that also renders judgment on it and integrates it into the life of the community that has permitted the researcher the privilege of researching. The graduate (and even undergraduate) student should be able to learn how their particular research influences the means by which they can and do act as university citizens. Researchers should in the long run be encouraged to give their research public significance by presenting it in such a way that indicates respect for the general audience. Researchers ought to remember that they can learn from this audience and write their reports accordingly.

In like manner, service activities can reinforce the teaching and learning functions of the university or college. As sites of action, servers do not merely assist, they perform on the public stage. This can help them build confidence in their own identity independent of the one tied inextricably to the university. They can thus take pride in articulating a public place in the world instead of being someone affiliated with the school that won the NCAA basketball championship, or someone who publishes this many articles in that many academic journals. It can also strengthen their own commitment to learning and teaching and help them transform the society-at-large into a learning society after they graduate or as representatives of their home institutions. University governance itself can become a self-conscious learning experience where people revel in discovery and the wonder of the world around them.

As I have tried to argue throughout the book, we can make steps toward this ideal. We do not need to re-structure the university radically to begin treating our students with the respect they deserve. Incorporating a few of these ideas would help make all university citizens more aware that they *are* university citizens. If our goal is to energize students, faculty members, and administrators and to help them act more communally, more civically, then we ought to put everyone on stage, if only for a few moments. As political and social science instructors we can make the world appear and disappear before our students' eyes. The more it appears the more opportunities we have to teach our students the art of leading a political life.

Hannah Arendt spent much of her life thinking about worlds in which she would never appear, worlds in which people had not appeared for ages. The Greek polis was one, revolutionary America another. If professors treat the historical event as a moment past or the political event as merely an object of rational inquiry, then they too present spaces that do not appear. But we can remember that though Hannah Arendt could not appear in these worlds, these worlds could appear in the mind of Hannah Arendt. In calling up the memory of these worlds in her written work, she helped bring to life spaces that might have otherwise disappeared in the public conversations of citizens. In so doing she permitted the world to continue talking, and learning, about the public spaces of the past. Those who still wonder about them can thank her, and those she learned from and who learned from her, for maintaining their permanence. Such spaces manifest themselves because people learn to make and attend to them. They learn to create public spaces ultimately because they have learned to learn, and for this they can thank their teachers. What better lesson can a teacher learn than this?

Notes

1.   A fifth argument, which I discuss here, is the religious one. I leave it to a footnote because it is not immediately relevant to all universities, but merely those with a formally religious, and specifically Christian, connection. I do not mean to efface differences between the various sorts of orders and denominations, but in presenting the general case, on Christian grounds, for community service, I can best suggest how and why my arguments here relate to these sorts of universities in general.

The Christian case for community service is rooted in the Gospels and the Epistles, and in the sentiment of helping others through Christ. In following the example of Jesus and ministering to those less fortunate individuals can in turn demonstrate their commitment to God, prepare themselves for salvation, share in the love of Christ and God, witness the work of Christ in the world, live within a Christian order, help save others for God, or live righteously according to biblical principles. Though there are many theological arguments for community service, all of them (necessarily) tie the server into a service for a higher order. It is an order that is constituted by citizens of a higher government, if we can employ the secular terms that we have used thus far.

I would suggest that, by extension, the arguments from judgment apply equally well to this realm. In so far as there is a Christian order, then its citizens ought to be able to render judgment as those of the secular world must. Admittedly, this is a different order of thinking, because Christian government is not always democratic, and the order of the church is based, not on (or not only on) the judgment of the congregant, but also on his or her faith. Faith is not an epistemological requirement for community service in the modern, secular world, nor is it defended by the sorts of philosophical argument I have recounted in this chapter. But many of the greatest thinkers in the Christian tradition, including for instance Augustine, Aquinas, John of Salisbury, and Duns Scotus, refer to reason as a necessary complement to faith in considering truth and falsity, good and evil. I would suggest that reason's civic partner, political judgment, must also be referenced in considering the benefits of community service.

Community service can contribute to the way a kind of Christian judgment can function at religious universities. It can be a way in which Christian universities, in considering their missions to the public at large, can teach students judgment in the context of this practice. This might be political judgment concerning this or that secular issue, or it might be teaching students how to judge Christian arguments for community service. That is, the practice of community service itself may help students judge whether that practice can and ought to be defended on theological grounds. The principles I have expounded here, then, need not apply only, or even primarily to, secular universities. Because all universities, including religious ones, have public commitments, that is commitments to the secular world in which they operate, all of them have some relevance to the teaching of public or political judgment.

In the context of the Christian university, this may be a specific public, but it is a public that creates its own spaces to appear. It is because a Jesuit priest is leading a demonstration against, say, the politics of the Guatemalan regime, that his role at his university is necessarily a public one. But the priest who is also a member of the board of trustees of the university can potentially create a space to appear as well. The question then is whether that priest will accede to a bureaucratic imperative (as I have termed it in the Introduction), or whether he will create a space in which others may appear. It is my argument here that community service is one way that both professors and students can learn how these sorts of spaces can be constituted. So that when they are confronted with the bureaucratic imperative at universities, they can then render good judgment about whether or not to accede to it. Given that Catholic universities have so many community service projects at any one time, this sort of learning can take special importance there. And the same can be said for universities of Mormon, Baptist, or other Christian denomination.

2.   For other observations on this matter see the relevant section in chapter 6.

3.   In this way it differs from the faculty seminar, which brings professors together in order to discuss some topic about which one of them is a specialist. The "committee seminar" I am describing is the one topic where nobody in the class is a specialist because everyone necessarily shares in the same subject matter.

4.   This can have direct benefits to departments of social science because professors in other departments might better appreciate the sort of observation and critical thinking that attends to social scientific reasoning.

5.   This could also be applied to members of the administration, but I am focusing on the professoriate here because they are responsible for teaching students and would thus benefit most from (re)learning how to be students.

6.   This might be one sort of requirement that comes after tenure, or after a certain number of years away from graduate school. Presumably tenure-track professors remember well their experience as students, so their mentality need not be enlarged. If tenure-track faculty members do not teach well, it is probably for reasons other than lacking an appreciation of what it means to be a student, and they might be candidates for other sorts of classes.

7.   Much of what follows results from research completed by my colleague Alexander Reichl (1999).

8.   Among other things, they might learn to observe political theater from the perspective of a critic in the audience, a perspective I have argued that teaches judgment to academic political scientists, as I have argued in chapter 3.

9.   For accounts of these programs see: Robert Koulish, "Citizenship Service Learning: Becoming Citizens by Assisting Immigrants," *PS: Political Science and Politics*, September 1998, 562-567; Glenn Beamer, "Service Learning: What's a Political Scientist Doing in Yonkers?" *PS: Political Science and Politics*, September 1998, 557-561; Vincent L. Marando and Mary Beth Melchior, "On Site, Not Out of Mind: The Role of Experiential Learning in the Political Science Doctoral Program," *PS: Political Science and Politics*, December 1997, 723-728; Harry C. Boyte, "Civic Education as

Public Leadership Development," *PS: Political Science and Politics*, December 1993, 763-769; George D. Kuh, John H. Schuh, Elizabeth J. Whitt and Associates, *Involving Colleges: Successful Approaches to Fostering Student Learning and Development Outside the Classroom*, San Francisco: Jossey Bass, 1991. See also the bibliography provided in Gorham (1992), as well as the websites of the National Center for Experiential Education (http://www.nsee.org/) and the American Association for Higher Education Service-Learning Project (http://www.aahe.org/).

10. In the fall 1998 one student in my honors seminar in social theory took it upon himself to investigate the development and institutional structure of the honors program at Loyola University. Not only did he teach the students in the class (and me) a great deal about the program, but he provided a great service to the program itself. His written analysis and critique of the program was examined by the honors program director, and some of his recommendations were considered by the honors advisory board.

Appendix

The Drama of the Space of Appearance

In chapter 2 I argued that one way to view Hannah Arendt's conception of the space of appearance is as emerging from an understanding of classical Greek theater. This is certainly not the only way to perceive the space of appearance, for some have rooted it in the philosophy of *Existenz* she learned from Jaspers, others contend it is an idea learned from Nietzsche's theory of tragedy, and still others note its Heideggerian roots. Clearly, she developed the conception from a number of sources and most probably integrated all her learning in developing the conception.

But as a practical matter, by perceiving the space of appearance as a concept rooted in the theater of ancient Greece, we can better understand the plurality and flexibility inherent in the concept. I want to suggest in this appendix that disputes arising over the concept of the space of appearance can be, if not resolved, then accommodated within this classical conception. We can explain further why the concept is so controversial, so open to interpretation.

On the academic stage constructed out of the work of Arendt, we can observe different representations of the space of appearance. Contemporary political theorists have interpreted Arendt to have meant one thing or another, and have judged Arendt's work correctly and incorrectly at the same time—for the space of appearance is many different things. Like the theater, political space can be different things to different people, and thus resists categorization. Both stages and political spaces come in many different varieties; they are plural by nature, just like the actors who disclose themselves within them. I argue that contemporary theorists misrecognize this fact, because they forget that the theater, like politics, is plural by nature. Whether or not Arendt herself understood this fact is irrelevant to my argument, because at the very least it helps explain how different contemporary theorists can build a variety of conceptions of the space of appearance from her insights.

The first group of theorists characterizes the formal properties of the space of appearance. One set of these theorists borrows concepts from critical theory to examine the space of appearance. Arendt's space is termed "communicative" and is based on Habermas' argument that the power that holds the space together rests not on the instrumentalization of the will of individuals, but on "the formation of a *common* will in a communication directed to reaching agreement" (Habermas 1994, 212). Habermas notes that for Arendt power is an end in itself, and that totalitarianism "destroys the communicative structure in which alone power can originate" (216). Arendt also demonstrates that communicative power helped topple old regimes in both France and America in the late eighteenth century. Both Habermas and Martin Jay (Jay and Botstein 1978) argue that in dissociating the social from the political in these spaces, Arendt misinterprets Marx, cannot account for economic power, and cannot recognize that structural violence inheres in capitalist institutions. Moreover, she fails to recognize that in order to be creative men must often be violent (Jay and Botstein 1978, 360). Jay charges her with elitism and claims that she does not understand the economic issues underlying political spaces, such as worker councils. Jay notes that unlike Arendt, "Habermas has been keenly aware of the social preconditions which may make such a utopian communicative situation possible" (367), and in doing so understands more completely the conditions under which political freedom can be realized.[1]

Seyla Benhabib (1995) justifies empirically communicative spaces in Arendt's work by deploying critical theory. Through an analysis of *Rahel Varnhagen: The Life of a Jewish Woman*, Benhabib argues that Arendt unites public and private realms in the space of the salon. She finds in the salon "a curious space that is of the home yet public, that is dominated by women yet visited and frequented by men, that is highly mannered and egalitarian, and that is hierarchical toward the 'outsiders' and egalitarian toward its members" (14). The salon space was one where women could find "visibility and self-expression," where they could discover the "joy of communication," and where women could "search for friendship" and cultivate intimacy (17-18). The salon, Benhabib contends, is precisely that space where women could appear in patriarchal nineteenth century society, without the agonal struggles or displays that Arendt argued characterized classical public spaces. Yet they too were spaces that cultivated equality and association friendship through the power of communication between women, and between women and men. Benhabib interrogates the traditional definitions of the public realm and asks "where must [the modern public] sphere be located, if not in civic and associational society?" (20). For Benhabib, then, the space of appearance in modern times can be communicative, associational, and a locale for procedural debate. Critical theory thus describes Arendtian space as connective, as full, as constituted by citizens united by discourse.

Benhabib (1996) emphasizes the narrative character of this communication. She distinguishes Arendt's conception of action from Heidegger's by arguing that Arendt, following Aristotle's *Politics*, conceived of action as interaction, something Heidegger lacked (105; see also Taminiaux 1996, 218). For Heidegger the space of appearance does not have a sense of "acting-with," and Arendt can account for Being as *Mitsein*, and not (merely) *Dasein*. This requires a narrative model of action—action embedded in a web of relationships and enacted stories, where individuals are with each other by sharing stories with others, and by inviting others to be part of their story (125ff). Benhabib makes clear that this is not simply reaching understanding among conversation partners, but also contrasts it with the agonal model of action I describe below. Narrative action demands a space of appearance, but this space need not be public (127)—for example, Rahel Varnhagen's salon.[2] In contrast, agonal action demands a public space, which citizens access only episodically and which forms out of a space of appearance "only under very specific historical and institutional conditions" (127). Politics, though, is "a certain quality of the life of speech and action . . . characterized by the willingness to give reasons in public, to entertain points of view and interests, even when they contradict one's own, and by the attempt to transform the dictates of self-interest into a common public goal" (146). Thus, whether as narration or communication, politics is a (sometimes conflictual) discourse that binds communities. Such community-building is ultimately rooted in Arendt's "anthropological universalism," the fact that "we are creatures immersed in a condition of plurality" (195). Such an account presupposes the sort of respect and civility that I have described in chapter 2.

In contrast to critical theory's characterization, a few theorists have emphasized Arendt's aesthetic coloring of the space of appearance. Bonnie Honig, for instance, describes the space of appearance as agonal, and the citizens who appear as creating their identities by acting.

> [The political actors] momentary engagement in action in the public realm engenders identities that are lodged forever in the stories told of their heroic performances by the spectators who witness them. Prior to or apart from action, this self has no identity; it is fragmented, discontinuous, indistinct, and most certainly uninteresting (Honig 1995, 140).

The space of appearance unites the self according to Honig, not necessarily the community. By acting (heroically), the individual quiets the site of what had been previously one of struggle and achieves an identity that is performative production. Yet in doing so, action also disrupts, for the selves who are now identified do so in contrast or in conflict with other selves. The citizen defines his identity in struggle with other citizens defining their identities. Thus, the *space* of appearance is not fundamentally associative or communicative, but disruptive. "Tormented by inner conflicts in the private realm, the self is released from its cycles of ordinariness by the rupture that is action. The self as subject is disrupted and the rupture creates the space for the emergence of the actor and his heroic identity" (Honig 1993, 117). The space is created out of rupture and one that permits the expression of civic identity by creating spaces between citizens. The space does not unite citizens, but separates them. In this way, action is an event, "an agonistic disruption of the ordinary sequence of things that makes way for novelty and distinction, a site of resistance of the irresistible, a challenge to the normalizing rules that seek to constitute, govern, and control various behaviors" (Honig 1995, 146). In this sense action politicizes spaces of appearance, even those spaces that Arendt had considered private. Honig subsequently criticizes Benhabib's analysis of the salon and suggests that these were sites of gossip, intrigue, and competition, and not merely communicative competence.

Dana Villa (1992a and 1996) argues that Arendt follows Nietzsche in characterizing the space of appearance as agonal, and thus aesthetic.[3] Action is performance, and as such is "self-contained, as immanently valuable in its greatness or beauty" (1992a, 276). Action is "end-constitutive"—"its goal does not stand apart from the process dominating it at every point, but is rather formed in the course of the 'performance' itself" (1996, 32). Theorists have traditionally distinguished Arendt's notion as being either heroic or deliberative (Kateb 1977; Passerin d'Entreves 1994, 152-154; Fuss 1979; Dallmayr 1984), but Villa argues that these are really "two moments in the theorization of self-contained action" (1992a, 279).[4] The principle that free action demands virtuosity renders political action contingent, phenomenal, and plural, and such qualities permit the actor to "gather together and display [the] uniqueness" of the self that would otherwise be dispersed or fragmented (282). Acting glorifies appearance and endows the world with meaning, and the self with identity, that without a space for action they would lack.

In this sense, Villa shares Honig's argument that action identifies citizens, creates their identity, but only where citizens struggle to do so. The site of this Nietzschean struggle is the space of appearance. Arendt "tames the agon," Villa argues, by presenting political judgment as taste, and by "reintroducing the connection between plurality and deliberation, by showing how the activity of judgment can, potentially, reveal to an audience what they have in common in the process of articulating their differences" (298). What they have in common is debate, not common purpose or consensus. Deliberation, then, unites individuals in the space of appearance and must do so for Arendt because she is a lover of the world. Arendt wants action-as-performance to illuminate the world through common sense, and thus breaks from Nietzsche's desire for the performance artist to overcome the world. In practice, such performing action is exemplified in "all speech that serves to preserve a constitution from internal or external erosion" (Villa 1996, 38). Political speech is always about itself, "in the sense that its primary concern much always be the health of the public sphere and the particular way of being together it makes possible" (41). So the content of political speech is always secondary to its form.

Both the critical theorists and the aesthetic theorists highlight either side of Arendt's dual conception of the formal space of appearance as I have described it. Either the space is associational and connective or it is disruptive and dissociable.[5] Space is either full or empty, it either unites citizens (through communication) or distances them (through struggle). Yet the genius of Arendt lies in her insight that spaces of appearance can be both simultaneously. Both the critical and aesthetic theorists declare that Arendt's theory is one based on pluralism, but in highlighting one side or the other they seem to forget its profound implications. Plural spaces mean that citizens can make their appearances in various forms, in various ways.[6] They can struggle *and* communicate, distance themselves *and* gather themselves together, at different times and simultaneously. Some spaces are sites of communicative deliberation, others of agonal struggle, and still others of agonal communication. This is why Arendt's theory is appropriate for social and political science, for it recognizes empirically a variety of spaces, seemingly different, but all permitting citizens to appear, and men and women to act. Such analysis is possible if we remember that Arendt uses the metaphor of the Greek theater to describe political spaces. Theatrical spaces are also plural. They come in many different varieties; stage many different plays; house many different actors, artists, and performers; and possess different formal properties. There are different types of stages and staging, thus rendering individual theaters plural.[7]

Arendt's commentators have also divided themselves on the substance of the space of appearances, namely the role and definition of the citizenry. Some have argued that Arendtian spaces are to be filled with a political elite, citizens who emphasize a collective tradition and look to the past for foundation. Others contend that, on the contrary, Arendt argues for participatory democracy, and political space is to be filled with active, equal citizens who intend to transform, in a revolutionary fashion, government and the public realm. I will argue that both conceptions are compatible with Arendt's dramaturgical understanding of the space of appearance.

In the 1970s Arendt's conception of the space of appearance and political action was termed elitist, and often conservative (Canovan 1974, Rich 1979, Kateb 1977, Parekh 1981, see also Levin 1979). Focusing on political space as agonal, a number of theorists claimed that Arendt reserved politics for a select few, and that those few participants were to mimic a fundamentally traditional, patriarchal public realm, the Greek polis. Feminists criticized her because she focused on classical public spaces, male spaces glorifying Greek hero-worship and because she ignored the contributions women made to the public realm. Participatory democrats claim that she forgets or ignores that councils, for instance, are public spaces created by the poor and dispossessed, the *animal laborans*—those who cannot possess the distinction and passion for excellence necessary to act publicly (Alejandro 1993, 176). Thus Arendt restricts political action to a (self-chosen) few and ties that action into a classical quest for excellence.

More recently, however, theorists have begun to characterize Arendt as a radical democrat and have appropriated the space of appearance as a participatory one (Isaac 1994 and 1996, Knauer 1992, Ring 1991, Passerin d'Entreves 1994, Canovan 1992, and Hinchman 1984). Many of these arguments derive from Arendt's analysis of council democracy (Arendt 1965, Sitton 1994). Councils are democratic spaces based territorially, organized around the principle of equality, autonomous, federated, and constituted by a self-selected political elite. Arendt noted that such councils are found in and around revolutions, for instance the Hungarian revolution of 1956 (Arendt 1958a), and the Jeffersonian ward system proposed during and after the American Revolution (Arendt 1965). She has been criticized for misunderstanding the economic nature of conciliar democracy (Sitton 1994, Wolin 1994), but praised for her commitment to public participation in politics.

Jeffrey Isaac (1994) praises her as radical and argues that those who term Arendt conservative do not understand the meaning of her term elite. A political elite is one "insulated from the many," not one that rules over others, and so is an "oasis" of public freedom (158). In the face of mass conformity, active citizens can form their own "elite" by providing public spaces where those who choose to enter can help create and maintain freedom. Thus councils are spaces of appearance, constituted by a self-selected citizenry, that break up mass society and counter its homogenizing tendencies (160). Moreover, her critique of parties and representative systems in *On Revolution* (Arendt 1965) further indicates Arendt's commitment to democratic politics. Isaac employs Arendt's analysis to explain, and justify, the Charter 77 movement in the former Czechoslovakia (163), and argues that feminists, environmentalists, consumer groups, religiously based action committees, and community development organizations exemplify spaces of appearance in contemporary American politics (165). The agonistic character of public spaces does not suggest "a mystique of heroic sacrifice" but rather a "conception of civic initiative that also can affirm basic human rights and dignities" (Isaac 1996, 65). Thus Arendt's theory can be applied to cases of international human rights, and organizations such as Amnesty International or the Helsinki Citizens' Assembly (Isaac 1996, 71).

I contend that spaces of appearance are both conservative and radical, elitist and participatory, and can be so at different times and simultaneously. Political space, given its plural nature (itself based on, among other things,[8] the theatrical model), differ from each other, and can be internally diverse as well. Consequently, given the circumstances, it is possible for the elite and "commoners" to create public spaces with the intention of instituting change. For instance, as I argue in chapter 6, the European Community was founded by both popular and elite groups who, working within their respective public spheres of influence, helped further the cause of a united Europe after World War II. It is also possible to appreciate the Environmentalist movement as catalyzed by radical and conservative groups seeking to transform public awareness of the Earth but with different ends in mind. What characterizes both groups is a commitment to action (Gundersen 1995).

I would like to represent the positions I have outlined so far:

Spaces of Appearance

Substance	Form	
	Agonal	**Associational**
Elitist	Jean Monnet's Action Committee	Rahel Varnhagen's Salon
Participatory	Alliance Quebec	Public Citizen, Inc.

I have delineated both the formal and substantive dimensions of the space of appearance as contemporary interpreters of Arendt's theory have understood her. I have also inserted "representative" or "typical" examples of political action that I have already mentioned in the text, corresponding to these dimensions.[9] To refresh the reader's memory, Jean Monnet's Action Committee (for a United States of Europe), founded in 1955, represented an agonistic space created by an elite for the purposes of transforming European public space (Winand 1994; Monnet 1978). Rahel Varnhagen's salon, as described by Seyla Benhabib, was an association of citizens of a particular class and status ("hierarchical to the outsiders") who created a space for women to act publicly. Alliance Quebec is a people's movement for the defense of anglophone rights in Quebec and attempts to raise the identity of English Quebecers by publicizing an oppositional stance to the Parti Quebecois government. Public Citizen is the organization founded by Ralph Nader whose purpose is to encourage the public to press for administrative reform (through the Center for Responsive Law) and to create a space for all consumers to act politically in the United States.

These political spaces typify the specific dimensions that contemporary theorists have circumscribed, and all these political action groups "count" as spaces of appearance because Arendt recognizes the plural nature of the space of appearance. Jean Monnet's Action Committee was restricted to a few individuals, but can be considered an agonistic space because it attempted to transform elite European politics in the process. The members viewed themselves as "good," even "great," Europeans who transcended nationalist or partisan identities in order to work for a new kind of (elite) European politics. In the context of post-war high politics—that is, on that particular stage—the Action Committee created a kind of freedom. In contrast, Nader's organization opens itself up to all, and makes no pretensions to establishing new regimes or in pursuing glory. In the context of late twentieth century American politics, it encourages citizens to deliberate on consumer issues, and offers a place where citizens can check the power of the pharmaceutical, utility, and automobile industries as it attempts to educate the general public. Within its "stage," Public

Citizen encourages action and the maintenance of civic freedom. The form and substance of both organizations differ quite radically, but given the different stages in which they have appeared, both exemplify Arendtian politics.

I want to go further, however, and suggest that all these political formations very often effect the different dimensions I have outlined here. I have already noted Bonnie Honig's observation that the nineteenth century salon could be a space of communicative power between women, but also a space of gossip and intrigue, one based on agonal struggle and display. Similarly, Alliance Quebec defies the Parti Quebecois government while it tries to encourage discussion of the issue of anglophone rights. It does so by both extending its membership, and publicizing its positions, so that more individuals can understand the plight of the anglophone Quebecer. In so doing, the organization encourages discourse on the language issue both within Quebec and in Canada generally.[10] The members of Alliance Quebec thus participate in both an agonal and an associational politics. Finally, Ralph Nader's campaign for president in 1996 reflects the agonal space he has tried to craft, in order to communicate the issues of Public Citizen and the Green Party to the citizens of the United States, and identify supporters. Again, the plural stages of appearance circumscribe the form and substance of political action and offer opportunities for actors to express themselves heroically and communicate at the same time. All of these movements have at least one thing in common—the creation of civility, the establishment of citizenship. But, as Arendt herself noted (and as I mentioned in chapter 2), civility connects and separates people, at times simultaneously. This duality, in some instances this paradox, is something we ought to expect when we try to change the world, or study it.

This duality is recognized by Mary Dietz in a recent essay (Dietz 1996). Dietz roots the concept of the space of appearance in *The Origins of Totalitarianism* (Arendt 1973)[11] and argues that Arendt's confrontation with its horrors explain the complex and plural nature of that space. Arendt was faced with the problem of relating the reality of Nazism and the Holocaust objectively without stripping them of their evil. She also had to represent the "factual territory" that totalitarianism created for Germans and Jews, a territory of "fanatical hatred" and one institutionalized by incomprehensible spaces— concentrations camps and gas chambers. Dietz argues that it is the space of Auschwitz that Arendt imagines when she reconstitutes spaces of appearance. Auschwitz was an abyss, the space emptied of all moral and political concern. Those who think about political spaces after Auschwitz, those who pull back from that abyss, peer into "an empty space where there are no longer nations and peoples but only individuals for whom it is now not of much consequence what the majority of peoples, or even the majority of one's own people, happens to think at any given moment" (Arendt, quoted in Dietz, 5; see also Arendt 1968, 13, 16). The problem for citizens after Auschwitz is how to repair this empty space and reconstruct a space where both Germans and Jews can live together. This is her purpose in *The Human Condition*, a book that attempts to "deal with the aftermath of hell," repair political spaces, and permit citizens to live together, after the radical emptiness of the concentration camps.

According to Dietz, then, her conception of political action and the space of appearance in *The Human Condition* was a "direct and personal" attempt at offering Germans and Jews a "way back from the abyss" and a way to be brought together (6-7). Dietz analogizes this book to Nietzsche's "transfiguring evening glow," an act of "creating a luminous and healing illusion . . . that allows for a kind of convalescence" (8). Arendt sought to create a "powerful, iridescent counterimage" that would disrupt the memory of the radical incurable evil of the concentration camps. This image was the space of appearance, and it is with this understanding of both political history and Arendt's personal and literary history that we can appreciate the power of that image. The space of appearance is Arendt's response, indeed her scream, to the voices in the abyss.[12]

Dietz defends her analysis here by examining carefully Arendt's distinctions between labor and work. As we know from Arendt's analysis both labor and work, held as organizing principles for society, dehumanize men. A laboring society reduces men to automatic processes and compulsive repetitions, while a fabricating society instrumentalizes and objectifies men. The only place where both extremes occurred simultaneously—where labor became routinized deathlessness and work became the objectified violation of life—was in the concentration camps. Thus, in affirming the existential superiority of action over labor and work, Dietz does not believe that she was extolling the glories of heroic sacrifice, or confronting death in a Nietzschean fashion; rather she was countering, quite specifically, the unreality, the abyss, of the concentration camps, the place where inmates were both dead and alive at the same time. Concentration camps emptied their spaces of men, Arendt attempted to conceive of spaces filled with them, in all their diversity. So Arendt emphasized the "who," not the "what," of persons in the space of appearance, as a confirmation that they do indeed exist, and can cherish their distinctiveness.

Dietz's insight here is invaluable. For she recognizes that for Arendt the only place where people cannot appear, where they cannot fill empty space, where they are emptied by a space, is the concentration camps. Thus the space of appearance is the "countermemory" to the non-space of those camps. But, and Arendt is consistently clear on this point, these spaces, as "luminous glows," as positive assertions of the identities of persons, as collected persons acting, are plural—they are everything the concentration camp was not, and they are, and cannot be, the concentration camp itself. In the world after Auschwitz, Arendt seems to be saying, *any* place people can act politically will permit them to appear. This means that any stage, except the concentration camp (or other analogous, incomprehensible stages), is *potentially* a space of appearance. Not all stages may permit actors to disclose themselves and appear as unique, but they offer the possibility of action. Concentration camps do not, and cannot.

But in the modern, post-Auschwitz world citizens must be concerned with how stages are constructed, and how people appear in them, for they are important where individuals are permitted to display themselves. Political spaces challenge the abyss of totalitarianism, but they also function as theaters. Yet Arendt might lament conditions of modernity that stage political space in such a way that actors, audience, and stagehands cannot initiate action, portray themselves, or meaningfully associate with others. Where political spaces are representational or where they are constructed spectacles, those spaces no longer behave like the classical theaters Arendt envisioned. For representational spaces or constructed spectacles do not permit initiative, creativity, or spontaneity. Arendt discussed the problem of political representation in *On Revolution* (1965, 236-239),[13] and we have been considering them in light of the problems of theatrical, or spatial, representation. Not only does political representation preclude direct action, but state institutions can also inhibit self-presentation and participation. In chapter 1 I raised the question of how one can participate in civic space where that civic space has been constructed as a spectacle, where the space itself is representational.[14] How do citizens truly appear in a space that is already enframed?[15] In this framework, the "transfiguring evening glow" begins to dim.

Notes

1. Heather and Stolz (1979) defend Arendt from the charges of critical theorists. They claim that Habermas misunderstands Arendt in a number of ways: (1) Arendt searches for rational standards, not communicative power or unending discourse. (2) She rejects the classical tradition because she dissociates philosophy from politics, thus the joys of political life have to do with the free and equal association of citizens, not philosophical or communicative truth. (3) Arendt's own political experience of totalitarianism sensitized her to the problems posed by collective action and human freedom, and she recognizes its role in the collapse of political space. In doing so she reminds us that political activity is necessary and essential for freedom to appear, and so is not the elitist that (and is more "radical" than) the critical theorists are willing to admit. Heather and Stolz conclude that political action "fashions among the participants a new public space" and comes together through power and association (17), and in doing so "save" Arendt for critical theory.

2. And so Benhabib (1996) reinterprets Arendt's notions of the social and the political. Politics may involve a transformation of the social sphere in order to achieve "enlarged mentality" (145-146). Benhabib adds that Arendt's notion of the private deepens her conception of a human life—for the home "provides the space that protects, nurtures, and makes the individual fit to appear in the public realm" (213). This is part of her larger project of reconstructing Arendt's distinctions for feminist and democratic theory.

3. In another essay, Villa critiques the perspective of critical theory by claiming that communicative space ultimately presupposes plurality and so permits a politics based on respect for difference (1992b). See also Villa 1996, 67-72. Moreover, "from Arendt's point of view, plurality is not just a condition, but also an *achievement* of political action and speech; these activities give public expression to difference" (717).

4. Deliberative speech is agonistic (Villa 1996, 30-40, 52, 56). "Where [our commitment to the world] animates debate and disagreement, the talk that results is genuinely political; it rises above the mere clash of interests or the willful assertion of identity. Thus, the deliberative politics she champions is a contentious, agonistic, and

often polemical exchange of opinion, one that stands in sharp contrast to the stately application of *phronesis*" (Villa 1996, 52). This is presumably in contrast to a Habermasian emphasis on practical reason. Villa later (56) argues that the "performative dimension has priority over the deliberative and dialogical." I have tried to argue that both positions seem reasonable if we take seriously the theatrical metaphor Arendt employs. Villa also argues that Habermas and Benhabib want to eliminate the performative dimension of political action by separating it from it deliberative dimension (71). In re-framing her argument in terms of narrative, and not communication, I think Benhabib (1996, cf., 125ff) recognizes that the two are not always distinct. On her part, Benhabib complains that Villa's argument "underestimates [Arendt's] major contribution to twentieth century philosophies of action, which is the radical discovery of the link between action, narration, and interpretation" (1996, 197). Though Villa claims that the deliberative, rational dimension must be cast alongside the performative dimension (1996, 71). I confess, that I do not fully understand the nature of this dispute, given what I assume to be Arendt's profound grasp of the classical world, and especially Greek theater. I would argue that both positions can be informed by examining the practice of classical theater underlying Arendt's theory of the space of appearance.

5.   Peter Fuss (1979) reconciles these positions by claiming that politics possesses two dimensions—substantive, filled with personal initiative, and procedural, as the realm of decision-making that accommodates different positions. I would argue, however, that both the agonal and accommodational dimensions of politics are formal dimensions, because politics as public display of the self is a different end than politics as the constitution of society or community. Fuss himself doubts that his scheme "will wash" (173) and suggests that the citizen must instead cultivate representative thinking, "the ability to view any given situation from as many different points of view as possible in order to arrive at the most informed opinion" (174). While this is undeniably important, it is possible only because the space of appearance itself is potentially not one thing, but many things. The plurality of spaces of appearance make the task of representative thinking even more difficult.

6.   According to Hanna Pitkin (1972), in the public space we find "the kind of simultaneous awareness of innumerable perspectives on a shared public enterprise we have been discussing, and in the common experience of participating in reconciling these perspectives for common action" (217).

7.   The case might also be made in comparing various types of theater. Classical theater, Elizabethan theater, dinner theater, street theater—these are diverse forms of theater all of which permit actors to act and identities to be performed. Yet the communicative competence engendered by classical theater (as the audience communicates with the actors and with each other), differs from the disruptive performances of street actors (who coerce individuals into expressing themselves, and thus their identities). And the agonal displays of classical actors contrast with the attempts by street performers to associate with the audience, and have members of that audience associate with each other.

8.   For instance, classical rhetoric. Remer (1996) and Vickers (1988) both note that classical rhetoricians created rules based on decorum—the "understanding that content (*res*) cannot be separated from form (*verba*), which is to say that human communication always occurs within a given context" (Remer 1996, 14). (Note that the word for speech content, *res*, is the same as that for space.) Decorum requires prudential knowledge which itself demands "an understanding of human nature" and an obligation on the part of orators to "familiarize themselves with the multiplicity of human personalities" (Remer

1996, 15; see also Vickers 1988, 24-25, 344). So rules of classical rhetoric also rested on the plurality of humankind. Peter Arnott (1991) recognizes the close affinities between classical rhetoric and drama (51-53). Benhabib (1996) suggests that Arendt's conception might also have been influenced by Heidegger's conception of *Erschlossenheit*, or "being-as-disclosure," which derives from Aristotle's notion of *aletheia*, that truth is disclosure. Though this conception returns us to the importance of classical poetics.

9.   Though, as will become clear, I believe the examples to be deceptive, because each can ultimately exemplify another ideal type. The dramaturgical theory of the space of appearance is conceptually powerful and so can account for how these examples appear simultaneously in a single space.

10.   And even in the United States—members of Alliance Quebec have brought their grievances to both Wall Street and members of Congress (who recently held hearings on the issue).

11.   Richard King (1984) argues that Arendt's theory of political space need not have followed her analysis of totalitarianism (236), but he recognizes that "the world she constructed in *Origins* was an antiworld" (240). Dietz, I think more correctly, would characterize the camps as not anti-world, but anti-space or anti-appearance. The world, Arendt reminds us in her essay on Lessing, "can form only in the interspaces between men in all their variety" (Arendt 1968, 31). King connects her early and middle thought in her essay "Ideology and Terror," published in 1953 and later appended to the second edition of *The Origins of Totalitarianism* (244). Barnouw (1990) and Benhabib (1996) also emphasize the centrality of her first published book to her later work.

12.   A related interpretation of the connection between Arendt's first two books in English is made by Paul Ricoeur in his preface to the French edition to *The Human Condition* (Ricoeur 1991, 43-66). In it he points out that Arendt concluded in *The Origins of Totalitarianism* that the hypothesis that "everything is possible" led to totalitarian domination and destruction. That is, totalitarian regimes are fundamentally grounded in constant social and political transformation. This realization, he believes, led her to wonder what creates a non-totalitarian universe, one that would not lead to constant change and disruption. From this, Ricoeur concludes, Arendt began to study the durable nature of the universe. And so she studied the permanent conditions of human existence—labor, work, and action—that could give rise to humane and civilized politics. Ricoeur frames these studies as problems of time—its malleability and short duration in the former, its stability and long duration in the latter—but in doing so connects both books to the same theme, and like Dietz, sees one as the inverse of the other.

13.   Arendt argues that political life demands discussion and deliberation, and representative democracy cannot provide the plurality of perspectives necessary for this. It disrupts proper opinion formation on political topics. Moreover, the vote is a private act which does not require political experience or thoughtful opinion, so representatives cannot create a meaningful relation between the individual and the body politic (see Sitton 1994).

14.   In the words of Dana Villa (1992b): "The Arendtian public space is a space of genuine public appearances, of signs whose play and self-referentiality is restricted by their being 'seen and heard by everyone'...Postmodernity, on the other hand, has left the 'order of appearance' behind: 'reality' (including the reality of appearances Arendt wants to preserve) is presently generated as a simulation effect" (717).

15.   Dana Villa (1992b) recognizes that Arendt and Foucault "are both concerned to tell the story of how an essentially theatrical space...is colonized by a new form of disciplinary or 'socializing' power, a power that substitutes an institutionally dispersed

and normalizing regime of panoptic visibility for a centralized space in which *action* is seen and heard by all" (718). While I disagree that Arendt has a "panoptic" vision of modernity, both critique modern, theatrical/political space as necessarily representational. Both Arendt and Foucault realize that modern politics is staged, and that such staging, rather than permitting free, spontaneous activity, directs actors to deliver their lines as they have been written and position themselves as the director requires.

References

Abensour, Miguel et al., eds. 1996. *Politique et Pensée: Colloque Hannah Arendt*. Paris: Payot.

Abramson, Jeffrey. 1994. *We, The Jury: The Jury System and the Ideal of Democracy*. New York: Basic Books.

Adenauer, Konrad. 1966. *Memoirs 1945-53*. Beate Ruhm von Oppen, trans. Chicago: Henry Regnery.

Alejandro, Roberto. 1993. *Hermeneutics, Citizenship, and the Public Sphere*. Albany: State University of New York Press.

Anderson, Charles W. 1993. *Prescribing the Life of the Mind*. Madison: University of Wisconsin Press.

Arendt, Hannah. 1957. "History and Immortality." *Partisan Review* 24, 1 (winter): 11-35.

———. 1958a. "Totalitarian Imperialism: Reflections on the Hungarian Revolution." *Journal of Politics* 20, 1: 5-43.

———. 1958b. *The Human Condition*. Garden City, N.Y.: Doubleday.

———. 1961. *Between Past and Future: Six Exercises in Political Thought*. Cleveland: Meridian Books.

———. 1964a. "*The Deputy*: Guilt by Silence?" In Eric Bentley, ed., *The Storm over* The Deputy. New York: Grove Press, 85-94.

———. 1964b. *Eichmann in Jerusalem: A Report on the Banality of Evil*. New York: Penguin Books.

———. 1965. *On Revolution*. New York: Penguin Books.

———. 1968a. "The Conquest of Space and the Stature of Man." In *Between Past and Future: Eight Exercises in Political Thought*. New York: Viking Press, 265-280.

———. 1968b. *Men in Dark Times*. San Diego: Harcourt Brace and Company.

———. 1968c. "Truth and Politics." In *Between Past and Future: Eight Exercises in Political Thought*. New York: Viking Press, 227-264.

———. 1970. *On Violence*. San Diego: Harcourt Brace Jovanovich.

———. 1973. *The Origins of Totalitarianism*. New York: Harcourt Brace Jovanovich.

———. 1978. *The Life of the Mind. Volume 1*. San Diego: Harcourt Brace.

———. 1979. "On Hannah Arendt." In Melvyn Hill, ed., *Hannah Arendt: The Recovery of the Public World*. New York: St. Martin's Press, 301-339.

———. 1982. *Lectures on Kant's Political Philosophy*. Ronald Beiner, ed., Chicago: University of Chicago Press.

———. 1994. *Essays in Understanding, 1930-1954*. Jerome Kohn, ed., New York: Harcourt Brace.

Arnott, Peter D. 1991. *Public and Performance in the Greek Theatre*. London: Routledge.

Bachelard, Gaston. 1964. *The Poetics of Space*. Maria Jolas, trans. Boston: Beacon Press.

Baird, George. 1995. *The Space of Appearance*. Cambridge: MIT Press.

Barber, Benjamin. 1984. *Strong Democracy*. Berkeley: University of California Press.

Barnouw, Dagmar. 1990. *Visible Spaces: Hannah Arendt and the German-Jewish Experience*. Baltimore: Johns Hopkins University Press.

Barraclough, Geoffrey. 1963. *European Unity in Thought and Action*. Oxford: Basil Blackwell.

Barthes, Roland. 1967. *Writing Degree Zero*. New York: Hill and Wang.

———. *S/Z*. 1974. Richard Miller, trans. New York: Hill and Wang.

Beacham, Richard C. 1992. *The Roman Theatre and its Audience*. Cambridge: Harvard University Press.

Beatty, Joseph. 1994. "Thinking and Moral Considerations: Socrates and Arendt's Eichmann." In Lewis P. Hinchman and Sandra K. Hinchman, eds., *Hannah Arendt: Critical Essays*. Albany: State University of New York Press, 57-74.

Beiner, Ronald. 1982. "Interpretive Essay." In Hannah Arendt, *Lectures on Kant's Political Philosophy*, Ronald Beiner, ed., Chicago: University of Chicago Press.

Bellah, Robert et al., 1985. *Habits of the Heart*. New York: Vintage.

Beloff, Max. 1957. *Europe and the Europeans: An International Discussion*. London: Chatto and Windus.

———. 1963. *The United States and the Unity of Europe*. Washington D.C.: Brookings.

Benhabib, Seyla. 1988. "Judgment and the Moral Foundations of Politics in Arendt's Thought." *Political Theory* 16, no. 1: 29-51.

———. 1995. "The Pariah and Her Shadow: Hannah Arendt's Biography of Rahel Varnhagen." *Political Theory* 23, no. 1: 5-24.

———. 1996. *The Reluctant Modernism of Hannah Arendt*. Thousand Oaks, Calif.: Sage.

Berger, Peter L. 1963. *Invitation to Sociology: A Humanistic Perspective*. Garden City, N.Y.: Doubleday.

Bernstein, Richard J. 1986. *Philosophical Profiles: Essays in a Pragmatic Mode.* Philadelphia: University of Pennsylvania Press.

Bickford, Susan. 1995. "In the Presence of Others: Arendt and Anzaldùa on the Paradox of Public Appearance." In Bonnie Honig, ed., *Feminist Interpretations of Hannah Arendt.* University Park: Pennsylvania State University Press, 313-335.

Biskowski, Lawrence J. 1993. "Practical Foundations for Political Judgment: Arendt on Action and World." *Journal of Politics* 55, no. 4: 867-887.

Blaut, J. M. 1993. *The Colonizer's Model of the World: Geographical Diffusionism and Eurocentric History.* New York: Guilford Press.

Bloom, Allan. 1987. *The Closing of the American Mind.* New York: Simon and Schuster.

Brightman, Carol, ed., 1995. *Between Friends: The Correspondence of Hannah Arendt and Mary McCarthy, 1949-1975.* New York: Harcourt Brace.

Brinkley, Douglas, and Clifford Hackett, eds., 1991. *Jean Monnet: The Path to European Unity.* New York: St. Martin's Press.

Brookfield, Stephen D. 1995. *Becoming a Critically Reflective Teacher.* San Francisco: Jossey Bass.

Buckley, William F. 1990. *Gratitude: Reflections on What We Owe Our Country.* New York: Random House.

Burgess, Michael. 1989. *Federalism and European Union: Political Ideas, Influences, and Strategies in the European Community, 1972-1987.* London: Routledge.

Canovan, Margaret. 1974. *The Political Thought of Hannah Arendt.* London: Dent and Sons.

———. 1992. *Hannah Arendt: A Reinterpretation of Her Political Thought.* Cambridge: Cambridge University Press.

Carter, W. Horsfall. 1966. *Speaking European: The Anglo-Continental Cleavage.* London: George Allen and Unwin.

Chamberlin, William Henry. 1947. *The European Cockpit.* New York: Macmillan.

Cohen, Raymond. 1987. *Theatre of Power: The Art of Diplomatic Signalling.* London: Longman.

Collin, Françoise, ed. 1986. *Hannah Arendt.* Paris: Les Cahiers du Grif.

Costa Bona, Enrica. 1988. "L'Italia e L'Integrazione Europea: Aspetti Storici e Diplomatici (1947-1957)." *Il Politico* LIII, no. 3: 467-481.

Coudenhove-Kalergi, Count Richard. 1926. *Pan Europe.* New York: Alfred A. Knopf.

———. 1953. *An Idea Conquers the World.* London: Hutchinson.

Courtine-Denamy, Sylvie. 1997. *Hannah Arendt.* Paris: Hachette.

Dallmayr, Fred R. 1984. *Polis and Praxis: Exercises in Contemporary Political Theory.* Cambridge: MIT Press.

de Rougemont, Denis. 1965. *The Meaning of Europe.* Alan Braley, trans. New York: Stein and Day.

Dietz, Mary G. 1994. "'The Slow Boring of Hard Boards': Methodical Thinking and the Work of Politics." *American Political Science Review* 88, no. 4: 873-886.

———. 1996. "A Transfiguring Evening Glow: Hannah Arendt's Space of Appearances in the Presence of Dark Times." Paper prepared for *Hannah Arendt Twenty Years Later: A German Jewess in the Age of Totalitarianism.* Conference at Harvard University, Cambridge, Massachusetts. March 22-23. Cited by permission of the author.

Disch, Lisa Jane. 1994. *Hannah Arendt and the Limits of Philosophy.* Ithaca: Cornell University Press.

Eaton, Judith S. 1991. *The Unfinished Agenda: Higher Education and the 1980s.* New York: MacMillan.

Edelman, Murray. 1964. *The Symbolic Uses of Politics.* Champaign. Illinois: University of Illinois Press.

———. 1988. *Constructing the Political Spectacle.* Chicago: University of Chicago Press.

Elon, Amos. 1997. "The Case of Hannah Arendt." *The New York Review of Books.* November 6: 25-29.

Euben, J. Peter. 1986. "Introduction." In J. Peter Euben, ed., *Greek Tragedy and Political Theory.* Berkeley: University of California Press, 1-41.

———. 1990. *The Tragedy of Political Theory: The Road Not Taken.* Princeton: Princeton University Press.

Finkielkraut, Alain. 1992. *Remembering in Vain: The Klaus Barbie Trial and Crimes Against Humanity.* Roxanne Lapidus with Sima Godfrey, trans. New York: Columbia University Press.

Florinsky, Michael T. 1955. *Integrated Europe?* New York: Macmillan.

Foucault, Michel. 1970. *The Order of Things: An Archaeology of the Human Sciences.* New York: Vintage.

Frampton, Kenneth. 1979. "The Status of Man and the Status of his Objects: A Reading of *The Human Condition.*" In Melvyn Hill, ed., *Hannah Arendt: The Recovery of the Public Realm.* New York: St. Martin's Press.

Fuss, Peter. 1979. "Hannah Arendt's Conception of Political Community." In Melvyn Hill, ed., *Hannah Arendt: Recovery of the Public World.* New York: St. Martin's Press.

Gillingham, John. 1991. *Coal, Steel, and the Re-Birth of Europe, 1945-1955: The Germans and French from Ruhr Conflict to Economic Community.* Cambridge: Cambridge University Press.

Gladwyn, Lord. 1966. *The European Idea.* London: Weidenfeld and Nicolson.

Glock, Charles Y., Gertrude J. Selznick, and Joe L. Spaeth. 1966. *The Apathetic Majority: A Study Based on Public Responses to the Eichmann Trial.* New York: Harper and Row.

Goffman, Erving. 1959. *The Presentation of Self in Everyday Life.* Garden City. New York: Doubleday.

———. 1971. *Relations in Public.* New York: Harper and Row.

Goldhill, Simon. 1990. "The Great Dionysia and Civic Ideology." In John J. Winkler and Froma I. Zeitlin, eds., *Nothing to do with Dionysos? Athenian Drama in its Social Context*. Princeton: Princeton University Press, 97-129.

Gorham, Eric. 1992. *National Service, Citizenship, and Political Education*. Albany: State University of New York Press.

———. 1993. "Democratic (Higher) Education: Inculcating Citizenship through Teaching at the University." *The Centennial Review* 37, no. 3: 605-627.

———. 1995. "Social Citizenship and its Fetters." *Polity* 28, no. 1 (fall): 25-47.

Gottsegen, Michael G. 1994. *The Political Thought of Hannah Arendt*. Albany: State University of New York Press.

Graham, Hugh Davis. 1989. "Structure and Governance in American Higher Education: Historical and Comparative Analysis in State Policy." *Journal of Policy History* 1, no. 1: 80-107.

Gray, J. Glenn. 1979. "The Abyss of Freedom—and Hannah Arendt." In Melvin Hill, ed., *Hannah Arendt: The Recovery of the Public World*. New York: St. Martin's Press.

Grotius Seminar. 1963. *Limits and Problems of European Integration: The Conference of May 30-June 2, 1961*. Proceedings and papers from the Grotius seminar. The Hague: Martinus Nijhoff.

Gundersen, Adolf. 1995. *The Environmental Promise of Democratic Deliberation*. Madison: University of Wisconsin Press.

Habermas, Jurgen. 1994. "Hannah Arendt's Communications Concept of Power." In Lewis P. Hinchman and Sandra K. Hinchman, eds., *Hannah Arendt: Critical Essays*. Albany: State University of New York Press, 211-229.

Hallstein, Walter. 1962. *United Europe: Challenge and Opportunity*. Cambridge: Harvard University Press.

Hansen, Phillip. 1993. *Hannah Arendt: Politics, History, and Citizenship*. Stanford, Calif.: Stanford University Press.

Hay, Denys. 1957. *Europe, the Emergence of an Idea*. Edinburgh: Edinburgh University Press.

Heather, Gerard P., and Matthew Stolz. 1979. "Hannah Arendt and the Problem of Critical Theory." *Journal of Politics* 41: 2-22.

Henderson, Jeffrey. 1990. "The *Demos* and the Comic Competition." in John J. Winkler and Froma I. Zeitlin, eds., *Nothing to do with Dionysos? Athenian Drama in its Social Context*. Princeton: Princeton University Press, 271-313.

Herriot, Edouard. 1930. *The United States of Europe*. Reginald J. Dingle, trans. New York: Viking.

Hinchman, Lewis P., and Sandra K. Hinchman. 1994. "Existentialism Politicized: Arendt's Debt to Jaspers." In Lewis P. and Sandra K. Hinchman, eds., *Hannah Arendt: Critical Essays*. Albany: State University of New York Press, 143-178.

Hinchman, Sandra K. 1984. "Common Sense and Political Barbarism in the Theory of Hannah Arendt." *Polity* 17, no. 2: 317-339.

Hoffman, Stanley. 1964. "Europe's Identity Crisis: Between the Past and America." *Daedalus*. No. 4 (fall): 1244-1297.

Hogan, Michael J. 1987. *The Marshall Plan: America, Britain, and the Reconstruction of Western Europe, 1947-1952*. Cambridge: Cambridge University Press.

Holborn, Hajo. 1951. *The Political Collapse of Europe*. New York: Knopf.

Honig, Bonnie. 1993. *Political Theory and the Displacement of Politics*. Ithaca: Cornell University Press.

————. 1995. "Toward an Agonistic Feminism: Hannah Arendt and the Politics of Identity." In Bonnie Honig, ed., *Feminist Interpretations of Hannah Arendt*. University Park: Pennsylvania State University Press, 135-166.

Hughes, H. Stuart. 1977. *Consciousness and Society: The Reorientation of European Social Thought, 1890-1930*. New York: Vintage.

Isaac, Jeffrey C. 1994. "Oases in the Desert: Hannah Arendt on Democratic Politics." *American Political Science Review* 88, no. 1: 156-168.

————. 1996. "A New Guarantee on Earth: Hannah Arendt on Human Dignity and the Politics of Human Rights." *American Political Science Review* 90, no. 1: 61-73.

Jay, Martin, and Leon Botstein. 1978. "Hannah Arendt: Opposing Views." *Partisan Review* XLV, no. 3: 348-380.

Kateb, George. 1977. "Freedom and Worldliness in the Thought of Hannah Arendt." *Political Theory* 5, no. 2: 141-182.

Keenan, Alan. 1994. "Promises. Promises: The Abyss of Freedom and the Loss of the Political in the Work of Hannah Arendt." *Political Theory* 22, no. 2: 297-322.

Kennan, George F. 1967. *Memoirs, 1925-1950*. Boston: Little Brown.

Kindleberger, Charles. 1987. *Marshall Plan Days*. Boston: Allen and Unwin.

King, Richard H. 1984. "Endings and Beginnings: Politics in Arendt's Early Thought. *Political Theory* 12, no. 2: 235-251.

Kirchheimer, Otto. 1961. *Political Justice: The Use of Legal Procedure for Political Ends*. Princeton. N.J.: Princeton University Press.

Knauer, James T. 1992. "Motive and Goal in Hannah Arendt's Concept of Political Action." In Joseph Losco and Leonard Williams, eds., *Political Theory: Classic Writings. Contemporary Views*. New York: St. Martin's Press, 636-648.

Knox, Bernard M. W. 1964. *The Heroic Temper: Studies in Sophoclean Tragedy*. Berkeley: University of California Press.

Kohler, Lotte, and Hans Saner, eds., 1992. *Hannah Arendt. Karl Jaspers: Correspondence, 1926-1969*. Robert and Rita Kimber, trans. San Diego: Harcourt Brace.

Kohr, Leopold. 1978. *The Breakdown of Nations*. New York: E. P. Dutton.

Lang, Berel. 1994. "Hannah Arendt and the Politics of Evil." In Lewis P. and Sandra K. Hinchman, eds., *Hannah Arendt: Critical Essays*. Albany: State University of New York Press, 41-54.

Lefort, Claude. 1988. *Democracy and Political Theory.* David Macey, trans. Minneapolis: University of Minnesota Press.

Levin, Martin. 1979. "On Animal Laborans and Homo Politicus in Hannah Arendt: A Note." *Political Theory* 7, no. 4: 521-531.

Ley, Graham. 1991. *A Short Introduction to the Ancient Greek Theater.* Chicago: University of Chicago Press.

Lindsay, Kenneth. 1960. *European Assemblies: The Experimental Period, 1949-1959.* London: Stevens and Sons.

Lipgens, Walter. 1982. *A History of European Integration. Volume 1. 1945-1947.* P. S. Falla and A. J. Ryder, trans. Oxford: Clarendon Press.

Longo, Oddone. 1990. "The Theater of the Polis." In John J. Winkler and Froma I. Zeitlin, eds., *Nothing to do with Dionysos? Athenian Drama in its Social Context.* Princeton: Princeton University Press, 12-19.

Losco, Joseph, and Leonard Williams, eds. 1992. *Political Theory: Classic Writings, Contemporary Views.* New York: St. Martin's Press.

Macmillan, Harold. 1969. *Tides of Fortune, 1945-1955.* London: Macmillan.

Malandrino, Corrado. 1988. "Fermenti Europeisti e Federalisti tra Guerra Mondiale e Primo Dopoguerra." *Il Politico* LIII, no. 3: 483-510.

Marjolin, Robert. 1989. *Architect of European Unity: Memoirs, 1911-1986.* London: Weidenfeld and Nicolson.

McKeon, Richard. 1973. *Introduction to Aristotle.* 2d ed. Chicago: University of Chicago Press.

Meier, Christian. 1993. *The Political Art of Greek Tragedy.* Andrew Webber, trans. Baltimore: Johns Hopkins University Press.

Miller, James. 1979. "The Pathos of Novelty: Hannah Arendt's Image of Freedom in the Modern World." In Melvyn Hill, ed., *Hannah Arendt: Recovery of the Public World.* New York: St. Martin's Press, 177-208.

Milward, Alan S. 1984. *The Reconstruction of Western Europe.* Berkeley: University of California Press.

———. 1992. *The European Rescue of the Nation-State.* Berkeley: University of California Press.

Mitchell, Timothy. 1988. *Colonising Egypt.* Cambridge: Cambridge University Press.

Monnet, Jean. 1978. *Memoirs.* Richard Mayne, trans. Garden City, N.Y.: Doubleday.

Moulakis, Athanasios. 1994. *Beyond Utility: Liberal Education for a Technological Age.* Columbia, Mo.: University of Missouri Press.

Nadler, Leonard, and Zeace Nadler. 1987. *The Comprehensive Guide to Successful Conferences and Meetings.* San Francisco: Jossey-Bass.

Nietzsche, Friedrich. 1993. *The Birth of Tragedy out of the Spirit of Music.* Shaun Whiteside, trans. London: Penguin.

Noelle-Neumann, Elisabeth. 1993. *The Spiral of Silence.* Chicago: University of Chicago Press.

Nussbaum, Martha C. 1997. *Cultivating Humanity: A Classical Defense of Reform in Liberal Education.* Cambridge: Harvard University Press.

Ober, Josiah, and Barry Strauss. 1990. "Drama. Political Rhetoric. and the Discourse of Athenian Democracy." In John J. Winkler and Froma I. Zeitlin, eds., *Nothing to do with Dionysos? Athenian Drama in its Social Context*. Princeton: Princeton University Press, 237-270.

Padel, Ruth. 1990. "Making Space Speak." In John J. Winkler and Froma I. Zeitlin, eds., *Nothing to do with Dionysos? Athenian Drama in its Social Context*. Princeton: Princeton University Press, 336-365.

Pangle, Thomas L. 1992. *The Ennobling of Democracy: The Challenge of the PostModern Age*. Baltimore: Johns Hopkins University Press.

Parekh, Bhikhu. 1981. *Hannah Arendt and the Search for a New Political Philosophy*. Atlantic Highlands, N.J.: Humanities Press International.

————. 1992. "Hannah Arendt." In Joseph Losco and Leonard Williams, eds., *Political Theory: Classic Writings, Contemporary Views*. New York: St. Martin's Press, 621-635.

Parri, F. et al. 1947. *Europa Federata*. Milano: Edizioni di Communità.

Passerin d'Entreves, Maurizio. 1994. *The Political Philosophy of Hannah Arendt*. London: Routledge.

Pickard-Cambridge, Arthur. 1968. *The Dramatic Festivals of Athens*. Oxford: Clarendon Press.

Pirro, Robert. 1996. *Putting the Imagination in Play for Critical and Connected Democratic Membership: Greek Tragedy and its Heroes in Hannah Arendt's Political Thought*. Ph.D. diss. University of California, Berkeley, 20-49.

Pitkin, Hanna Fenichel. 1972. *Wittgenstein and Justice*. Berkeley: University of California Press.

Rappard, William. 1930. *Uniting Europe: The Trend of International Cooperation since the War*. New Haven: Yale University Press.

Redfield, James. 1990. "Drama and Community: Aristophanes and Some of his Rivals." In John J. Winkler and Froma I. Zeitlin, eds., *Nothing to do with Dionysos? Athenian Drama in its Social Context*. Princeton: Princeton University Press, 314-335.

Rehm, Rush. 1992. *Greek Tragic Theatre*. London: Routledge.

Reichl, Alexander J. 1999. "Learning from St. Thomas: Community, Capital, and the Redevelopment of Public Housing in New Orleans." *Journal of Urban Affairs* 21, no. 2: 169-187.

Remer, Gary. 1996. *Humanism and the Rhetoric of Toleration*. University Park: The Pennsylvania State University Press.

Reynaud, Paul. 1951. *Unite or Perish: A Dynamic Program for a United Europe*. New York: Simon and Schuster.

Rich, Adrienne. 1979. *On Lies, Secrets and Silences*. New York: W. W. Norton.

Ricoeur, Paul. 1991. *Lectures 1: Autour du Politique*. Paris: Seuil.

Rijksbaron, A., W. H. Roobol, and M. Weinglas, eds. 1987. *Europe from a Cultural Perspective: Historiography and Perceptions*. The Hague: Nijgh and Van Ditmar Universitair.

Ring, Jennifer. 1991. "The Pariah as Hero: Hannah Arendt's Political Actor." *Political Theory* 19, no. 3: 433-452.

Rogat, Yosal. 1961. *The Eichmann Trial and the Rule of Law*. Santa Barbara: Center for the Study of Democratic Institutions.

Rosenstock-Huessy, Eugen. 1969. *Out of Revolution: Autobiography of Western Man*. Norwich, Vt.: Argo Books.

Salkever, Stephen G. 1986. "Tragedy and the Education of the *Demos*: Aristotle's Response to Plato." In J. Peter Euben, ed., *Greek Tragedy and Political Theory*. Berkeley: University of California Press, 274-303.

Saxonhouse, Arlene W. 1986. "Myths and the Origins of Cities: Reflections on the Autochthony Theme in Euripides' *Ion*." In J. Peter Euben, ed., *Greek Tragedy and Political Theory*. Berkeley: University of California Press, 252-273.

Sayre, Henry. 1990. "Performance." In Frank Lentricchia and Thomas McLaughlin, eds., *Critical Terms for Literary Study*. Chicago: University of Chicago Press, 91-104.

Scalingi, Paula. 1980. *The European Parliament: The Three Decade Search for a United Europe*. Westport, Conn.: Greenwood Press.

Seabury, Paul. 1967. *The Rise and Decline of the Cold War*. New York: Basic Books.

Selznick, Philip. 1992. *The Moral Commonwealth: Social Theory and the Promise of Community*. Berkeley: University of California Press.

Sennett, Richard. 1974. *The Fall of Public Man*. New York: Vintage Books.

Sennholz, Hans F. 1955. *How Can Europe Survive?* Toronto: D. Van Nostrand.

Sforza, Count Carlo. 1936. *Europe and Europeans: A Study in Historical Psychology and International Politics*. Indianapolis: Bobbs Merrill.

Simon, Erika. 1982. *The Ancient Theatre*. C. E. Vafopoulou-Richardson, trans. London: Methuen.

Sitton, John F. 1994. "Hannah Arendt's Argument for Council Democracy." In Lewis P. Hinchman and Sandra K. Hinchman, eds., *Hannah Arendt: Critical Essays*. Albany: State University of New York Press, 307-329.

Slater, Niall W. 1990. "The Idea of the Actor." In John J. Winkler and Froma I. Zeitlin, eds., *Nothing to do with Dionysos? Athenian Drama in its Social Context*. Princeton: Princeton University Press, 384-395.

Smith, Howard K. 1950. *The State of Europe*. New York: Knopf.

Spaak, Paul-Henri. 1971. *The Continuing Battle: Memoirs of a European, 1936-1966*. Henry Fox, trans. London: Weidenfeld and Nicolson.

Spinelli, Altiero, and Ernesto Rossi. 1988. *The Ventotene Manifesto*. Ventotene: The Altiero Spinelli Institute for Federalist Studies.

Strong, Tracy B. 1990. "The Promise and Lure of Aesthetics: Political Theory and the Recognition of Persons." In *The Idea of Political Theory: Reflections on the Self in Political Time and Place*. Notre Dame: University of Notre Dame Press, 39-71.

Taminiaux, Jacques. 1986. "La Vie de Quelqu'un." In Françoise Collin, ed., *Hannah Arendt*. Paris: Les Cahiers du Grif.

———. 1996. "*Bios politikos* and *bios theoretikos* in the Phenomenology of Hannah Arendt." *International Journal of Philosophical Studies* 4, no. 2: 215-232.

Taylor, Charles. 1979. "Action as Expression." In Cora Diamond and Jenny Teichman, eds., *Intention and Intentionality*. Ithaca: Cornell University Press, 73-89.

———. 1985a. *Human Agency and Language: Philosophical Papers 1*. Cambridge: Cambridge University Press.

———. 1985b. *Philosophy and the Human Sciences: Philosophical Papers 2*. Cambridge: Cambridge University Press.

Tropman, John E., Harold R. Johnson, and Elmer Tropman. 1979. *The Essentials of Committee Management*. Chicago: Nelson-Hall.

Urwin, Derek W. 1991. *The Community of Europe: A History of European Integration since 1945*. London: Longman.

Vercelli, Cinzia Rognoni. 1991. "La Prima Organizzazione Internazionale dei Federalisti: L'UEF." *Il Politico* LVI, no. 1: 57-76.

Vickers, Brian. 1988. *In Defence of Rhetoric*. Oxford: Clarendon Press.

Villa, Dana. 1992a. "Beyond Good and Evil: Arendt. Nietzsche. and the Aestheticization of Political Action." *Political Theory* 20, no. 2: 274-308.

———. 1992b. "Postmodernism and the Public Sphere." *American Political Science Review* 86, no. 3: 712-721.

———. 1996. *Arendt and Heidegger: The Fate of the Political*. Princeton: Princeton University Press.

von Lang, Jochen, and Claus Sibyll, eds. 1983. *Eichmann Interrogated: Transcripts from the Archives of the Israeli Police*. Ralph Manheim, trans. New York: Farrar Straus and Giroux.

Wahlke, John C. 1991. "Liberal Learning and the Political Science Major: A Report to the Profession." *PS: Political Science and Politics* (March): 48-60.

Wales, Peter. 1963. *Europe is My Country: The Story of West European Cooperation since 1945*. London: Methuen.

Walton, Clarence C. 1952. "The Fate of New-Federalism in Western Europe." *Western Political Quarterly* 5, no. 3 (September): 366-390.

Walton, J. Michael. 1990. *Greek Theatre Practice*. London: Methuen.

Wilkinson, James D. 1981. *The Intellectual Resistance in Europe*. Cambridge: Harvard University Press.

Willis, F. Roy. 1971. *Italy Chooses Europe*. New York: Oxford University Press.

Winand, Pascaline. 1994. "Monnet's Action Committee for the U.S. of Europe. Its Successor and the Network of Europeanists." Presented at the European Community Studies Association Conference, Washington, D.C.

Winkler, John J. 1990. "The Ephebes' Song: *Tragoidia* and *Polis*." In John J. Winkler and Froma I. Zeitlin, eds., *Nothing to do with Dionysos? Athenian Drama in its Social Context*. Princeton: Princeton University Press, 20-62.

Woetzel, Robert K. 1962. *The Nuremburg Trials in International Law.* New York: Frederick Praeger.

Wolin, Sheldon S. 1994. "Hannah Arendt: Democracy and the Political." In Lewis P. Hinchman and Sandra K. Hinchman, eds., *Hannah Arendt: Critical Essays.* Albany: State University of New York Press, 289-306.

Yarbrough, Jean, and Peter Stern. 1981. "*Vita Activa* and *Vita Contemplativa*: Reflections on Hannah Arendt's Political Thought in *The Life of the Mind.*" *Review of Politics* 43, no. 3: 323-354.

Young-Bruehl, Elisabeth. 1982. *Hannah Arendt: For Love of the World.* New Haven: Yale University Press.

Zeitlin, Froma I. 1986. "Thebes: Theater of Self and Society in Athenian Drama." In J. Peter Euben, ed., *Greek Tragedy and Political Theory.* Berkeley: University of California Press, 101-141.

———. 1990. "Playing the Other: Theater, Theatricality, and the Feminine in Greek Drama." In John J. Winkler and Froma I. Zeitlin, eds., *Nothing to do with Dionysos? Athenian Drama in its Social Context.* Princeton: Princeton University Press, 63-96.

Zurcher, Arnold J. 1958. *The Struggle to Unite Europe, 1940-1958.* New York: New York University Press.

Index

About the Author

Eric Gorham is associate professor, Department of Political Science, Loyola University, New Orleans, Louisiana. He is the author of *National Service, Citizenship, and Political Education* (SUNY Press, 1992), as well as articles in journals such as *Polity, Social History, Soundings* and *The Centennial Review*. He teaches courses in the history of political thought, political economy, the philosophy of social science, and contemporary social theory, and has been visiting associate professor at Concordia University in Montreal. He adores traveling and recommends Quebec and Spain to anyone who will listen.